CROSSWORDS WORD SEARCHES
LOGIC PUZZLES & SURPRISES!

mind STRETCHERS

PAPAYA EDITION

EDITED BY STANLEY NEWMAN

Reader's Digest

The Reader's Digest Association, Inc.
Pleasantville, NY / Montreal

Project Staff

EDITORS
Neil Wertheimer, Sandy Fein

PUZZLE EDITOR
Stanley Newman

PRINCIPAL PUZZLE AUTHORS
George Bredehorn, Stanley
Newman, Dave Phillips,
Peter Ritmeester

SERIES ART DIRECTOR
Rich Kershner

DESIGNERS
Tara Long, Erick Swindell

ILLUSTRATIONS
©Norm Bendel

COPY EDITOR
Diane Aronson

PROOFREADER
Adam Cohen

Reader's Digest Home & Health Books

**PRESIDENT, HOME & GARDEN
AND HEALTH & WELLNESS**
Alyce Alston

EDITOR IN CHIEF
Neil Wertheimer

CREATIVE DIRECTOR
Michele Laseau

EXECUTIVE MANAGING EDITOR
Donna Ruvituso

**ASSOCIATE DIRECTOR,
NORTH AMERICA PREPRESS**
Douglas A. Croll

MANUFACTURING MANAGER
John L. Cassidy

MARKETING DIRECTOR
Dawn Nelson

The Reader's Digest Association, Inc.

**PRESIDENT AND
CHIEF EXECUTIVE OFFICER**
Mary Berner

**PRESIDENT,
GLOBAL CONSUMER MARKETING**
Dawn Zier

**VICE PRESIDENT,
CONSUMER MARKETING**
Kathryn Bennett

ISBN 978-1-60652-993-5

Address any comments about *Mind Stretchers*, *Papaya Edition* to:

The Reader's Digest Association, Inc.
Editor in Chief, Books
Reader's Digest Road
Pleasantville, NY 10570-7000

To order copies of this or other editions of the *Mind Stretchers* book series,
call 1-800-846-2100.

Visit our online store at **rdstore.com**

For many more fun games and puzzles, visit www.rd.com/games.

Printed in the United States of America

1 3 5 7 9 10 8 6 4 2

US 4967/L-11

Contents

Dear Puzzler,

Does the name Arthur Wynne ring a bell? What about the name Howard Garns?

These two gentlemen were the inventors of America's two favorite puzzles, crosswords and sudoku, respectively. I think it's really sad that Wynne and Garns aren't better known by the puzzle-solving public, because we owe both of them a debt of thanks for all the challenge and fun their creations have brought us.

Liverpool-born Arthur Wynne was working for the old *New York World* when he was asked to invent a new game for the paper's Sunday "Fun" supplement in 1913. His "Word-Cross" puzzles were an immediate hit, and spread rapidly to most of the nation's newspapers in less than 10 years. But unfortunately for Wynne, he never trademarked or patented his invention. It's said that he thought crosswords' popularity would be a mere fad that would soon blow over.

Side note: Several years ago, I had the pleasure of meeting Wynne's grandson, Arthur Wynne Vaast, in Washington, D.C., at the first-day ceremonies for the issuance of a crossword postage stamp.

As for Indiana native Garns, who was a 74-year-old retired architect when his first sudoku puzzle appeared in print in 1979, if not for *New York Times* puzzle editor Will Shortz, the name of sudoku's inventor might still be a mystery. That's because Garns' first puzzle—and, as far as we know, all the sudokus he ever published—appeared anonymously in an American pulp crossword-magazine series, under the title "Number Place."

Here's how Will used his legendary puzzle skills to unearth Garns' identity. While the puzzle-magazine series in question didn't give individual puzzle bylines, it did list all of a particular issue's puzzle authors at the front. Will's massive collection of puzzle magazines happens to include that series, and he discovered that Garns' name appeared at the front of every issue that had a sudoku, but was missing from issues without one. Luckily for puzzle history, the only puzzle Garns ever created for that magazine was sudoku!

That was pretty solid circumstantial evidence for bestowing the title Father of Sudoku, but not exactly proof. That proof came soon after Will's discovery, when architect colleagues of Garns came forward with their memories of his working on the puzzles while at his office desk.

As you work your way through the easy-to-tough crosswords and sudokus in this edition of *Mind Stretchers*, may I suggest that you join me in raising your cup of coffee (or a glass of whatever your favorite beverage might be), and toasting the creative talents of Arthur Wynne and Howard Garns.

Stanley Newman
Mind Stretchers Puzzle Editor

■ Foreword

Meet the Puzzles!

Mind Stretchers is filled with a delightful mix of classic and new puzzle types. To help you get started, here are instructions, tips, and examples for each.

WORD GAMES

Crossword Puzzles

Edited by Stanley Newman

Crosswords are arguably America's most popular puzzles. As presented in this book, the one- and two-star puzzles test your ability to solve straightforward clues to everyday words. "More-star" puzzles have a somewhat broader vocabulary, but most of the added challenge in these comes from less obvious and trickier clues. These days, you'll be glad to know, uninteresting obscurities such as "Genus of fruit flies" and "Famed seventeenth-century soprano" don't appear in crosswords anymore.

Our 60 crosswords were authored by more than a dozen different puzzle makers, all nationally known for their skill and creativity.

Clueless Crosswords

by George Bredehorn

A unique crossword variation invented by George, these 7-by-7 grids primarily test your vocabulary and reasoning skills. There is one simple task: Complete the crossword with common uncapitalized seven-letter words, based entirely on the letters already filled in for you.

EXAMPLE	SOLUTION

Hints: *Focusing on the last letter of a word, when given, often helps. For example, a last letter of G often suggests that IN are the previous two letters. When the solutions aren't coming quickly, focus on the shared spaces that are blank—you can often figure out whether it has to be a vowel or a consonant, helping you solve both words that cross it.*

Split Decisions

by George Bredehorn

Crossword puzzle lovers also enjoy this variation. Once again, no clues are provided except within the diagram. Each answer consists of two words whose spellings are the same, except for two consecutive letters. For each pair of words, the two sets of different letters are already filled in for you. All answers are common words; no phrases or hyphenated or capitalized words are used. Certain missing words may have more than one possible solution, but there is only one solution for each word that will correctly link up with all the other words.

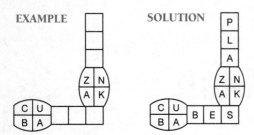

EXAMPLE   SOLUTION

Hints: *Start with the shorter (three- and four-letter) words, because there will be fewer possibilities that spell words. In each puzzle, there will always be a few such word pairs that have only one solution. You may have to search a little to find them, since they may be anywhere in the grid, but it's always a good idea to fill in the answers to these first.*

Triad Split Decisions

by George Bredehorn

This puzzle is solved the same way as Split Decisions, except you are given three letters for each word instead of two.

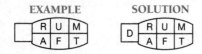

EXAMPLE   SOLUTION

Word Searches

Kids love 'em, and so do grownups, making word searches perhaps the most widely appealing puzzle type. In a word search, the challenge is to find hidden words within a grid of letters. In the typical puzzle, words can be found in vertical columns, horizontal rows, or along diagonals, with the letters of the words running either forward or backward. Usually, a list of words to search for is given to you. But

ANSWERS!

Answers to all the puzzles are found beginning on page 233, and are organized by the page number on which the puzzle appears.

to make word searches harder, puzzle writers sometimes just point you in the right direction, such as telling you to find 25 foods. Other twists include allowing words to take right turns, or leaving letters out of the grid.

Hints: *One of the most reliable and efficient searching methods is to scan each row from top to bottom for the first letter of the word. So if you are looking for "violin" you would look for the letter "v." When you find one, look at all the letters that surround it for the second letter of the word (in this case, "i"). Each time you find a correct two-letter combination (in this case, "vi"), you then scan either for the correct three-letter combination ("vio") or the whole word.*

NUMBER GAMES

Sudoku

by Conceptis Ltd.

Sudoku puzzles have become massively popular in the past few years, thanks to their simplicity and test of pure reasoning. The basic Sudoku puzzle is a 9-by-9 square grid, split into 9 square regions, each containing 9 cells. Each puzzle starts off with roughly 20 to 35 of the squares filled in with the numbers 1 to 9. There is just one rule: Fill in the rest of the squares

EXAMPLE

8	4						7	1
3			7	1	8			9
		5	9		3	6		
	9	7	8		1	2	3	
	6						9	
	3	1	2		9	7	6	
		4	3		2	9		
1			5	9	4			6
9	8						5	3

SOLUTION

8	4	9	6	2	5	3	7	1
3	2	6	7	1	8	5	4	9
7	1	5	9	4	3	6	8	2
5	9	7	8	6	1	2	3	4
2	6	8	4	3	7	1	9	5
4	3	1	2	5	9	7	6	8
6	5	4	3	8	2	9	1	7
1	7	3	5	9	4	8	2	6
9	8	2	1	7	6	4	5	3

with the numbers 1 to 9 so that no number appears twice in any row, column, or region.

Hints: Use the numbers provided to rule out where else the same number can appear. For example, if there is a 1 in a cell, a 1 cannot appear in the same row, column, or region. By scanning all the cells that the various 1 values rule out, you often can find where the remaining 1 values must go.

Hyper-Sudoku

by Peter Ritmeester

Peter is the inventor of this unique Sudoku variation. In addition to the numbers 1 to 9 appearing in each row and column, Hyper-Sudoku also has four 3-by-3 regions to work with, indicated by gray shading.

EXAMPLE

1	4	5	9			7		
		7	5	8	4	1		
3				7	2		5	
5	9		4	2	7			
	6		8					7
	7	4				2	9	5
	1					8		
	5		2			6		
6			7			5		

SOLUTION

1	4	5	9	3	6	7	2	8
9	2	7	5	8	4	1	3	6
3	8	6	1	7	2	9	5	4
5	9	3	4	2	7	8	6	1
2	6	1	8	5	9	3	4	7
8	7	4	6	1	3	2	9	5
7	1	9	3	6	5	4	8	2
4	5	8	2	9	1	6	7	3
6	3	2	7	4	8	5	1	9

LOGIC PUZZLES

Find the Ships

by Conceptis Ltd.

If you love playing the board game Battleship, you'll enjoy this pencil-and-paper variation! In each puzzle, a group of ships of varying sizes is provided on the right. Your job: Properly place the ships in the grid. A handful of ship "parts" are put on the board to get you started. The placement rules:

1. Ships must be oriented horizontally or vertically. No diagonals!

2. A ship can't go in a square with wavy lines; that indicates water.

3. The numbers on the left and bottom of the grid tell you how many squares in that row or column contain part of ships.

4. No two ships can touch each other, even diagonally.

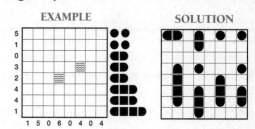

EXAMPLE   SOLUTION

Hints: The solving process involves both finding those squares where a ship must go and eliminating those squares where a ship cannot go. The numbers provided should give you a head start with the latter, the number 0 clearly implying that every square in that row or column can be eliminated. If you know that a square will be occupied by a ship, but don't yet know what kind of ship, mark that square, then cross out all the squares that are diagonal to it—all of these must contain water.

ABC

by Peter Ritmeester

This innovative new puzzle challenges your logic much in the way a Sudoku puzzle does. Each row and column in an ABC puzzle contains exactly one A, one B, and one C, plus one blank (or two, in harder puzzles). Your task is to figure out where the three letters go in each row. The clues outside the puzzle frame tell you the first letter encountered when moving in the direction of an arrow.

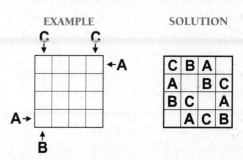

EXAMPLE   SOLUTION

Hints: If a clue says a letter is first in a row or column, don't assume that it must go in the first square. It could go in either of the first two squares (or first three, in the harder puzzles). A good way to start is to look for where column and row clues intersect (for example, when two clues look like they are pointing at the same square). These intersecting clues often give you the most information about where the first letter of a row or column must go. At times, it's also possible to figure out where a certain letter goes by eliminating every other square as a possibility for that letter in a particular row or column.

Fences

by Conceptis Ltd.

Lovers of mazes will enjoy these challenges. Connect the dots with vertical or horizontal lines, so that a single loop is formed with no crossings or branches. Each number indicates how many lines surround it; squares with no number may be surrounded by any number of lines.

EXAMPLE   SOLUTION

Hints: Don't try to solve the puzzle by making one continuous line—instead, fill in the links (that is, spaces between two dots) you are certain about, and then figure out how to connect those links. To start the puzzle, mark off any links that can't be connected. That would include all four links around each 0. Another good starting step is to look for any 3 values next or adjacent to a 0; solving those links is easy. In time, you will see that rules and patterns emerge, particularly in the puzzle corners, and when two numbers are adjacent to each other.

Number-Out

by Conceptis Ltd.

This innovative new puzzle challenges your logic in much the same way a Sudoku puzzle does. Your task is to shade squares so that no number appears in any row or column more than once. Shaded squares may not touch each other horizontally or vertically, and all unshaded squares must form a single continuous area.

EXAMPLE   SOLUTION

Hints: First look for all the numbers that are unduplicated in their row and column. Those squares will never be shaded, so we suggest that you circle them as a reminder to yourself. When there are three of the same number consecutively in a row or column, the one in the middle must always be unshaded, so you can shade the other two. Also, any square that is between a pair of the same numbers must always be unshaded. Once a square is shaded, you know that the squares adjacent to it, both horizontally and vertically, must be unshaded.

Star Search

by Peter Ritmeester

Another fun game in the same style of Minesweeper. Your task: find the stars that are hidden among the blank squares. The numbered squares indicate how many stars are hidden in squares adjacent to them (including diagonally). There is never more than one star in any square.

EXAMPLE   SOLUTION

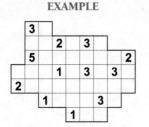 

Hint: If, for example, a 3 is surrounded by four empty squares, but two of those squares are adjacent to the same square with a 1, the other two empty squares around the 3 must contain stars.

123

by Peter Ritmeester

Each grid in this puzzle has pieces that look like dominoes. You must fill in the blank squares so that each "domino" contains one each of the numbers 1, 2, and 3, according to these two rules:

EXAMPLE   SOLUTION

			1					2	1	2	3	1	3
		3						3	2	3	1	2	1
								1	3	1	2	3	2
3				2				3	1	2	3	2	1
	2							1	2	3	1	3	2
		1		1				2	3	1	2	1	3

1. No two adjacent squares, horizontally or vertically, can have the same number.

2. Each completed row and column of the diagram will have an equal number of 1s, 2s, and 3s.

Hints: Look first for any blank square that is adjacent to two different numbers. By rule 1 above, the "missing" number of 1-2-3 must go in that blank square. Rule 2 becomes important to use later in the solving process., For example, knowing that a 9-by-9 diagram must have three 1s, three 2s, and three 3s in each row and column allows you to use the process of elimination to deduce what blank squares in nearly filled rows and columns must be.

Throughout *Mind Stretchers* you will find unique mazes, visual conundrums, and other colorful challenges, each developed by maze master Dave Phillips. Each comes under a new name and has unique instructions. Our best advice? Patience and perseverance. Your eyes will need time to unravel the visual secrets.

In addition, you will also discover these visual puzzles:

Line Drawings

by George Bredehorn

George loves to create never-before-seen puzzle types, and here is another unique Bredehorn game. Each Line Drawing puzzle is different in its design, but the task is the same: Figure out where to place the prescribed number of lines to partition the space in the instructed way.

Hint: Use a pencil and a straightedge as you work. Some lines come very close to the items within the region, so being straight and accurate with your line-drawing is crucial.

One-Way Streets

by Peter Ritmeester

Another fun variation on the maze. The diagram represents a pattern of streets. A and B are parking spaces, and the black squares are stores. Find a route that starts at A, passes through all the stores exactly once, and ends at B. (Harder puzzles use P's to indicate parking spaces instead of A's and B's, and don't tell you the starting and ending places.) Arrows indicate one-way traffic for that block only. No

EXAMPLE   SOLUTION

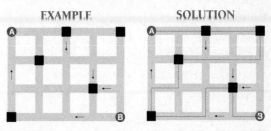

block or intersection may be entered more than once.

Hints: The particular arrangement of stores and arrows will always limit the possibilities for the first store passed through from the starting point A and the last store passed through before reaching ending point B. So try to work both from the start and the end of the route. Also, the placement of an arrow on a block doesn't necessarily mean that your route will pass through that block. You can also use arrows to eliminate blocks where your path will not go.

BRAIN TEASERS

To round out the more involved puzzles are more than 150 short brain teasers, most written by our puzzle editor, Stanley Newman. Stan is famous in the puzzle world for his inventive brain games. An example of how to solve each puzzle appears in the puzzle's first occurrence (the page number is noted below). You'll find the following types scattered throughout the pages.

* Invented by and cowritten with George Bredehorn
** By George Bredehorn

But wait...there's more!

At the top of many of the pages in this book are additional brain teasers, organized into three categories:

• **QUICK!**: These tests challenge your ability to instantly calculate numbers or recall well-known facts.

• **DO YOU KNOW** ...: These more demanding questions probe the depth of your knowledge of facts and trivia.

• **HAVE YOU** ...: These reminders reveal the many things you can do each day to benefit your brain.

For the record, we have deliberately left out answers to the **QUICK!** and **DO YOU KNOW...** features. Our hope is that if you don't know an answer, you'll be intrigued enough to open a book or search the Internet for it!

■ Meet the Authors

STANLEY NEWMAN (puzzle editor and author) is crossword editor for *Newsday*, the major newspaper of Long Island, New York. He is the author/editor of over 125 books, including the autobiography and instructional manual *Cruciverbalism* and the best-selling *Million Word Crossword Dictionary*. Winner of the First U.S. Open Crossword Championship in 1982, he holds the world's record for the fastest completion of a *New York Times* crossword—2 minutes, 14 seconds. Stan operates the website www.StanXwords.com and also conducts an annual Crossword University skill-building program on a luxury-liner cruise.

GEORGE BREDEHORN is a retired elementary school teacher from Wantagh, New York. His variety word games have appeared in the *New York Times* and many puzzle magazines. Every week for the past 20 years, he and his wife, Dorothy, have hosted a group of Long Island puzzlers who play some of the 80-plus games that George has invented.

CONCEPTIS (www.conceptispuzzles.com) is a leading supplier of logic puzzles to printed, electronic, and other gaming media all over the world. On average, ten million Conceptis puzzles are printed in newspapers, magazines and books each day, while millions more are played online and on mobile phones each month.

DAVE PHILLIPS has designed puzzles for books, magazines, newspapers, PC games, and advertising for more 30 years. In addition, Dave is a renowned creator of walk-through mazes. Each year his corn-maze designs challenge visitors with miles of paths woven into works of art. Dave is also codeveloper of eBrainyGames.com, a website that features puzzles and games for sale.

PETER RITMEESTER is chief executive officer of PZZL.com, which produces many varieties of puzzles for newspapers and websites worldwide. Peter is also general secretary of the World Puzzle Federation. The federation organizes the annual World Puzzle Championship, which includes difficult versions of many of the types of logic puzzles that Peter has created for *Mind Stretchers*.

■ Master Class: **Anagrams**

How to Solve Letter-Rearrangement and Word-Formation Puzzles

A scene from the crossword documentary film *Wordplay* features eminent crossword author Merl Reagle driving his car near his Florida home, relating how he can't help but mentally rearrange the words that he sees while behind the wheel. One example he gives in the film makes me laugh out loud whenever I think of it—the letters in "Dunkin'," as in "Dunkin' Donuts," can be anagrammed to spell "Unkind." Merl used UNKIND DONUTS as an answer in one of his crosswords and, although I don't know exactly what the clue was, you can be sure it made use of outrageous-but-suitable wordplay.

Yes, Merl is a master anagrammer. Besides his "driving discoveries," another of Merl's specialties is rearranging the names of celebrities to form words or everyday phrases. Among his remarkable finds in this area are actor EDDIE ALBERT/DELIBERATED, and TV media critic GENE SHALIT/ENGLISH TEA. While Merl does make professional use of many of his anagrams, the truth is that he loves mixing up the letters in words to form new words. He just can't help himself, because it's so much fun for him to do.

This obsession is something your humble puzzle editor completely understands. I must admit that I practice it regularly, although with nowhere near the skill or success of Mr. Reagle. I think of it as "letter acrobatics," making the letters in a word jump around every which way, in pursuit of a new word or words. Once in a great while, I do come up with what I think is an interesting find. A few years ago, I was in an elevator of an office building managed by Olympia and York, whose name was on the wall. While standing there with nothing else to do, I began to mentally rearrange the letters in "Olympia." And, before I got to my floor, I realized that "Olympian" is an anagram of "palimony."

Anagramming is not only fun, it can also help to keep your mind flexible and sharp. That's why there are quite a few games in each *Mind Stretchers* edition that involve letter rearrangement and word formation, such as the National Treasure, Opposite Attraction, Transdeletion, and Two-by-Four puzzles.

So, in this Master Class, it will be my pleasure to share with you some anagram skill-building tips and techniques that you'll be able to use right away, and to provide you with additional resources that will help you to continue honing your abilities on your own.

Warm-Up

To get started, see how well you do with these. Find the common word that is an anagram of the words below. If more than one answer is indicated, be sure to find them all. Take all the time you need. Answers are at the end of this section, but if you get stuck, don't look at them just yet.

1. ONCE (1 answer)

_____

2. POOL (2 different answers)

_____

_____

3. PALE (3 different answers)

_____

_____

_____

4. STOP (5 different answers)

_____

_____

_____

_____

_____

5. CAUSE (1 answer)

_____

6. OCEAN (1 answer)

_____

7. EARLY (2 different answers)

_____

_____

8. METEOR (1 answer)

_____

9. AMENITY (1 answer)

_____

10. MARGINAL (1 answer)

_____

How well did you do?

No matter how you got your answers, you should have found the shorter words easier to anagram than the longer ones, even where multiple answers were asked for. The reason, of course, is a matter of math. Assuming no duplicate letters, there are only 23 different ways that the letters in any particular four-letter word can be rearranged. When there's a double letter in the word (as in POOL above), there are less than half as many possible rearrangements—only 11.

When you have only a four-letter word to work with, you should have no trouble finding all its anagrams by using what I call the "brute force" method. That is, try all the possibilities until you find the answer(s). To do this most methodically, start with the first letter in the word, and see if rearranging the remaining three letters after it will form a new word. Then try the second letter of the word as the starting letter, and so on. For four-letter words, this should never take you very long, especially since you'll be able to quickly skip past letter combinations that don't form words. In the case of ONCE above, for example, you could safely reject OE and NC as possible starts for an anagram.

"Brute force" becomes less and less useful as a solving technique as you increase the number of letters you're working with. It's that pesky math of all the possibilities. For five-letter words with no repeated letters, there are 119 possible rearrangements; for six-letter words, there are a daunting 719 of them! How many for the longer words? You don't want to know!

Clearly, we need more thoughtful ways to search for anagrams of longer words.

Letter-Grouping Tips

Here's advice from my friend and colleague Trip Payne, a nationally known crossword author who is also a world-class Scrabble player. As of this writing, he is one of the 100 top-ranked players in the United States. That means he must be a great anagrammer, and he is.

• Since it's easiest to think of words from their initial letters, you should look first for letter combinations that are most likely to start words, and then try to form the rest of a word from the letters that remain. Trip recommends looking for common prefixes such as RE- and DIS-, as well as consonant pairs like ST- , SC-, and CH-.

• If that doesn't work, try to find frequently seen word endings next, such as the suffixes –ING, -ED, -EST and –ION, and consonant pairs such as –NT and –SH.

• Paying attention to the relative vowel/consonant mix may also be of help. If, for example, it's a longish word with one vowel, count on that vowel being somewhere in the middle of the word.

If there are many vowels relative to consonants, look for common vowel groupings like EAU, AI, and OO. If there are roughly the same number of vowels and consonants, it's most likely that the vowels and consonants in the word will more or less alternate.

An additional pointer from my own experience: Look for shorter words that might be used to form compound words, like HOUSE/BOAT, SONG/BIRD, and TEAM/MATE.

If you had trouble anagramming any of the Warm-Up words above, now's the time for you to try again, keeping these tips in mind. One or more of these pointers will point you in the right direction, especially for words 8-10: METEOR, AMENITY, and MARGINAL.

Visualization Methods

Now that you've got a leg up on the "what to do" of anagramming, let's talk about the "how to do it."

When looking for a word to play on a Scrabble rack, most experienced players will rearrange the letters repeatedly, reordering the letters into sensible groupings (as suggested above), rather than just "mentally moving" the tiles. Obviously, each new ordering of the letters helps to give the mind a fresh look at them.

The letters on a *Mind Stretchers* page aren't portable, of course, but you should use your pencil to make your own rearrangements. In particular, many word gamers have found that it's easier to spot anagrams when the letters in question are arranged in a two-dimensional pattern of some kind, rather than in the straight line in which they appear on a printed page.

Will Shortz, puzzle editor of *The New York Times*, is partial to a pyramid pattern like this:

```
        A
      B   C
    D   E   F
  G   H   I   J
```

I prefer something a little more random-looking for my letters, a roughly square shape like this:

```
      I   C
   A    H    E
      J    F    G
        D   B
```

Other shapes you might like to try include a circle or an "X."

Whatever two-dimensional shape you use, you'll likely agree that looking at your arrangement makes it easier for the eye to "flow" from one letter to the next than just looking at a "straight line" of letters.

More Practice

Now, let's use what you've learned so far: Find the one common word that is an anagram of each of the words below. There's a hint next to each one to help get you started.

1. ALIGNS (keep the vowels apart)

_____

2. ATTICS (try the starting consonant pairs mentioned above)

_____

3. RAWNESS (think "plural")

_____

4. BOREDOM (think "compound word")

_____

5. SUPERSONIC (try the suffixes mentioned above)

_____

Additional Skill-Building Suggestions

There are many fine commercial word games that will give you good practice in anagramming. Two of the best known are Scrabble and Boggle, both of which I've enjoyed playing for many years. Each has its own advantages in anagram skill-building. As mentioned above, in Scrabble, you can rearrange the letter tiles on your rack, which is a great help in finding the best words to play. With Boggle, the letters aren't moved; but since you and your opponents play the same letters at the same time and compare the words you've all found when time is up, you're able to see words you may have missed.

If your local daily newspaper has the Jumble syndicated word game, that's another good source of anagram practice. While the Jumble words don't exceed six letters in length, the "bonus" answer to the cartoony question is often 10 letters long or more.

When playing any "low-tech" board game such as Scrabble or Boggle, I always find myself wondering if there are any better plays than the ones that I (or the other players) actually found. My natural curiosity would like to be satisfied by knowing what words we've missed.

If you've got Internet access, you can scratch that itch by playing some of the many interactive word games available on the World Wide Web. Here are a few of my favorites, all of which are free to download or use:

• www.wordtwist.org has a Boggle-like game in which you play the same letter grids that many others have already played. When time is up, you'll see all the words that everyone else has found.

• www.quackle.org has the Scrabble-like game Quackle available for free download. Developed by some folks at MIT, it has many useful features, from "rack shuffling" to an artificial-intelligence mechanism that will show you the best moves at any point.

• The company that produces the Jumble newspaper game has a great Web site, www.jumble.com, which features numerous word-unscrambling games.

• Trip Payne likes www.jumbletime.com for anagram practice. It includes many daily challenges for words of various lengths.

Three-time National Scrabble Champion Joe Edley, who has written many books and spoken extensively on Scrabble, recommends this simple-but-effective practice method: Take any long word you like and find all the shorter words that can be formed from its letters. Once you've done that, you can get immediate feedback at the aptly named Web site www.anagrammer.com, which will give you a complete list of shorter words found in any word you enter. Joe also likes the free downloadable program available at www.zyzzyva.net, which many Scrabble experts use for training.

Final DWOSR

Make use of the hints presented here and, with a little practice, you're sure to become a better anagrammer; and you'll be able to knock off the bottom-of-the-page *Mind Stretchers* letter-mix challenges with more success, and have a lot more fun.

So I wish you DUCK LOGO!

—Stanley Newman

Warm-Up Answers
1. CONE 2. LOOP, POLO 3. LEAP, PEAL, PLEA 4. OPTS, POST, POTS, SPOT, TOPS 5. SAUCE 6. CANOE 7. LAYER, RELAY
8. REMOTE 9. ANYTIME 10. ALARMING
More Practice Answers
1. SIGNAL 2. STATIC 3. ANSWERS 4. BEDROOM 5. PERCUSSION

★ Body Language by Gail Grabowski

ACROSS

1 Lasso
5 Smash into
8 Spaghetti or ravioli
13 Battery fluid
14 Hourly pay
15 Pale
16 Not on time
17 Of unknown authorship: Abbr.
18 Use watercolors
19 Geometry subject
22 Scoreboard postings: Abbr.
23 Great bother
24 Spheres
26 Pleasant smells
30 "Yikes!"
33 Go quickly
37 Pesters
38 Gone With the Wind estate
39 Steed or stallion
40 Historical period
41 Mar. 17 honoree
42 Alan of M*A*S*H
43 Speaker's platform
44 Shoe parts
45 Wall-calendar line
46 Pass, as time
48 "Darn it!"
50 Sharp-eyed birds
55 Clumsy one
57 Where a pane is inserted
61 Show to be true
63 Office assistant
64 Israeli diplomat Eban
65 Spooky
66 Settled the bill
67 Limerick, for example
68 Specified
69 Pub serving
70 Makes mistakes

DOWN

1 Essayist __ Waldo Emerson
2 Florida city
3 Breads with pockets
4 Perfect places
5 Hindu princess
6 Highly excited
7 Bistro handout
8 Copier insert
9 Dry __ bone
10 Trim and tidy
11 Circus structure
12 Aardvarks' snacks
14 Thin cookie

20 Fill with joy
21 Flagmaker Betsy
25 Montana city
27 Tatum or Ryan
28 Santa __ (ship of 1492)
29 Shocked
31 Type of exam
32 Berets and bonnets
33 Playwright George Bernard
34 Old king of rhyme
35 Catalog page to fill in
36 Japanese city

41 Bundle of wheat
43 TV star Arnaz
47 Assembled, as a blouse
49 Suit material
51 Jelly flavor
52 Plug away
53 Fireplace remnant
54 Stitched lines
55 Ready for customers
56 General vicinity
58 California wine valley
59 Clock face
60 Garfield dog
62 Compete

★ Square Links

Find the three squares that are not linked to any of the others.

CENTURY MARKS

Inserting plus signs and minus signs, as many as necessary, in between the nine digits below, create a series of additions and subtractions whose final answer is 100. Any digits without a sign between them are to be grouped together as a single number.

Example: 4 7 - 5 + 2 2 + 8 - 1 + 2 9 = 100

$$8 \quad 3 \quad 2 \quad 9 \quad 2 \quad 7 \quad 3 \quad 7 \quad 4 \quad = \quad 100$$

★ Where to Now?

Find these worldwide place names, all containing the letters TO, that are hidden in the diagram, either across, down, or diagonally.

```
T  O  R  Y  B  A  K  E  P  O  T  N
O  P  T  O  R  O  N  T  O  O  D  O
N  O  T  N  I  O  N  T  G  C  V  T
G  R  O  O  S  O  M  N  O  I  E  R
V  T  R  Y  T  T  M  R  C  G  T  E
E  K  Q  S  O  R  L  T  E  J  O  V
E  S  U  O  L  U  O  T  B  B  S  E
C  O  A  W  E  R  H  P  G  G  O  A
H  A  Y  O  I  G  K  U  O  I  I  T
E  L  P  A  A  P  C  T  T  N  S  O
T  I  V  E  R  T  O  N  O  O  I  G
O  Y  K  O  T  U  T  T  L  T  O  A
E  T  O  X  L  O  S  Z  E  S  T  B
F  Y  K  O  T  E  W  Q  D  E  R  O
T  O  N  G  A  M  G  N  O  T  A  T
```

ARTOIS
BRISTOL
CAPE TOWN
ESTONIA
ETON
EVERTON
HOUSTON
OPORTO
STOCKHOLM
TIVERTON
TOBAGO
TOBERMORY
TOGO
TOKYO
TOLEDO
TONGA
TOPEKA
TORONTO
TORQUAY
TOULON
TOULOUSE
VICTORIA

INITIAL REACTION

Identify the well-known proverb from the first letters in each of its words.
Example: L. B. Y. L. Answer: Look Before You Leap

T. I. C. _____

★ Sudoku

Fill in the blank boxes so that every row, column, and 3x3 box contains all of the numbers 1 to 9.

	6	4			7	3		5
9			5		4			
2		7			8			9
	1				5	2	8	3
				8				
7	9	8	4				6	
3			8			4		6
			1		3			2
1		5	2			9	3	

MIXAGRAMS

Each line contains a five-letter word and a four-letter word that have been mixed together (the order of the letters in each word has not been changed). Unmix the two words on each line and write them in the spaces provided. When you're done, find a two-part answer to the clue by reading down the letter columns in the answers. Example: D A R I U N V E T = DRIVE + AUNT

CLUE: High-paying proposition

S A L N O G A B E = _ _ _ _ _ + _ _ _ _

C O L A L O D Y N = _ _ _ _ _ + _ _ _ _

D I N P O D O U T = _ _ _ _ _ + _ _ _ _

A V A G A S I N E = _ _ _ _ _ + _ _ _ _

★ Capital B by Sally R. Stein

ACROSS

1 Arizona Indian
5 Prepare, as potatoes
9 Recedes
13 Major kitchen appliance
14 Best-selling cookie
15 Of the moon
17 Asian capital
20 __ days (time long past)
21 Addition result
22 Untruths
23 By oneself
26 Make angry
28 Computer games, for example
32 Placed in order
36 Ages __ (time long past)
37 Astronauts' org.
39 Largest artery
40 European capital
44 Actress Zellweger
45 Percolate
46 Fruity drink
47 High regard
49 Church tops
52 Don't include
54 Stamp of approval
55 Take a crack __ (try)
58 __ Vegas
60 King or emperor
64 European capital
68 Sleeper's sound
69 Hot beverages
70 USC rival
71 Helper: Abbr.
72 Arsenal supply
73 Ball-__ hammer

DOWN

1 "King of the road"
2 Elliptical shape
3 Remain unsettled
4 Swallow
5 Cow comment
6 Noah creation
7 Solidifies
8 Sound of a yawn
9 Inventor Whitney
10 Large croaker
11 __ B'rith
12 Of sound mind
16 Highways: Abbr.
18 Be sure of
19 French friends
24 Bowling place
25 Graduate-school exams
27 Young horse
28 British sword
29 Mean ones
30 Wellspring
31 Slalom curves
33 Courtroom activity
34 Piano piece
35 Knights' female equivalents
38 Assists in wrongdoing
41 Be dazed
42 Search for
43 Fencing weapon
48 1,760 yards
50 Deserve
51 Stop, as a leak
53 Salad ingredient
55 Belly muscles
56 Sandwich filler
57 Wedding-ceremony exchanges
59 Arise (from)
61 Shoestring
62 __ Stanley Gardner
63 Actress Meg
65 Goldfish or gerbil
66 Sandwich filler
67 GI hangout

★ Fences

Connect the dots with vertical or horizontal lines, so that a single loop is formed with no crossings or branches. Each number indicates how many lines surround it; squares with no number may be surrounded by any number of lines.

```
.  .  .  .  .  .  .  .  .
   3  2  2        1
.  .  .  .  .  .  .  .  .
               3     0
.  .  .  .  .  .  .  .  .
      0  2     2
.  .  .  .  .  .  .  .  .
 3  3     3  2     1
.  .  .  .  .  .  .  .  .
   2     3  1     2  2
.  .  .  .  .  .  .  .  .
      2     0  2
.  .  .  .  .  .  .  .  .
 2     2
.  .  .  .  .  .  .  .  .
 2           2  3  3
.  .  .  .  .  .  .  .  .
```

ADDITION SWITCH

Switch the positions of two of the digits in the incorrect sum at right, to get a correct sum.
Example: 955+264 = 411. Switch the second 1 in 411 with the 9 in 955 to get: 155+264 = 419

$$\begin{array}{r} 8\,6\,2 \\ +\,6\,2\,5 \\ \hline 8\,9\,3 \end{array}$$

★★ Line Drawing

Draw two straight lines, each from one edge of the square to another edge, so that the letters in each of the four regions spell a word of a different length.

THREE OF A KIND

Find the three hidden words in the sentence that, read in order, go together in some way.
Example: I s<u>old</u> Nor<u>ma</u> <u>new</u> screwd<u>rivers</u> (answer: "old man river").

Their diners' catsup is too watery, some owners claim.

★ Piercing

Find these words, all relating to various meanings of the title word
(including the title itself), that are hidden in the diagram, either across,
down, or diagonally.

```
E  K  G  O  G  A  S  T  U  T  E  T
T  H  C  N  N  P  R  A  H  S  D  R
U  I  G  N  I  B  O  R  P  E  G  A
C  N  S  L  T  C  D  E  H  D  N  N
A  T  H  E  T  M  R  C  W  B  I  S
R  E  R  K  I  E  T  E  N  U  B  F
G  N  I  L  L  I  R  D  I  F  B  I
A  S  L  P  P  H  Z  E  I  P  A  X
K  E  L  H  S  X  Y  E  V  F  T  I
G  E  G  V  R  J  R  E  V  E  S  N
Q  I  E  S  A  C  L  O  U  D  S  G
H  P  E  N  E  T  R  A  T  I  N  G
```

ACUTE
ASTUTE
DRILLING
EAR-SPLITTING
FIERCE
HIGH-PITCHED
INTENSE
KEEN
LOUD
PENETRATING
PIERCING
PROBING
SEVERE
SHARP
SHREWD
SHRILL
STABBING
TRANSFIXING

WHO'S WHAT WHERE?

The correct term for a resident of Melbourne, Australia, is:

A) Melburnian   B) Burnisite

C) Melbourner   D) Melbie

★ Meet the Presidents by Sally R. Stein

ACROSS

1 Fourth planet from the Sun
5 Mediterranean fruits
9 Hide away
14 Bassoon relative
15 "What's __ for me?"
16 It's not allowed
17 13th president
20 Sword metal
21 Raison d'__
22 At any time
23 Persuade
25 Right-hand person
27 Like sailboats
30 DVD player ancestors
32 "__ seen enough!"
35 Start of a play
36 Business transaction
38 Had a meal
40 22nd and 24th president
43 Bogged down
44 Stereo system
45 American flag color
46 Orange drink
47 Digital music player
49 Closed, as an envelope
51 Babe of baseball
53 Anti-drug officer
54 Victor's cry
56 *Othello* villain
59 Whole bunch
63 Third president
66 Promising one
67 Neighborhood
68 Exxon's former name
69 Quickness
70 14 Across accessory
71 Beef dish

DOWN

1 Some PTA members
2 Slightly
3 Performer's part
4 Choosy
5 Kind of Christmas tree
6 Back-of-book reference
7 Natural talent
8 Agitate
9 Gateway Arch city: Abbr.
10 Brought under control
11 Aloof
12 Feeling miffed
13 Farmer, at times
18 Lotion ingredient
19 Shakespearean king
24 Envelope line: Abbr.
26 Phrase of understanding
27 Molten rock
28 Foul-smelling
29 Attics, often
30 Bona fide
31 Music-score marking
33 Location
34 All finished
37 Reverberate
39 Some tunas
41 Do newspaper work
42 Passport stamp
48 Greek letters
50 Author __ Stanley Gardner
52 Not completed, as obligations
53 Kind of checking account
54 Craving
55 Horse-stopping exclamation
57 Not quite shut
58 *Chicago* actor
60 Right-hand person: Abbr.
61 Medicinal amount
62 Winter forecast
64 Exist
65 Brief craze

★ Number-Out

Shade squares so that no number appears in any row or column more than once. Shaded squares may not touch each other horizontally or vertically, and all unshaded squares must form a single continuous area.

5	3	1	2	1
4	4	2	3	2
1	3	2	4	4
3	2	2	5	4
3	5	4	1	4

OPPOSITE ATTRACTION

Unscramble the letters in the phrase SLY BLUE to form two common words that are opposites of each other. Example: The letters in SLED INFO can be rearranged to spell FIND and LOSE.

_____   _____

★ Straight Ahead

Enter the grid; pass through all of the blue squares, then exit. You must travel horizontally or vertically in a straight line, and turn only to avoid passing through a black square. It is okay to retrace your path.

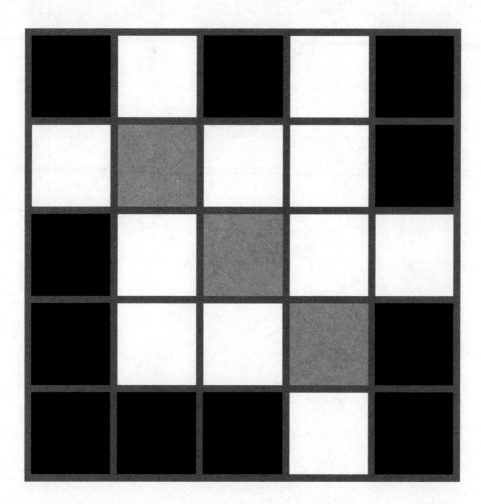

THREE AT A RHYME

Rearrange these letters to form three one-syllable words that rhyme.
Example: A A A B C E K S W X X = AXE, BACKS, WAX

E E L O O O T W

_____ _____ _____

★ Wraparounds by Gail Grabowski

ACROSS

1 Sharif of film
5 In the neighborhood
10 Con game
14 Broad valley
15 Nonpoetic writing
16 Soft drink
17 Versatile musician
19 Highways: Abbr.
20 Pose again
21 Editor's notation
22 Draw with acid
23 Cry audibly
25 Wild West show
27 Some TV anchors
31 __ tube (tire part)
34 Boxer nicknamed "The Greatest"
35 Place of worship
39 Stinging insect
40 __ Tin Tin
41 Like a bright evening sky
42 Before, in poems
43 Massachusetts fish
44 Human being
45 Coffee-to-go topper
46 Piece of gravel
48 Small sizes
51 Cake serving
54 VCR button
55 Bothersome one
57 Swiss peaks
60 Question again
64 Jump
65 County-fair prize
67 *Born Free* lioness
68 Fall zodiac sign
69 Hand-cream ingredient
70 Very pale
71 High-school composition
72 Hackman of Hollywood

DOWN

1 Scent
2 Horse's hair
3 Stein fillers
4 Negligent
5 Hosp. employee
6 Spheres
7 Parka, for one
8 *Lou Grant* actor
9 Resulted in
10 Storm-door insert
11 Southern region
12 Actor Baldwin
13 Prepare, as potatoes
18 Molecule part

24 Singer Midler
26 Cut calories
27 DEA agents
28 Writer T.S.
29 Frame holding a pane
30 Within reach
32 Spooky
33 Marsh growths
36 "Is it Miss or __?"
37 Raindrop sound
38 Cruise ship
41 Went fast
47 Employee check amount

49 Actress Garr
50 Sore-ankle soother
52 *Gone With the Wind* actor
53 Immigration island
55 Not guilty, for one
56 Snakelike swimmers
58 Taverns
59 Blood components
61 Competent
62 Part of ASAP
63 Leg joint
66 Bit of sun

★ One-Way Streets

The diagram represents a pattern of streets. A and B are parking spaces, and the black squares are stores. Find the route that starts at A, passes through all stores exactly once, and ends at B. Arrows indicate one-way traffic for that block only. No block or intersection may be entered more than once.

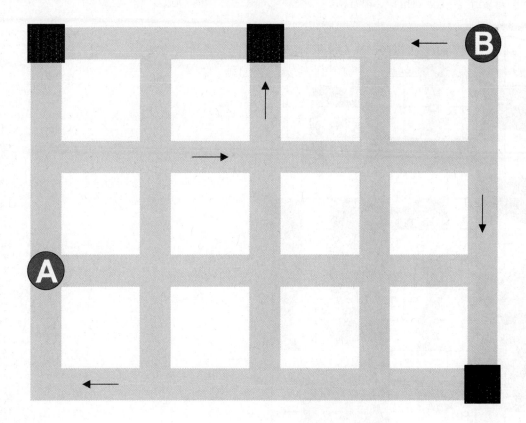

SOUND THINKING

There are two common uncapitalized words whose only consonant sounds are S, N, B, R, and D, in that order. SIGNBOARD is one of them. What's the other?

_____

★★ Split Decisions

In this clueless crossword puzzle, each answer consists of two words whose spellings are the same, except for the consecutive letters given. All answers are common words; no phrases or hyphenated or capitalized words are used. Some of the clues may have more than one solution, but there is only one word pair that will correctly link up with all the other word pairs.

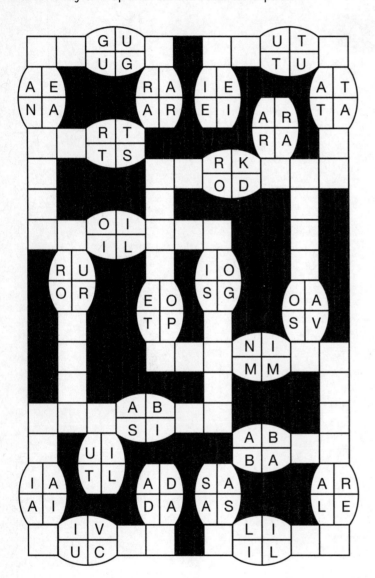

TRANSDELETION

Delete one letter from the word IRREVERENT and rearrange the rest, to get a type of popular pet.

★ Star Search

Find the stars that are hidden in some of the blank squares. The numbered squares indicate how many stars are hidden in the squares adjacent to them (including diagonally). There is never more than one star in any square.

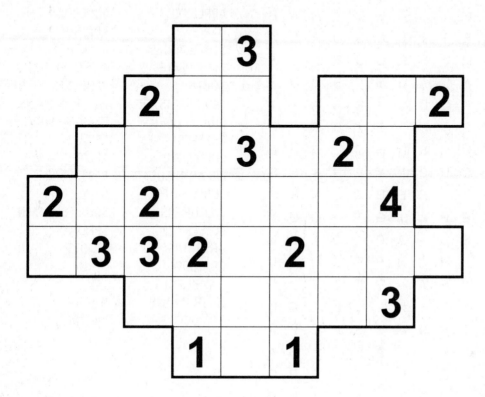

TELEPHONE TRIOS

Using the numbers and letters on a standard telephone, what three seven-letter words or phrases from the same category can be formed from these telephone numbers?

332-8779   _ _ _ _ _ _ _

782-2464   _ _ _ _ _ _ _

787-2877   _ _ _ _ _ _ _

★ At the Diner

Find these words associated with diners that are hidden in the diagram, either across, down, or diagonally.

```
C A S H R E G I S T E C T G W B
I S I L E R E F I L L S O A L W
R A G U S N M A E R C D F U G A
F P A N C A K E A U T F E P D I
Y T I U T A R G B O L B S A X T
V Q X S G T S I H E E Z B R O R
C A M B N F R H S R H B I K B E
T U R I S I C U R L Y F R I E S
A S T I L P K I E E B A J N K S
M T R L W K E P W I G T B G U Y
T O P E E S S C A A P I O L J R
O O R U M R L H I N F E S O S U
P L T A H O Y E A A R F L T B Q
E S B A R C T E Y K L E L P E D
E Y S D R A T S U M E S P E P R
F S N I K S J E U T A E E A B A
F X W R T O O B K C A T B S P O
O S O D A F O U N T A I N I K B
C E R O D O L R N L L I F E R K
S R B Z T K E G P X K P P E M L
K T H H U L R E G R U B M A H A
I I S H I R U R E R U O D T O H
N A A S S L Y H Y V E L T U C C
O W H P B W G S P A N C A K E S
```

APPLE PIE
BAR
BLUEBERRIES
BLUE PLATE
BOOTH
CASH REGISTER
CHALKBOARD
CHEESEBURGER
COFFEE POT
CREAM N SUGAR
CURLY FRIES
CUSTOMERS
CUTLERY
GHERKINS
GRATUITY
HAMBURGER
HASH BROWNS
HOT DOG

JUKEBOX
KETCHUP
MILKSHAKE
MUSTARD
PANCAKES
PAPER NAPKINS
PARKING LOT
REFILLS
RELISH
RIBS
SKINS
SODA FOUNTAIN
SPECIALS
STOOLS
SYRUP
TAX
WAFFLES
WAITRESS

IN OTHER WORDS

There is only one common uncapitalized word that contains the consecutive letters WTS. What is it?

———————————————————

★ Be Quick by Gail Grabowski

ACROSS

1 Metal corrosion
5 Air-traffic controller's device
10 Psychic reader
14 Prefix meaning "against"
15 Get away from
16 Heavenly headwear
17 Guys-only party
18 Some dress sizes
19 Desertlike
20 Hurry
22 Leg joint
23 Slow down, as rainfall
24 Small taste
26 Church-tower feature
29 Wandered around
33 Sharp taste
37 Start a card game
39 San Antonio shrine
40 Standoffish
42 *Much __ About Nothing*
43 Jeans fabric
44 Sheriff's group
45 At a snail's pace
47 Richard of *Chicago*
48 Fretted
50 Sporting sword
52 Checklist line
54 "Am not!" response
58 Wild canine
61 Hurry
65 Landed (on)
66 Dickens' Heep
67 __ Lee (cake company)
68 Fishing-rod attachment
69 Washer cycle
70 Chapters of history
71 Small bouquet
72 Enthusiastic
73 Not as much

DOWN

1 Poison-ivy reaction
2 "__ we meet again"
3 Performer's platform
4 Too small, as clothing
5 Recorded again
6 Jai __
7 Boring
8 Stray from the script
9 Mix the soup again
10 Hurry
11 Get, as a salary
12 Author Wiesel
13 Took the train
21 Place for a bath
25 Frog relative
27 Meadows
28 Soup server
30 Lion's hair
31 Middle East ruler
32 Round roof
33 Bugler's evening call
34 Tremendously
35 Facial feature
36 Hurry
38 Airshow stunt
41 Many inches
46 TV news segment
49 Bashful
51 Mess up
53 *Santa __* (ship of Columbus)
55 Artist's stand
56 Frighten
57 Gumbo veggies
58 Bend out of shape
59 Bread spread
60 Doesn't tell the truth
62 Princess' dad
63 Make simpler
64 Talk back to

★ Hyper-Sudoku

Fill in the blank boxes so that every row, column, 3x3 box, *and* each of the four 3x3 gray regions contains all of the numbers 1 to 9.

		1					7	9
						3	2	
5	9		1	3		6	4	
6	3						1	2
		7		5				6
1		9		6	2	7		
9		3	2	8	4	1		
2							8	
			9				3	

MIXAGRAMS

Each line contains a five-letter word and a four-letter word that have been mixed together (the order of the letters in each word has not been changed). Unmix the two words on each line and write them in the spaces provided. When you're done, find a two-part answer to the clue by reading down the letter columns in the answers.

CLUE: Risky investment

E N D J O E B Y T = _ _ _ _ _ + _ _ _ _

A R E U S M O K E = _ _ _ _ _ + _ _ _ _

M A M I N G N O D = _ _ _ _ _ + _ _ _ _

F R A U K D E E R = _ _ _ _ _ + _ _ _ _

★★ Close Shave

Which of the nine is the correct mirror image?

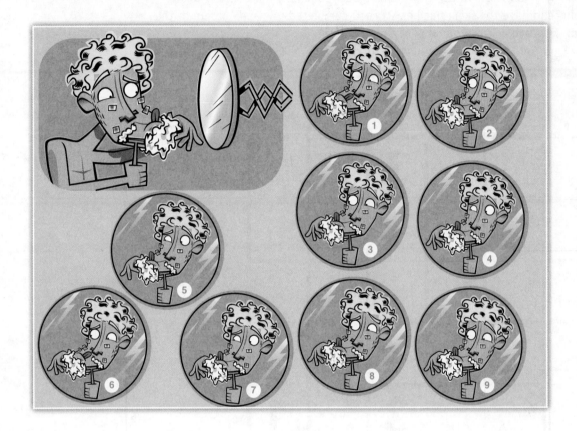

BETWEENER

What three-letter word belongs between the word at left and the word at right, so that the first and second word, and the second and third word, each form a common compound word?

FIRE __ __ __ CHAIR

★ 123

Fill in the diagram so that each rectangular piece has one each of the numbers 1, 2, and 3, under these rules: 1) No two adjacent squares, horizontally or vertically, can have the same number. 2) Each completed row and column of the diagram will have an equal number of 1s, 2s, and 3s.

			3		
	2			2	
			3		1

SUDOKU SUM

Without repeating any digits, complete the sum at right, by filling one digit in each of the five blanks.

```
    3  1  _
+   _  _  6
   _____
    _  _  5
```

★ Chophouse by Norma Steinberg

ACROSS

1 Identical
5 Belt site
10 Fat-free milk
14 "I cannot tell __"
15 Where to say "I do"
16 Stack
17 Unit of heredity
18 Hotelier Helmsley
19 Big-eyed birds
20 Circle segment
21 Breakfast pastry
23 Leave the office for a sec
25 School subj.
26 Takes the gold
27 Shields
32 Like a rock
34 Dog sounds
35 Tear apart
36 Add to the payroll
37 Part of a bookcase
38 A few
39 Unmatched, as a sock
40 Condition
41 Dealt (with)
42 Cakes and pies
44 Snitched
45 Split __ soup
46 All finished
49 Predictable
54 Caribbean, e.g.
55 Mimicked
56 Pulls from behind
57 Address abbr.
58 Auctioneer's call
59 Flood-control structure
60 Be in front
61 Finishes
62 Washstand pitchers
63 Music and the dance

DOWN

1 Heroic tales
2 Warning
3 Avoid speaking bluntly
4 Wide shoe
5 Tusked marine mammal
6 Native Alaskan
7 Take __ the chin
8 Of sound mind
9 Quid pro quo
10 Spill absorber
11 New Zealand bird
12 Troubles
13 Open fabric
21 Small horse
22 Cupboard invaders
24 Yearn (for)
27 Yeats and Keats
28 Dramatic part
29 Plane that sprays
30 Use a stopwatch
31 Hurried
32 Wearing sneakers
33 Ocean phenomenon
34 "Huh?"
37 Fence-sitter's position
38 By oneself
40 Perceived
41 Bundle binding
43 Card suit
44 Dissertations
46 Fierce feline
47 Imply
48 Rounds of applause
49 Parakeet's home
50 Fairy tale's second word
51 Be inclined (to)
52 Actress Barrymore
53 Rant and __
57 In the style of

★ ABC

Enter the letters A, B, and C into the diagram so that each row and column has exactly one A, one B, and one C. The letters outside the diagram indicate the first letter encountered, moving in the direction of the arrow. Keep in mind that after all the letters have been filled in, there will be one blank box in each row and column.

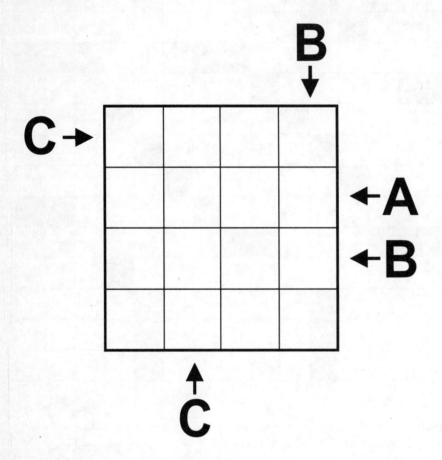

CLUELESS CROSSWORD

Complete the crossword with common uncapitalized seven-letter words, based entirely on the letters already filled in for you.

J	U		G			R
	■		■	U	■	
		I		R		P
T	■		■	K	■	
	V				V	
	■		■		■	S
S		E			H	S

★ Find the Ships

Determine the position of the 10 ships listed to the right of the diagram. The ships may be oriented either horizontally or vertically. A square with wavy lines indicates water and will not contain a ship. The numbers at the edge of the diagram indicate how many squares in that row or column contain parts of ships. When all 10 ships are correctly placed in the diagram, no two of them will touch each other, not even diagonally.

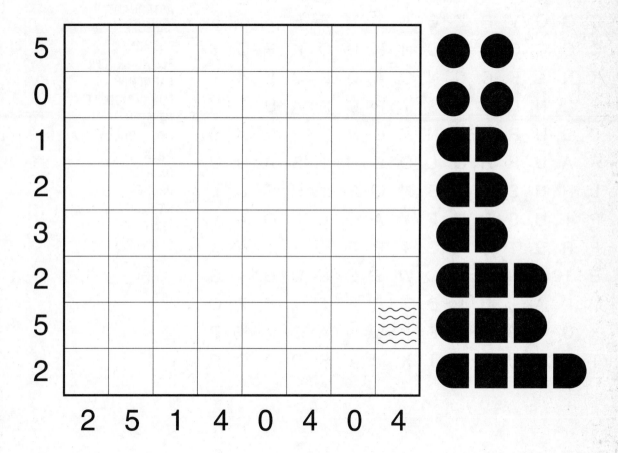

TWO-BY-FOUR

The eight letters in the word NOCTURNE can be rearranged to form a pair of common four-letter words in three different ways, if no four-letter word is repeated. Can you find all three pairs of words?

— — — —   — — — —   — — — —   — — — —

— — — —   — — — —

★ Taking Up Space

Find these terms associated with outer space that are hidden in the diagram, either across, down, or diagonally. (The individual words of all multiple-word answers are hidden separately.) There's one additional six-letter answer in the category, not listed below, that's also hidden in the diagram. What's that word?

```
R  M  N  A  S  A  U  R  S  E  U  D  U  M  F
O  O  G  V  P  Z  E  A  T  L  E  F  Z  O  L
C  O  C  O  A  H  U  H  F  U  O  K  F  O  Y
K  N  L  K  C  C  N  C  A  D  R  C  L  A  I
E  L  N  N  E  A  S  T  R  O  N  A  U  T  N
Q  L  U  R  S  T  N  H  C  M  E  P  N  A  G
S  A  U  R  H  O  L  O  E  U  T  S  A  U  U
L  H  N  S  I  U  S  N  C  C  I  U  S  J  L
P  I  U  S  P  M  F  Y  A  O  L  L  O  P  A
F  R  S  T  O  A  G  T  P  F  L  Y  I  N  J
E  I  O  N  T  G  C  W  S  O  E  C  U  A  S
M  P  A  B  U  L  D  T  R  E  T  I  B  R  O
X  U  Y  B  E  Y  E  L  U  N  A  S  M  N  B
T  S  P  U  T  N  I  K  M  I  S  S  I  O  R
```

APOLLO
ASTRONAUT
CAPSULE
COSMONAUT
FLYING SAUCER
LAUNCHER
LUNAR MODULE
MISSION
MOON BUGGY
NASA
ORBITER
PROBE
SATELLITE
SHUTTLE
SPACECRAFT
SPACESHIP
SPUTNIK
UFO

INITIAL REACTION

Identify the well-known proverb from the first letters in each of its words.

G. M. T. A. _____

★ Marching Along by Sally R. Stein

ACROSS

1 Bullets, for example
5 Seep
9 Better qualified
14 __ in the neck (pest)
15 Army group
16 Feeling of accomplishment
17 Mom's sister
18 Army-camp structure
19 Prepared for a photo
20 Drill sergeant's command
22 Gives temporarily
23 Spruce up prose
24 Sturdy tree
25 In the center of
28 Rights org.
30 Actor's negotiator: Abbr.
33 Crooner Perry
34 Whole bunch
35 Install, as carpet
36 Drill sergeant's phrase
40 Compass pt.
41 Poet T.S.
42 Cry of dread
43 Gateway Arch city: Abbr.
44 Prefix for nautical
45 Gem measures
47 Money player
48 Alphabetize
49 Mrs. George W. Bush
52 Drill sergeant's command
57 One-way sign
58 Sandwich cookie
59 Singer Fitzgerald
60 Pebbles Flintstone's mom
61 Pots' partners
62 Hog food
63 Impudent

64 Vending-machine opening
65 Looks at

DOWN

1 On __ with (equivalent to)
2 Hawaiian island
3 __ vase (Chinese collectible)
4 Precisely
5 Clothing ensemble
6 __ a time (individually)
7 Metal in pennies
8 Diminutive ending
9 Sign of audience approval
10 "Babbling" water
11 The Simpsons girl
12 Biblical paradise
13 Cherry and carmine
21 NFL six-pointers
24 Ye __ Shoppe
25 Charley horses
26 Everest or McKinley
27 Drive forward
28 Sound of a sneeze
29 Golf vehicle
30 2 Down welcome
31 Too skinny
32 Beginners

34 Recipe direction
37 Erode
38 Butter substitute
39 Defensive structure
45 Talk-show associate
46 Exist
47 High-school dances
48 Shorthand expert
49 Attorney's expertise
50 Opera solo
51 Internet addresses, for short
52 Spinning toys
53 Kind of vaccine
54 Fashion magazine
55 Spiny houseplant
56 Strikes sharply

★ Go With the Flow

Enter the maze, pass through all the yellow circles exactly once, and then exit.
You must go with the flow, making no sharp turns, and you may use paths more
than once.

THREE AT A RHYME

Rearrange these letters to form three one-syllable words that rhyme.

A E E E E F R T W

_____   _____   _____

★ Fences

Connect the dots with vertical or horizontal lines, so that a single loop is formed with no crossings or branches. Each number indicates how many lines surround it; squares with no number may be surrounded by any number of lines.

```
0 2       3

          3 2 3 2
                  3

  1 3 2       2
    2     3 0 3
1
2 1 3 3
        1       3 3
```

ADDITION SWITCH

Switch the positions of two of the digits in the incorrect sum at right, to get a correct sum.

```
  6 0 8
+ 1 9 0
-------
  7 1 7
```

★ Outdoor Cooking

Find these terms associated with outdoor cooking that are hidden in the diagram, either across, down, or diagonally. (The individual words of all multiple-word answers are hidden separately.) There's one additional eight-letter answer in the category, not listed below, that's also hidden in the diagram. What's that word?

```
B S B I R O I T A P S S F O N Y C
E R S O O T C O V A C I A E I H E
R U I S E G A S U A S A D U A I M
A T L Q H O F C E H N R R R C E B
P E R T U O I G W R A O C V K E E
S N E E R E N S E G F O R O I O R
K S D K W I T T U E A L M P I N S
E I A E L E O T C L U S A G A F G
B L N L F N K W E O U T D O O R S
A S I O G I O S B S E C I P S K K
B R R S I L N Z R C H I C K E N R
G D A C G L S K A E T S X N O T O
Q M M C H O P S B A R B E C U P P
```

ALFRESCO
APRON
BRIQUETTES
CARVING
CHARCOAL
CHICKEN
EMBERS
FISH
FORK
GARDEN
GLOW
GRILLING
KEBAB
KNIFE
MARINADE

OIL
OUTDOORS
PATIO
PORK CHOPS
SAUCE
SAUSAGES
SKEWER
SMOKE
SOOT
SPARE RIBS
SPICES
STEAKS
TONGS
UTENSILS

WHO'S WHAT WHERE?

The correct term for a resident of the African nation of Swaziland is:

A) Swazilander
B) Swazilian
C) Swazi
D) Swazilese

★ Washday Woes by Gail Grabowski

ACROSS

1 Hasty escapes
5 Pretzel covering
9 Shopping center
13 Toledo's lake
14 On the ocean
15 *Star Wars* weapon
16 First-class
17 Sits in the sun
18 Get out of bed
19 Fruit-tree protector
21 Glide on ice
22 Bother
23 Sunrise direction
25 Football positions
28 After-bath application
32 Wear away
36 Hotel price
38 German automaker
39 Long skirt
40 Dinner course
41 Rural stopovers
42 Hardly __ (rarely)
43 Army offense: Abbr.
44 Move stealthily
45 Video-store offering
47 March Madness org.
49 Nile queen, for short
51 Purple flowers
56 Like a gymnast
59 Stage lamp
62 Theater employee
63 Sugar shape
64 Diva's performance
65 Football-shoe feature
66 Part of U.S.A.
67 Depend (on)
68 Hang onto
69 Sunbeams
70 Dates regularly

DOWN

1 Dog walker's gear
2 Pleasant scent
3 Arithmetic sign
4 Watermelon throwaways
5 Glossy fabric
6 Pronto, in memos
7 Former Tonight Show host
8 Take a bite of
9 Tom Sawyer's creator
10 China's continent
11 Remainder
12 Family diagram
15 Rodeo rope
20 Joy
24 Acted like
26 Make a sketch
27 Hair stylist's shop
29 Sandy hill
30 Author Ferber
31 Hazard
32 Part of EMT: Abbr.
33 Speak wildly
34 Yoked animals
35 Very inexpensive
37 After-bath application
40 After-Christmas event
44 Go yachting
46 Watchful
48 Changes, as a hemline
50 Hollywood award
52 Deceitful ones
53 Come to the same conclusion
54 Argentina neighbor
55 Hangs around
56 Good fortune
57 Spot in the ocean
58 You, Biblically
60 Mountain lion
61 Follow orders

★ Sudoku

Fill in the blank boxes so that every row, column, and 3x3 box contains all of the numbers 1 to 9.

8	2							
	4		1	9			2	
1			3		6			
	9	5		3		2		
	2		4	6	5		1	
		6		8		7	5	
			2		9			8
	6			7	4		3	
						1		9

MIXAGRAMS

Each line contains a five-letter word and a four-letter word that have been mixed together (the order of the letters in each word has not been changed). Unmix the two words on each line and write them in the spaces provided. When you're done, find a two-part answer to the clue by reading down the letter columns in the answers.

CLUE: They may be sown

S A W N O R D O N = _ _ _ _ _ + _ _ _ _

V I S T A W A L T = _ _ _ _ _ + _ _ _ _

F O A L T O H U R = _ _ _ _ _ + _ _ _ _

A M D I S A T G E = _ _ _ _ _ + _ _ _ _

★ 123

Fill in the diagram so that each rectangular piece has one each of the numbers 1, 2, and 3, under these rules: 1) No two adjacent squares, horizontally or vertically, can have the same number. 2) Each completed row and column of the diagram will have an equal number of 1s, 2s, and 3s.

					3
3			2		
			3		
	3				

SUDOKU SUM

Without repeating any digits, complete the sum at right, by filling one digit in each of the five blanks.

```
   2 _ _
 + _ 7 9
 -------
   _ _ 5
```

★ Water Carriers by Gail Grabowski

ACROSS

1 Location
5 Antlered animal
10 Omelet ingredients
14 Sweater material
15 Singer Baker
16 Humdinger
17 Molecule part
18 Floor installer
19 List entry
20 Type of stockings
22 Casts a ballot
23 Destroy
24 Table-setting part
26 File-folder attachments
29 __ *Misérables*
30 Kitchens and parlors: Abbr.
33 See eye to eye
34 Actor Hackman
35 Scrooge's cross word
36 Espionage org.
37 Gather up
39 Chimp, for one
40 Inventor Whitney
41 Spring flower
42 Oscar winner Berry
44 Bear's abode
45 Bro's kin
46 BB, for one
47 Homeowners' documents
49 Aquatic mammal
50 Not wordy
52 Pie-in-the-sky hope
57 Tax-deferred accts.
58 Olympic award
59 The Emerald __ (Ireland)
60 Director Kazan
61 Kukla and Fran's friend
62 Name for a Dalmatian
63 Declare untrue

64 Mix together
65 Optometrist's concerns

DOWN

1 Make a trade
2 Small amount
3 Roger Rabbit, e.g.
4 Shade provider
5 "Chances Are" singer Johnny
6 Burger topping
7 Lubricates
8 Church spires
9 Corn portion
10 T-man Ness
11 Bowling error
12 Happiness
13 Addition answers
21 Christmas season
22 Florist's vessel
25 Camera part
26 Secured, as a skate
27 Nimble
28 Loss of skilled personnel
31 Syrup source
32 Piece of bedding
34 Tank filler
37 Desertlike
38 Write "recieve"
41 "Now it's clear!"

42 Lettuce unit
43 Courtroom directive
46 Prepared, as potatoes
48 High-school composition
49 Portugal neighbor
50 Not winning or losing
51 __ Stanley Gardner
53 Just sitting around
54 Catch sight of
55 Hand-cream ingredient
56 Citi Field players
58 Disorderly crowd

★ One-Way Streets

The diagram represents a pattern of streets. A and B are parking spaces, and the black squares are stores. Find the route that starts at A, passes through all stores exactly once, and ends at B. Arrows indicate one-way traffic for that block only. No block or intersection may be entered more than once.

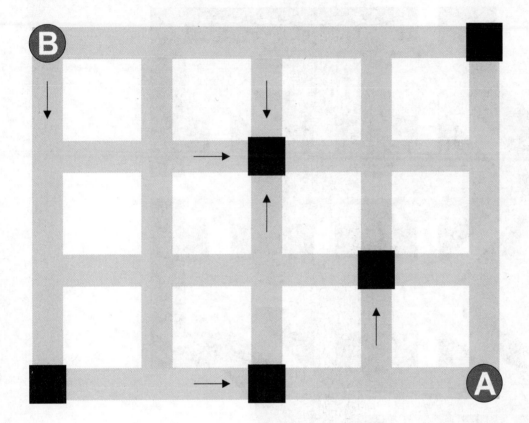

SOUND THINKING

There is only one common uncapitalized word whose only consonant sounds are Z, K, and N, in that order. What is it?

_____

★ No Three in a Row

Enter the maze, pass through all the squares exactly once, and then exit, all without retracing your path. You may not pass through three squares of the same color consecutively.

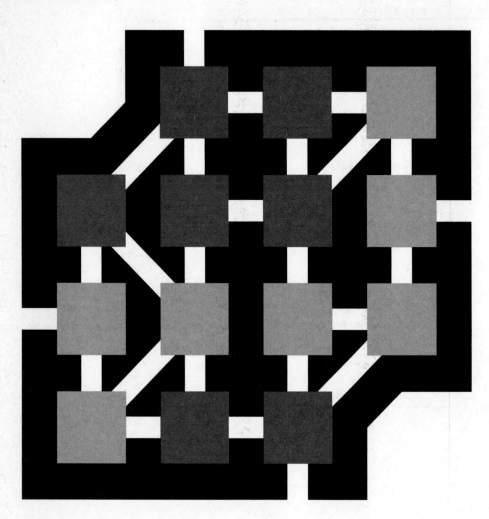

SAY IT AGAIN

What three-letter word seen on theater tickets, when pronounced differently, is also a word meaning "quarrel"?

— — —

★ Star Search

Find the stars that are hidden in some of the blank squares. The numbered squares indicate how many stars are hidden in the squares adjacent to them (including diagonally). There is never more than one star in any square.

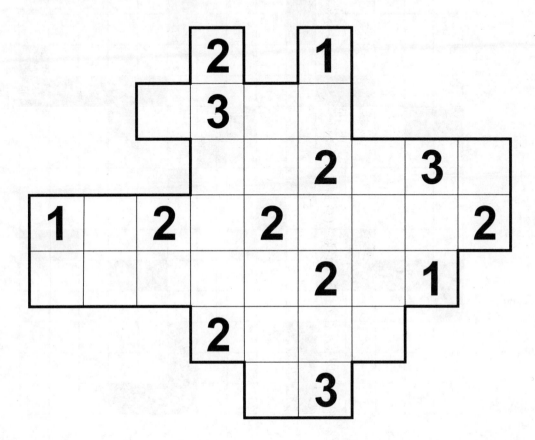

TELEPHONE TRIOS

1	ABC 2	DEF 3
GHI 4	JKL 5	MNO 6
PRS 7	TUV 8	WXY 9
*	0	#

Using the numbers and letters on a standard telephone, what three seven-letter words or phrases from the same category can be formed from these telephone numbers?

338-6833　　_ _ _ _ _ _ _

327-6378　　_ _ _ _ _ _ _

746-2373　　_ _ _ _ _ _ _

★ Easy As Pie by Sally R. Stein

ACROSS

1 Conclude
4 Music disks before CDs
7 Cat sounds
12 Shake out of slumber
15 Wide shoe
16 Any '50s tune
17 Preface, for short
18 Tic-___-toe
19 Unaccompanied
20 Pie flavor
23 Fireplace residue
24 Plaintiffs
25 Ancient Mexican
28 Sci-fi creatures: Abbr.
30 Bikini part
33 Calmed
36 Obtained illegally
38 Himalayan nation
39 Respectful title
41 Halt, at sea
42 Betray
44 Pays no attention to
46 Before, in poems
47 After taxes
49 Store employee
50 ___ Antoinette
52 Fam. member
55 Pie flavor
61 Caribbean island
62 Ecology agcy.
63 Sad song
64 Unconfirmed report
65 Zero
66 Actress Sophia
67 Kick out
68 Quarterback stats.
69 Fractions of a mi.

DOWN

1 Author Jong
2 They're taboo
3 Pie flavor
4 Iceberg and romaine
5 United Nations goal
6 Make safe
7 Castle surrounder
8 Singer Fitzgerald
9 Limburger feature
10 Kite mover
11 Get the point of
13 Sign of a hit show
14 Very long time

21 Puts to work
22 Former Mach 2 fliers: Abbr.
26 Enthusiasm
27 Eagle claw
29 No longer fresh
30 Pie flavor
31 Take a break
32 Colonizing insects
33 Poker starter
34 Jury member
35 Noise
37 Higher than
40 Music students' performances

43 Jules Verne captain
45 Happiness
48 Special skill
51 Quick
53 Acted angry
54 Signs of the future
55 Main point
56 Camel feature
57 Woodwind instrument
58 Poet Sandburg
59 450, in old Rome
60 River, to Ricardo
61 "___ we there yet?"

★ Mythically Speaking

Find these characters from Greek mythology that are hidden in the diagram, either across, down, or diagonally.

```
B P X L P S E A N S A R P E D O N N A N O
A R O J A N U E R H I P S U S E O R C P S
E I I T T W S H O T N G S C L E I K R U V
O E R T R T U S T G E Y P L A A U O E K F
R L E A O Q H K N N G M E A D M M R I O S
U E P R C M C I E L I H I N N E A N O U I
E C Y Z L A A N M R H C E S T D A N E P S
P T H E U P M R O Y P T A H N R O S D E A
P R V P S A E U T I I H E Y T I R R L E R
I A C H I L L E S I R U T S H E K C A E R
S A K Y S L E T X P S E E U P H O T T P N
Y P I R U A T I O V O N P B C M E E A I P
L S E L L K E L C O M A D Y A S M L K E I
P Y G M A L I O N E C W S D H E F A R I I
N I K R D T G P T H I P P O D A M I A O N
T H E S E S S Y A I E P O I S S A C B P N
Q E D N A E L A X E P O S I B N Z A L O S
R Z Z J D C W M C H E E B U D Y T E I S U
E C Y L A P R A H C R D N E S E Q L M E S
G A L A T E A D I A S I R H S S A K E I S
A N D R O M E D A M E P L T P C I X H D O
S P C N H P A D B O P U I A U A Z C T O L
E E H M H Q I A W R H S J E X G D G R N O
T H D R J A S T E D O D D N A A A C U A M
I C I F O S G P T N N A I N O M R A H O N
L Y O S A D O A T A E L Y W R E D N A E L
O S M R U L I E M K C M H S I M E H T P U
P P E P E R L T J E E U A R D N A S S A C
M U D N P A O R E D D A S F R O L E P L V
S T E F M D Z L E E B E O H P N U D H L N
S P S O S U E S E H T G S P H A E D R A M
C Y N O C Y C L O P S E L E N E B E S S P
```

ACHILLES
AGAMEDES
AGAMEMNON
ANDROMACHE
ANDROMEDA
APHRODITE
ARIADNE
ARTEMIS
BASSAREUS
BRITOMARTIS
CASSANDRA
CASSIOPEIA
CASTALIA
CLYTEMNESTRA
CROESUS
CYCLOPS
DAEDALUS
DAMOCLES
DAPHNE
DEMETER
DEUCALION
DIOMEDES
ELECTRA
EUROPA
GALATEA
GANYMEDE
HARMONIA
HARPALYCE
HELLEN
HIPPODAMIA
HYACINTHUS
HYPERION
IOBATES
IPHIGENIA
LEANDER
LYSIPPE
MACARIA
MENTOR
MOLOSSUS
NARCISSUS
NESTOR
NIKE
OEDIPUS
PALLAS
PANDORA
PATROCLUS
PELORUS
PENELOPE
PERIANDER
PERSEPHONE
PERSEUS
PHAEDRA
PHOEBE
PITTACUS
POLITES
POSEIDON
PROMETHEUS
PSYCHE
PYGMALION
SARPEDON
SCAMANDER
SELENE
TELAMON
TELEMACHUS
THEMIS
THESEUS
TYNDAREUS
ZEPHYR

IN OTHER WORDS

There is only one common uncapitalized word that contains the consecutive letters SSK. What is it?

_____

bRain BREatHER
ENERGY CONSERVATION MYTHS DEFLATED

We're becoming more and more aware of the importance of energy conservation but sometimes it's hard to tell what's fact and what's fiction. Here are four widely touted energy-saving myths that you should know the full facts about:

Programmable thermostats save you money Well, they actually do—but only if you program them for savings. Many people mistakenly think that the computer-chip-driven electronic devices *automatically* calculate efficient temperatures. But they don't. You must program them to lower the thermostat temperature—at night when you're asleep or during the day when you're at work, or in whatever way fits your schedule. Do that, and you'll save an average of 15 percent on your monthly bills.

It takes more energy to turn a computer on than to let it idle This may be true with a car (it depends on how long you idle it), but it's certainly not true with a computer. For the biggest energy savings, shut your computer off at night or when you'll be away from it for a long period of time. As an alternative, choose an energy-saving mode. Go into your operating system software's control panel and explore your computer's power management options. For example, setting your computer to go into "standby" mode ("sleep" for a Mac) after a set amount of time significantly cuts down on the energy it uses; choosing "hibernate" reduces energy use even further.

Computer screen savers save energy Screen savers prolong the life of your monitor by displaying a moving image to prevent a fixed image from being burned into the phosphor of the screen. But they do nothing to save power. Instead, they burn up electricity. To make your computer as energy-efficient as possible, see the item above.

Ceiling fans cool a room They don't cool the room, but they do cool the people in it by creating a wind-chill effect on the skin. That's a good thing, because it allows you to raise the temperature of your air conditioner thermostat or turn the AC off altogether. But where people go wrong is leaving those fans on when they leave the room. Instead, treat the fan like a light and turn it off. Otherwise, it will waste electricity.

★★ Line Drawing

Draw two straight lines, each from one edge of the square to another edge, so that the total of the numbers in each of the four regions is the same.

2

4

2

3

6

1

2

2

1

3

10

2

1   1

THREE OF A KIND

Find the three hidden words in the sentence that, read in order, go together in some way.

In football, overtime will extend erratic play.

★ ABC

Enter the letters A, B, and C into the diagram so that each row and column has exactly one A, one B, and one C. The letters outside the diagram indicate the first letter encountered, moving in the direction of the arrow. Keep in mind that after all the letters have been filled in, there will be one blank box in each row and column.

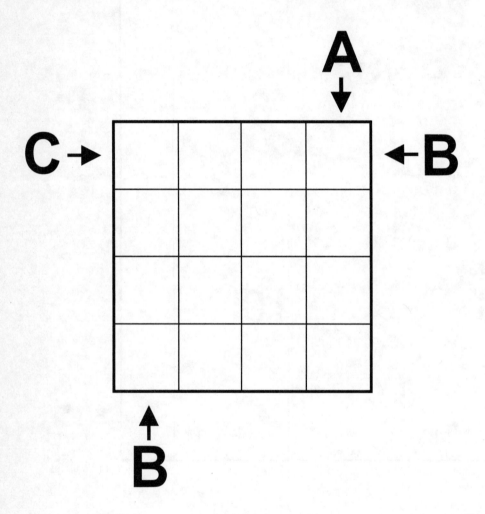

NATIONAL TREASURE

Rearrange the letters in GERMANY to get the first and last names of a well-known actress.

_____

★ Go West by Sally R. Stein

ACROSS

1 Sloppy situation
5 Dutch cheese
9 Dressed (in)
13 Supply-and-demand sci.
14 Pleasant
15 Make angry
16 "Get lost!"
17 Shaker contents
18 Type of exam
19 Aloha State city
22 "The Raven" writer
23 Peculiar
24 Leaves the path
28 Walk through water
30 Commercial-free TV network
33 Pigeon sounds
34 Internet auction site
36 Once more
38 Last Frontier city
41 Spoken for
42 Minus
43 Short distance
44 Cunning
45 Slippery fish
47 Comes to a point
49 America's Uncle
50 Sty dweller
51 Beaver State city
59 Woodwind instrument
60 Promissory notes
61 Slangy refusal
62 St. __ (city near Tampa)
63 Canoeing locale
64 Maple or mahogany
65 Looked at
66 Backyard building
67 Mail off

DOWN

1 Fly-swatter material
2 Sonic bounce
3 Any day now
4 *Peanuts* dog
5 Come next
6 Dashboard gauge
7 Rights org.
8 Procedure
9 Bunch of people
10 Former Italian money
11 Jai __
12 Local food shop
20 Last-place finisher
21 *Let's Make* __ (game-show oldie)
24 Hurries away
25 Melodic
26 Stallone's boxer role
27 Arthur of tennis
28 Salaries
29 Affirmative votes
30 Scrapbooker's adhesive
31 Motorcycle owner
32 Breaks suddenly
35 Sphere
37 Sound of fright
39 Basketball star Shaquille
40 Up and about
46 Computer messages
48 Authors' representatives
49 War horse
50 Masqueraded (as)
51 __ Benedict XVI
52 Do as told
53 Repetitive learning method
54 Ark builder
55 British noble
56 Clinton's vice president
57 Unwrap
58 Have to have

★★ Digital Display

Which of the numbered fingerprints matches each of the fingertips?

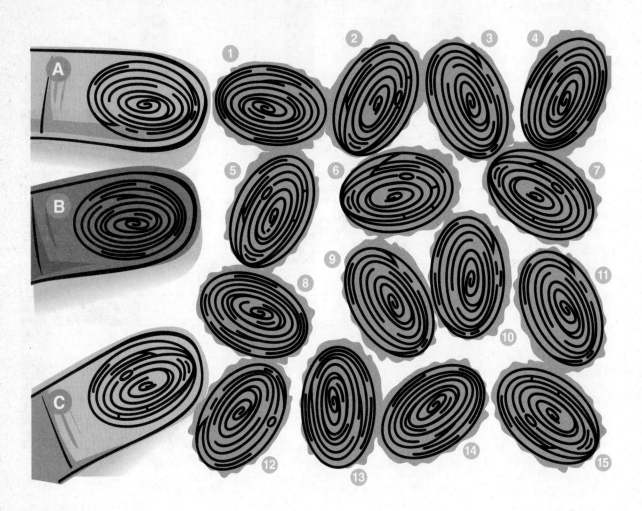

BETWEENER

What three-letter word belongs between the word at left and the word at right, so that the first and second word, and the second and third word, each form a common compound word?

DAY __ __ __ SPREAD

★★ Far From Forward

Try to find these "unbold" adjectives that are hidden in the diagram, either across, down, or diagonally, and you'll find that one of them has quietly slipped away. What's the missing word?

```
U  M  D  R  D  U  G  N  I  R  I  T  E  R  E
N  O  M  E  E  P  N  M  U  E  I  U  Q  L  C
S  D  T  B  R  N  O  S  V  Y  R  I  B  A  L
O  E  N  Z  A  U  E  I  O  N  T  M  U  D  U
C  S  A  J  S  S  S  R  X  C  U  T  C  I  F
I  T  T  Y  M  U  H  S  V  H  I  V  O  M  H
A  F  I  H  L  W  R  F  A  O  Q  A  C  I  S
H  H  S  C  O  O  I  H  U  N  U  U  L  T  A
M  E  E  K  T  C  N  S  I  A  U  S  I  M  B
S  R  H  M  K  E  K  R  E  S  E  R  V  E  D
C  C  T  N  E  C  I  T  E  R  B  Y  W  E  W
M  O  D  E  O  T  N  U  O  S  R  S  A  S  M
S  G  Y  V  E  O  G  E  Q  A  A  H  R  H  I
F  E  A  R  F  U  L  D  W  A  W  Y  L  Q  T
```

BASHFUL
CAUTIOUS
COY
FEARFUL
HESITANT
HUMBLE
MEEK
MODEST
MOUSY
NERVOUS
QUIET
RECLUSIVE
RESERVED
RETICENT
RETIRING
SHEEPISH
SHRINKING
SHY
TIMID
UNASSURED
UNSOCIAL
WARY

INITIAL REACTION

Identify the well-known proverb from the first letters in each of its words.

T. N. P. L. H. _____

★ Find the Ships

Determine the position of the 10 ships listed to the right of the diagram. The ships may be oriented either horizontally or vertically. A square with wavy lines indicates water and will not contain a ship. The numbers at the edge of the diagram indicate how many squares in that row or column contain parts of ships. When all 10 ships are correctly placed in the diagram, no two of them will touch each other, not even diagonally.

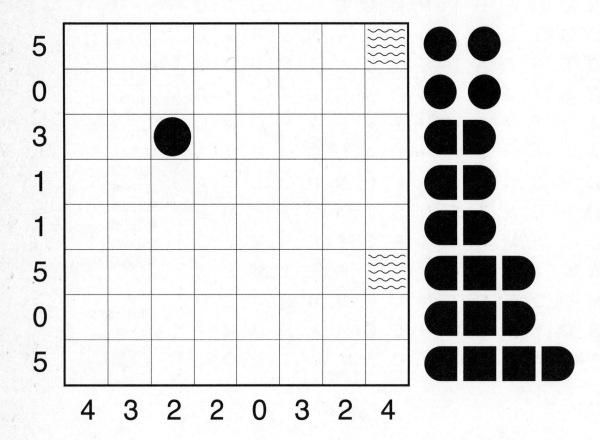

TWO-BY-FOUR

The eight letters in the word ORGANIZE can be rearranged to form a pair of common four-letter words in two different ways. Can you find both pairs of words?

_ _ _ _   _ _ _ _

_ _ _ _   _ _ _ _

★★ Sudoku

Fill in the blank boxes so that every row, column, and 3x3 box contains all of the numbers 1 to 9.

	2						1	
3	5		7		6		9	
	6		1		4	7		
	6		3		7			
	5		4	8	7		6	
	4			2		8		
	8		2		5	9		
7	9		1		4		2	
	4					8		

MIXAGRAMS

Each line contains a five-letter word and a four-letter word that have been mixed together (the order of the letters in each word has not been changed). Unmix the two words on each line and write them in the spaces provided. When you're done, find a two-part answer to the clue by reading down the letter columns in the answers.

CLUE: Oldster of song

S A G M I L U G E = _ _ _ _ _ + _ _ _ _

L A B R U V I N A = _ _ _ _ _ + _ _ _ _

A P A R T I S A Y = _ _ _ _ _ + _ _ _ _

B R E Y E L F A W = _ _ _ _ _ + _ _ _ _

★ Stunning by Gail Grabowski

ACROSS

1 Makes mistakes
5 Ascend, as a ladder
10 Short skirt
14 Gather, as crops
15 In a little while
16 Spring flower
17 Golda of Israel
18 Houston baseballer
19 Take it easy
20 Earthquake postscript
22 Leg joint
23 Prepare, as tea
24 Affirmative votes
26 Bumper mishap
29 Divide equally
33 Office aide: Abbr.
37 Song for two
39 Eiffel Tower locale
40 Elevator alternative
42 Summer shirt
43 Cut corners
44 Phone answerer's word
45 Nylon problem
47 "Piece of cake!"
48 Fencing blades
49 Urban haze
51 Dread
54 Singer Midler
58 List-ending abbr.
61 Arkansas capital
65 Folk singer Guthrie
66 Like a lot
67 Jane in a Brontë novel
68 Change the style of, as a room
69 Earn
70 Person, place, or thing
71 Bartlett or Bosc
72 Black-and-white cookies

73 Do some housecleaning

DOWN

1 Author Bombeck
2 Coral structures
3 Singer Bonnie
4 Shopping binge
5 Held on to
6 Eyelid attachment
7 Leave __ Beaver
8 "Heavens to Betsy!"
9 Out of money
10 Soda-fountain drink
11 Golf club
12 Cairo's river
13 Spot in the ocean
21 Stop-sign color
25 Poisonous snakes
27 Cashews, e.g.
28 Most high schoolers
30 Opera highlight
31 Cup edges
32 Catch sight of
33 Tennis champ Arthur
34 Dance move
35 December 26th event
36 Kitchen surface, perhaps
38 Group of athletes
41 Valentine flower
46 Wine glasses
50 "Golly!"
52 Texas landmark
53 Passenger
55 Current fashion
56 "Happy Birthday __"
57 Hosiery colors
58 Marshal Wyatt
59 Oak or apple
60 Alan of M*A*S*H
62 Pulled apart
63 Threesome
64 Daily Planet reporter Clark

★ Fences

Connect the dots with vertical or horizontal lines, so that a single loop is formed with no crossings or branches. Each number indicates how many lines surround it; squares with no number may be surrounded by any number of lines.

```
3 2       2     2 2
                    1       2
1     2 3 1 1
    3                 2
    0                 3
        1 2 2 0     3
  2     3
  2 1   3       2 1
```

ADDITION SWITCH

Switch the positions of two of the digits in the incorrect sum at right, to get a correct sum.

```
  3 6 9
+ 6 3 1
───────
  9 1 2
```

★★ Triad Split Decisions

In this clueless crossword puzzle, each answer consists of two words whose spellings are the same, except for the consecutive letters given. All answers are common words; no phrases or hyphenated or capitalized words are used. Some of the clues may have more than one solution, but there is only one word pair that will correctly link up with all the other word pairs.

TRANSDELETION

Delete one letter from the word SPLINTERED and rearrange the rest, to get a term for someone in charge.

_____

★ 123

Fill in the diagram so that each rectangular piece has one each of the numbers 1, 2, and 3, under these rules: 1) No two adjacent squares, horizontally or vertically, can have the same number. 2) Each completed row and column of the diagram will have an equal number of 1s, 2s, and 3s.

3					2
			2		
1					3
		3			

SUDOKU SUM

Without repeating any digits, complete the sum at right, by filling one digit in each of the five blanks.

```
    _ _ _
  + 1 7 3
  ─────────
    5 _ _
```

★ All Eyes by Gail Grabowski

ACROSS

1 Talk back to
5 Eve's mate
9 Bird in a Poe poem
14 Camel's bulge
15 Sandwich shop
16 High-society group
17 Opera solo
18 Prayer ending
19 Paid out
20 Pouch in a vest
23 "As I __ saying ..."
24 Piece of paper
25 Drink noisily, as soup
27 Filled completely
30 Soup utensil
32 Everyone
35 *Wheel of Fortune* purchase
37 Life stories, briefly
39 Not tight
41 Pollution control org.
42 Heavy, as fog
43 "Cut it out!"
44 Nomad
46 Hot drink
47 Glide on the ice
50 IRS payments
52 Gather up
54 Window parts
57 Friend
59 Dry cleaner's solvent
63 Newspaper notices
65 Mortgage, for example
66 How some order steak
67 Type of 46 Across
68 Rural hotels
69 Border
70 Sword metal
71 Flood prevention structure
72 Gardener's purchase

DOWN

1 Playwright George Bernard
2 Subtle glows
3 Common surname
4 Parking-lot openings
5 Get comfortable with, as changes
6 Test-driven vehicle
7 Actor Baldwin
8 Fancy furs
9 Get some sleep
10 Swiss peak
11 Opinion
12 Sicilian volcano
13 Tennis-court dividers
21 Throw with force
22 Overhead trains
26 After-bath garment
28 Water pitcher
29 Train station
31 Facial feature
32 Capone and Pacino
33 Oodles
34 Dead ringer
36 Volcano outflow
38 Baltic or Bering
40 Computer junk mail
42 Sleep image
45 Cash outlay
48 Graduation-cap attachment
49 Sixth sense: Abbr.
51 Sleeper's sounds
53 Well-built
55 Escape from
56 Suit material
57 Bursts, as a balloon
58 Aid in a crime
60 Singer Braxton
61 Private or captain
62 Oboe insert
64 Foot part

★ Number-Out

Shade squares so that no number appears in any row or column more than once. Shaded squares may not touch each other horizontally or vertically, and all unshaded squares must form a single continuous area.

5	4	4	4	3
4	3	5	2	1
1	3	3	3	5
2	1	2	4	5
3	5	2	3	4

OPPOSITE ATTRACTION

Unscramble the letters in the phrase NEW SOIL to form two words that are opposites of each other.

_____   _____

★★ Round and Round

Enter the maze at bottom, pass through all spheres exactly once, and then exit.
You may not retrace your path.

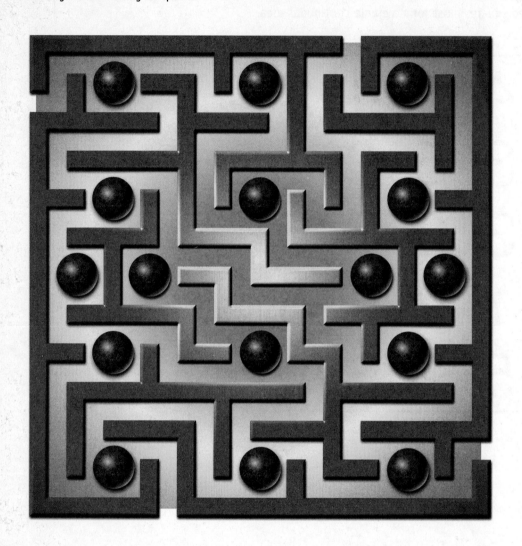

SAY IT AGAIN

What four-letter word for a type of singer, when pronounced differently, is also a type of fish?

— — — —

★ Fit

Find these words, all relating to various meanings of the title word
(including the title itself), that are hidden in the diagram, either across,
down, or diagonally.

```
P S A R E W R K C S P O R T T
R I P L E I E O H A L E W N R
E A I O G L M L E P A H S A I
P G T H R P E L L C Y M B V D
A I T N E T B V B S L D L E A
R L X T E A Y T A R U K A L P
E S E I P I R D C N C I H E E
D N O A F J D A I O S G T R R
T V C E M O S E L O H W H E P
H E A L T H Y R P F A T C T D
R I G H P R E T P X E O T O F
A T H L E T I C A F E N A N I
F Y T O N E Q M F I H E M E U
N N E I D E P X E T Z D A E R
```

AGILE
APPLICABLE
ATHLETIC
CAPABLE
COMPETENT
EXPEDIENT
FIT
HALE
HEALTHY
INTERLOCK
MATCH
PREPARED
READY
RELEVANT
RIGHT
SHAPE
SPORTY
TONED
TRIM
WELL-SUITED
WHOLESOME

WHO'S WHAT WHERE?

The correct term for a resident of the Mideast nation of Qatar is:

A) Qatarian   B) Qatari

C) Qatarer   D) Qatarite

★ Here, Kitty by Sally R. Stein

ACROSS

1 One-celled creature
6 Humorous poet Ogden
10 Web auction center
14 Sahara beast
15 Notion
16 __ of the above
17 Songbird sound
18 Fish's breathing organ
19 Smitten
20 Type of instant lottery ticket
22 Part of the eye
23 Inning enders
24 First stage
25 Talk nonsense
29 Small dog, familiarly
31 Andrew __ Webber
32 Sudden declines
37 *Gone With the Wind* mansion
38 Chicken throwaways
39 "Yikes!"
40 They winter in Florida
42 Ordinary language
43 Visibility problem
44 Reiterated, with "on"
45 Batman's sidekick
48 Top-billed performer
50 Former spouses
51 Carpentry tool
57 Swindle
58 Tube-shaped pasta
59 Distributed
60 Doing nothing
61 Hertz competitor
62 Author Zola
63 Bambi, for one
64 Monthly payment
65 Shoe bottoms

DOWN

1 Parts of a play
2 __ Antony
3 Ruler of Kuwait
4 Lugosi of films
5 Considering everything
6 Dusk-to-dawn period
7 Fernando's farewell
8 __-centered (egotistical)
9 50%
10 Sound of a well-tuned car
11 Wild pigs
12 Actress Dickinson
13 Bread baker's ingredient
21 Billiards stick
24 Approves
25 Diner sandwiches: Abbr.
26 Alda of *The Aviator*
27 Brooklyn or Manhattan, for short
28 Barely
29 Fruit-filled desserts
30 Golfer Ernie
32 Ripped up
33 Also
34 Flapjack franchise
35 Tip of an airplane
36 Lose fur
38 "That's show __!"
41 Make illegal
42 Veterans Day events
44 "That's what you think!"
45 Make a second offer
46 Rust, for example
47 Charming woman
48 Fine sheet fabric
49 Novel-plot surprise
51 Business bigwig
52 Not on tape
53 Office note
54 Send, as a postcard
55 *Vogue* rival
56 Hwys.

★★ One-Way Streets

The diagram represents a pattern of streets. A and B are parking spaces, and the black squares are stores. Find a route that starts at A, passes through all stores exactly once, and ends at B. Arrows indicate one-way traffic for that block only. No block or intersection may be entered more than once.

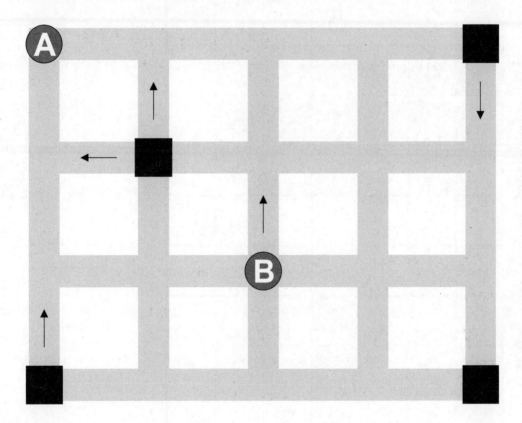

SOUND THINKING

There is only one common uncapitalized word whose only consonant sounds are V, S, and V, in that order. What is it?

_____

★ Hyper-Sudoku

Fill in the blank boxes so that every row, column, 3x3 box, *and* each of the four 3x3 gray regions contains all of the numbers 1 to 9.

7			2		5			
	3	1	4					
	5				1	9	8	
	9			5		7	3	
	4							
3		6		1		5	4	
6		3		4	8			
	1	4				6	2	
5			1		2	3		4

CENTURY MARKS

Inserting plus signs and minus signs, as many as necessary, in between the nine digits below, create a series of additions and subtractions whose final answer is 100. Any digits without a sign between them are to be grouped together as a single number.

2 4 4 5 8 9 1 1 3 = 100

★ Star Search

Find the stars that are hidden in some of the blank squares. The numbered squares indicate how many stars are hidden in the squares adjacent to them (including diagonally). There is never more than one star in any square.

		2		**2**		
	2			**3**		**2**
2		**2**	**2**		**4**	**2**	**2**
	1		**2**			
		1			**3**	

TELEPHONE TRIOS

	ABC	DEF
1	**2**	**3**
GHI **4**	JKL **5**	MNO **6**
PRS **7**	TUV **8**	WXY **9**
*	**o**	**#**

Using the numbers and letters on a standard telephone, what three seven-letter words or phrases from the same category can be formed from these telephone numbers?

538-2487　　＿ ＿ ＿ ＿ ＿ ＿ ＿

687-8273　　＿ ＿ ＿ ＿ ＿ ＿ ＿

822-2726　　＿ ＿ ＿ ＿ ＿ ＿ ＿

★ Sky-High by Gail Grabowski

ACROSS

1 Read quickly
5 Poker tokens
10 Nile queen, for short
14 Game on horseback
15 Brother of Moses
16 Pork cut
17 Legal rights grp.
18 Song syllables
19 Fairy-tale monster
20 Maker of illegal liquor
22 Takes advantage of
23 On the ocean
24 Drop in the mail
26 Out of control
29 Roadside eateries
33 Soufflé ingredients
37 Gather, as crops
39 Jet flier
40 What something is worth
42 Be incorrect
43 Sarcastic
44 Edit, as text
45 Hang onto
47 Sunrise direction
48 Believe appropriate
50 Catch sight of
52 Meadows
54 Flies high
58 Norway's largest city
61 Captivated by celebrities
65 Once more
66 Giggling sound
67 Golf-bag club
68 Speeder's penalty
69 Smooths (out)
70 Sensible
71 Practice for a bout
72 Floor models
73 Gen. Robt. __

DOWN

1 Computer junk mail
2 Beverage served with marshmallows
3 Dole out
4 Parts of speech
5 What a Siamese sheds
6 Mata __ (infamous spy)
7 Teheran's country
8 Flag holders
9 Entangled
10 Place of bliss
11 Fireplace fillers
12 Dublin's country
13 Small bills
21 Use a needle
25 Small bites
27 Onion relative
28 Takes a risk
30 Director Kazan
31 Curtain holders
32 Editor's notation
33 Days before holidays
34 Checkers or chess
35 Happiness
36 Tall yellow-petaled plant
38 Get ready, for short
41 Falco of The Sopranos
46 Have
49 Sampled, as soup
51 Preschooler
53 Martin of Shopgirl
55 Get out of bed
56 Like farm country
57 British biscuit
58 Clumsy ones
59 Scissors sound
60 Singer Horne
62 "Might I interrupt?"
63 Nevada city
64 Leg joint

★ ABC

Enter the letters A, B, and C into the diagram so that each row and column has exactly one A, one B, and one C. The letters outside the diagram indicate the first letter encountered, moving in the direction of the arrow. Keep in mind that after all the letters have been filled in, there will be one blank box in each row and column.

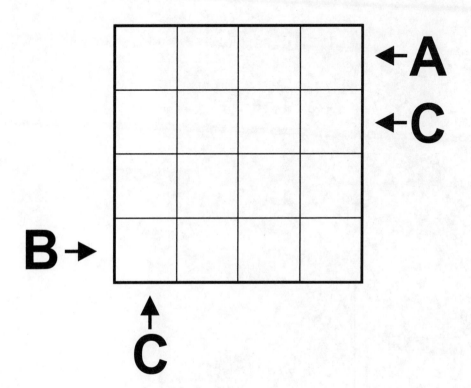

CLUELESS CROSSWORD

Complete the crossword with common uncapitalized seven-letter words, based entirely on the letters already filled in for you.

★ Friendship Chains

Which chain was laid down in the middle of the pile, having the same number of chains below it as above it?

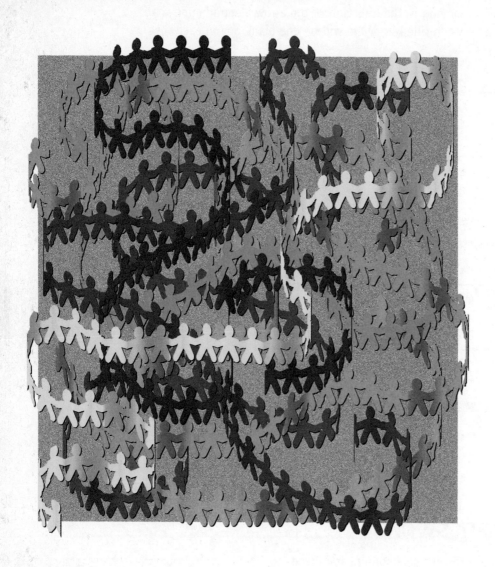

BETWEENER

What three-letter word belongs between the word at left and the word at right, so that the first and second word, and the second and third word, each form a common compound word?

COPY __ __ __ WALK

★★ Sudoku

Fill in the blank boxes so that every row, column, and 3x3 box contains all of the numbers 1 to 9.

	7	8		2			9	
3			6				4	7
9				8		3		
	9							
6		1				2		5
						6		
		5		7				6
4	6				8			3
	2			5		1	7	

MIXAGRAMS

Each line contains a five-letter word and a four-letter word that have been mixed together (the order of the letters in each word has not been changed). Unmix the two words on each line and write them in the spaces provided. When you're done, find a two-part answer to the clue by reading down the letter columns in the answers.

CLUE: Frogs' hangouts

P O L E G R A L E = _ _ _ _ _ + _ _ _ _

A I M B U R M E Y = _ _ _ _ _ + _ _ _ _

L I D L A U C E S = _ _ _ _ _ + _ _ _ _

S P Y O D O T E L = _ _ _ _ _ + _ _ _ _

★ On the Keyboard by Sally R. Stein

ACROSS

1 Hidden valleys
6 Behaves
10 Algebra, trig, etc.
14 Disprove
15 Chimney dust
16 Follow instructions
17 Silly
18 Long story
19 Reward for Rover
20 Buys everyone dinner
22 Metal that rusts
23 Occupied a couch
24 Prefix for violet
25 Sundial's "moving part"
29 Minor error
32 Discover, as an idea
33 *Jeopardy!* and *Wheel* ...
37 Shakespeare's river
38 West Florida city
39 Forget to mention
40 Learns by heart
42 Maytag competitor
43 Copy-machine powder
44 Group of priests
45 Clipped a lawn
48 Motorists' org.
49 Ayatollah's country
50 Wee-hour work group
57 Ship pole
58 Friend in battle
59 1950s battleground
60 Ending for major or novel
61 Sky color
62 59 Across native, for one
63 Prophet
64 Grounded planes: Abbr.
65 Homes for hatchlings

DOWN

1 Firm hold
2 Singer Horne
3 Internet auction site
4 Convent dwellers
5 Cowboy hat
6 Selling point
7 Blazer or parka
8 Formal wear in old Rome
9 Wild guess
10 Large house trailer
11 Cancel, as a rocket launch
12 Male voice
13 "Laughing" beast

21 Hem and __
24 Aircraft-carrier letters
25 Hoax
26 Bee's home
27 Building block of matter
28 Highway warning sign
29 Less plausible, as an excuse
30 Units of current
31 Split-__ soup
33 Stare, as at stars
34 Actor Sharif
35 Building add-on
36 Hang around

38 Metal in pewter
41 Fishing pole
42 Nome native
44 Purring pet
45 Silent performers
46 Give a speech
47 Squander
48 Light-dawning remark
50 Puts the collar on
51 Misfortunes
52 Oversupply
53 Hydrant attachment
54 Part of the eye
55 Heroic deed
56 Basks in the sun

★★ Line Drawing

Draw four straight lines, each from one edge of the square to another edge, so that the words in each of the eight regions have something in common.

MEZZANINE

EBBS

OOZE

BUZZ

MUTT

FLOOD

SKIING

BATTER   ABBEY

ASSAY   RADII

CHEESE

ERR

CHESS

FEED

SPARROW

THREE OF A KIND

Find the three hidden words in the sentence that, read in order, go together in some way.

Wash a velvet glove with a small brush.

★ Find the Ships

Determine the position of the 10 ships listed to the right of the diagram. The ships may be oriented either horizontally or vertically. A square with wavy lines indicates water and will not contain a ship. The numbers at the edge of the diagram indicate how many squares in that row or column contain parts of ships. When all 10 ships are correctly placed in the diagram, no two of them will touch each other, not even diagonally.

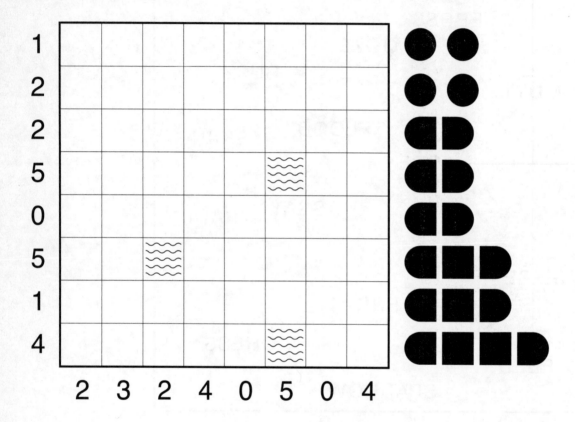

TWO-BY-FOUR

The eight letters in the word POIGNANT can be rearranged to form a pair of common four-letter words in two different ways. Can you find both pairs of words?

— — — —   — — — —

— — — —   — — — —

★★ Fences

Connect the dots with vertical or horizontal lines, so that a single loop is formed with no crossings or branches. Each number indicates how many lines surround it; squares with no number may be surrounded by any number of lines.

```
3   0   2 3   1
1     1   3   3
2 3
            3   3
2   3
                3 3
1   2 1       2
0   3 3   1   2
```

ADDITION SWITCH

Switch the positions of two of the digits in the incorrect sum at right, to get a correct sum.

```
  238
+726
-----
  604
```

★ Somewhat Sassy by Gail Grabowski

ACROSS

1 Baking utensils
5 Ocean vessel
9 Wetland
14 On the peak of
15 *Gone With the Wind* estate
16 Die down
17 Living-room furniture
18 Actor Alda
19 Game with straights and flushes
20 Knowledgeable investors, so to speak
23 Late-night TV host
24 Knapsack part
25 Light-bulb inventor
27 Light-switch positions
28 Grade below a B
30 Eject, as lava
33 Presentation prop
37 Iron source
38 Anti
40 Lamb's cry
41 Attention-getting lettering
43 Give temporarily
44 At an angle
45 Get a look at
47 Complimentary comment
50 Necklace fastener
53 High tennis shots
54 Produce-section display
59 Keep clear of
61 Just sitting around
62 California wine valley
63 "When pigs fly!"
64 Football coach's responsibility
65 Tied, as a score
66 Lock of hair
67 Pay to play 19 Across
68 Classroom furniture

DOWN

1 Free ticket
2 Molecule parts
3 Like Mr. Sprat's diet
4 Small bird
5 Post-office purchases
6 Angelic symbol
7 Iraq neighbor
8 Window section
9 Traveler's guide
10 Make illegal
11 Lawn tools
12 Dictation-taking pro
13 Long-billed bird
21 Light brown
22 Kennel sounds
26 Ventilation carrier
28 Actor Eastwood
29 Half a quart
30 Bawl
31 Tennis instructor
32 Snakelike fish
33 Come up short
34 Lincoln nickname
35 Competed in a marathon
36 Little bit
38 Rental units: Abbr.
39 Hassle, slangily
42 "She loves me not" flowers
43 Found out
45 Plan
46 Santa Claus aide
47 Shrub or bush
48 Nomad
49 Higher than
51 Debonair
52 Plumber's concerns
55 Hayworth or Moreno
56 Biblical paradise
57 Blind unit
58 Armored vehicle
60 AMA members

★★ Paisley Puzzler

Which piece has been snipped from the paisley material?

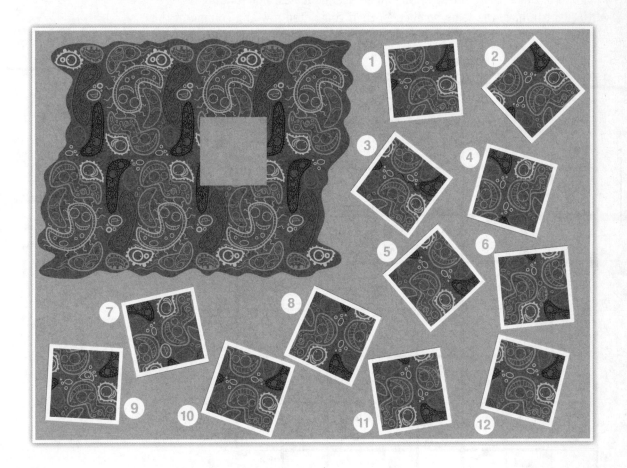

THREE AT A RHYME

Rearrange these letters to form three one-syllable words that rhyme.

G G G H H M S U U U

_____ _____ _____

★★ 123

Fill in the diagram so that each rectangular piece has one each of the numbers 1, 2, and 3, under these rules: 1) No two adjacent squares, horizontally or vertically, can have the same number. 2) Each completed row and column of the diagram will have an equal number of 1s, 2s, and 3s.

				1				1
2						3		
			1					
				2				
						1		
			3					
3						2		
				1				1

SUDOKU SUM

Without repeating any digits, complete the sum at right, by filling one digit in each of the five blanks.

$$
\begin{array}{r}
3\ 0\ 9 \\
+\ \underline{\ }\ \underline{\ }\ 6 \\
\hline
\underline{\ }\ \underline{\ }\ \underline{\ }
\end{array}
$$

★ Number-Out

Shade squares so that no number appears in any row or column more than once. Shaded squares may not touch each other horizontally or vertically, and all unshaded squares must form a single continuous area.

3	4	1	3	2
5	5	5	2	3
4	2	3	5	1
1	2	2	2	5
5	3	5	4	2

OPPOSITE ATTRACTION

Unscramble the letters in the phrase DO CLOTH to form two common words that are opposites of each other.

_____   _____

★ Sweet Talk by Sally R. Stein

ACROSS

1 Parcel out
6 "Terrible" infant stage
10 Tavern
13 Freak out
14 Nary a soul
15 Fuss
16 Roof overhangs
17 Marsh bird
18 Waiter's reward
19 Shrewd one
21 Garden tool
22 Sailor's assent
23 Cunning quality
25 Racetrack circuits
28 Poorly lit
31 Summer zodiac sign
32 Urban thoroughfare: Abbr.
33 Receded
35 Sneaker bottoms
39 Chances are
42 Toil, so to speak
43 Short putt
44 Mural, for example
45 President pro __
47 Suffix for book
48 Club member's payment
49 Three or four
53 Also
55 Bullfight cheer
56 Something easy
62 Repair
63 Nostalgic tune
64 Seiko competitor
65 Devoured
66 Copier paper size
67 Run off to wed
68 American flag color
69 Black-and-white cookie
70 Homes for robins

DOWN

1 Matures
2 Rich soil
3 Volcanic outflow
4 Dramatic musical works
5 In a bad mood
6 Drive-thru order
7 Is in operating condition
8 Playwright Eugene
9 Look at
10 Get into a tub
11 Felipe's farewell
12 Learning the __ (getting trained)
14 Prefix meaning "recent"
20 Aromatic tree
24 Midday
25 Young fellows
26 Give testimony
27 Brazilian soccer great
29 "Meet Me __ Louis"
30 Tin or titanium
33 Aquatic sport
34 Knucklehead
36 Waikiki feast
37 Raison d'__
38 Retired airplanes: Abbr.
40 Past due
41 "Me too!"
46 One sending a letter
48 Mild-mannered
49 Up to now
50 Exclusive group
51 Annoyed
52 Window projection
54 Frequently
57 Giuseppe's goodbye
58 Electrified fish
59 Singer Tori
60 Retained
61 Former spouses

★★ Tri-Color Maze

Enter the maze, pass through all the color squares exactly once, then exit, all without retracing your path. You must pass through the color squares in this sequence: red, blue, yellow, red, blue, etc.

SAY IT AGAIN

What common four-letter verb, when pronounced differently, is also a plural noun for a specific type of female barnyard animal?

— — — —

★★ Split Decisions

In this clueless crossword puzzle, each answer consists of two words whose spellings are the same, except for the consecutive letters given. All answers are common words; no phrases or hyphenated or capitalized words are used. Some of the clues may have more than one solution, but there is only one word pair that will correctly link up with all the other word pairs.

TRANSDELETION

Delete one letter from the word GENEROUS and rearrange the rest, to get a health-care occupation.

_____

★ Hyper-Sudoku

Fill in the blank boxes so that every row, column, 3x3 box, *and* each of the four 3x3 gray regions contains all of the numbers 1 to 9.

		3					1	8
	2		6				4	
1	9		3				5	6
2	5	4	1			6		
3				2	4	8		
			4			3		1
		1						2
	6		2	3			7	9
	7		8			3		

MIXAGRAMS

Each line contains a five-letter word and a four-letter word that have been mixed together (the order of the letters in each word has not been changed). Unmix the two words on each line and write them in the spaces provided. When you're done, find a two-part answer to the clue by reading down the letter columns in the answers.

CLUE: Card-carrying group

T E R O N T H O M = _ _ _ _ _ + _ _ _ _

P O V I L S A K A = _ _ _ _ _ + _ _ _ _

T R E V O L L E R = _ _ _ _ _ + _ _ _ _

L U V R I T A L K = _ _ _ _ _ + _ _ _ _

★ That's Easy by Gail Grabowski

ACROSS

1 Clarinet insert
5 "Woe is me!"
9 Ziti or rigatoni
14 Roof overhang
15 Throw of the dice
16 Nixon vice president
17 Roofed passage between buildings
19 Construction-site machine
20 "Finished!"
21 Pager sounds
22 Hoarse sound
24 Pre-owned
25 Loose-leaf filler
29 Those people
31 Faucet problem
34 Magazine executive
36 Swiss peak
37 Dentists' org.
38 Chinese side dish
39 Spooky
41 Matures, as wine
42 Barbie's beau
43 Lyricist Gershwin
44 Apply more paint to
46 Office attire
48 Become taller
50 Thickly packed
51 Iowa crop
53 LP player
55 Phone-book listings
56 Original inhabitants
61 Compel
62 Tight waistband
64 Shaquille of basketball
65 Military group
66 Author __ Stanley Gardner
67 Barnyard animals
68 Just manages, with "out"
69 Recipe amount: Abbr.

DOWN

1 Singer McEntire
2 British noble
3 Daredevil Knievel
4 Homeowner's document
5 Sports complex
6 Best, as a golf score
7 Pie __ mode
8 Cunning
9 Walks back and forth
10 Saw eye to eye
11 Garden flower
12 Change for a $20 bill
13 Dazzle
18 Masked swordsman of fiction
21 Front or rear edge of an auto
23 Ancient Egyptian ruler
25 Fringe benefits
26 "Au revoir!"
27 Site for park dining
28 Summer, in France
30 Inventor Whitney
32 Notions
33 Adhesive substance
35 Wears the crown
40 Get it wrong
41 Top poker card
45 Archie Bunker's wife
47 Alley feline
49 __-the-Pooh
52 Fishing-line holders
54 True things
55 Something prohibited
57 Skeptical remark
58 Part of speech
59 Em preceders
60 Dance move
61 Visibility problem
62 Pool stick
63 Pen filler

★ Where You Live

Find these places to live that are hidden in the diagram, either across, down, or diagonally. (The individual words of CRASH PAD are hidden separately.) There's one additional eight-letter answer in the category, not listed below, that's also hidden in the diagram. What's that word?

```
R G L J Q C A H S C R S M T W
E P N O F P A U A E S H A C K
S R A I D C A S T P E A N A S
I O U L L G T L T C A C S B R
D P C H A L E T N L O V I I C
E E Y O H H E E D P E D O B Q
N R G D S E D W O L A G N U B
C T H A C I E N D A T B A O H
H Y N A S B G Z G C A R O O C
A C L E I H A R O K T M M D X
L P R L O S T O C E I E A E E
E O L M A A T O R P B D A P L
I E H O H R O S M G A T T O C
T N I B A C C T Y C H A L E R
```

ABODE
BILLET
BUNGALOW
CABIN
CASTLE
CHALET
CONDO
COTTAGE
CRASH PAD
HABITAT
HACIENDA
HOME
LODGE
MANSION
PLACE
PROPERTY
QUARTERS
RESIDENCE
ROOST
SHACK
SHELTER

IN OTHER WORDS

There is only one common uncapitalized word that contains the consecutive letters UMQ. What is it?

_____

bRain BReatHer
THE NOT-SO-GRIM REAPER

Dying is certainly the most universal experience there is. And it's long been understood that humor helps to provide relief from our anxieties about death. So it shouldn't be surprising that so many humorists have written and said so much on the subject. Here are some of our favorite observations:

HE'S SO OLD THAT WHEN HE ORDERS A THREE-MINUTE EGG, THEY ASK FOR THE MONEY UP FRONT.

—MILTON BERLE

On the plus side, death is one of the few things that can be done as easily lying down.

—WOODY ALLEN

Immortality is a long shot, I admit. But somebody has to be first.

—BILL COSBY

It's a sobering thought that when Mozart was my age, he'd been dead for two years.

—TOM LEHRER

If life was fair, Elvis would be alive and all the impersonators would be dead.

—JOHNNY CARSON

They say such nice things about people at their funerals that it makes me sad that I'm going to miss mine by just a few days.

—GARRISON KEILLOR

If you live to be one hundred, you've got it made. Very few people die past that age.

—GEORGE BURNS

That would be a good thing for them to cut on my tombstone:
Wherever she went, including here, it was against her better judgment.

—DOROTHY PARKER

★★ One-Way Streets

The diagram represents a pattern of streets. P's are parking spaces, and the black squares are stores. Find the route that starts at a parking space, passes through all stores exactly once, and ends at the other parking space. Arrows indicate one-way traffic for that block only. No block or intersection may be entered more than once.

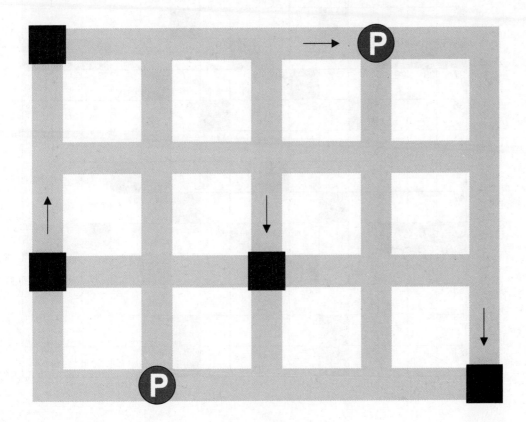

SOUND THINKING

There is only one common uncapitalized word whose only consonant sounds are P, B, and T, in that order. What is it?

_____

★ Scattered Showers by Sally R. Stein

ACROSS

1 Duck hunter's lure
6 Olden days
10 Rental dwellings: Abbr.
14 Make amends
15 Rams' mates
16 Modest response to a compliment
17 Tension
20 Listen to
21 Approximately
22 Answer to "Who's there?"
23 Hardens
25 *The Sun __ Rises*
27 Signed, as a contract
30 "Diana" singer Paul
32 Sore spot
36 Slip into
37 *Othello* villain
39 Carpenter, often
41 Computer processor
44 Free from care
45 Top draft rating
46 __ Lanka
47 Offer in a store
48 Loch __ monster
50 Run out, as a subscription
52 Very narrow shoe
54 Misfortunes
56 Not very reputable
59 Display anger
61 Carryall bag
65 Harshly
68 Cavalry outpost
69 Took a photo of
70 Oohed and __
71 Get a look at
72 Bugler's evening tune
73 Becomes hazy

DOWN

1 100-yard race
2 Suffix for kitchen
3 Apple center
4 Feeling tense
5 "Okay!"
6 Way back when
7 Possesses
8 Hardwood tree
9 Tee preceder
10 Type of missile
11 Public sch. auxiliaries
12 Quick haircut
13 "Auld Lang __"
18 Our sun's name
19 Scale notes after las
24 Polishes a manuscript
26 Jousting weapon
27 Results of brainstorming
28 Actor Nick
29 Prepare to be knighted
31 They're prohibited
33 Hold tightly
34 Legacy recipients
35 Bert's *Sesame Street* pal
38 Sports stadium
40 Have __ (enjoy yourself)
42 Disaster
43 Thoughtful views
49 Singer Kitt
51 Of the stars
53 Author Rand
55 Civil War general
56 Out of danger
57 Swelled heads
58 Org. for seniors
60 On the summit of
62 Honolulu's island
63 Wedding-cake layer
64 Wraps things up
66 Former Air France flier: Abbr.
67 Chitchat

★★ Bully For You

Enter the maze at bottom, pass through all the stars exactly once, and then exit at top. You may not retrace your path.

THREE AT A RHYME

Rearrange these letters to form three one-syllable words that rhyme.

C D E E O P U U W Y

_____ _____ _____

★★ Star Search

Find the stars that are hidden in some of the blank squares. The numbered squares indicate how many stars are hidden in the squares adjacent to them (including diagonally). There is never more than one star in any square.

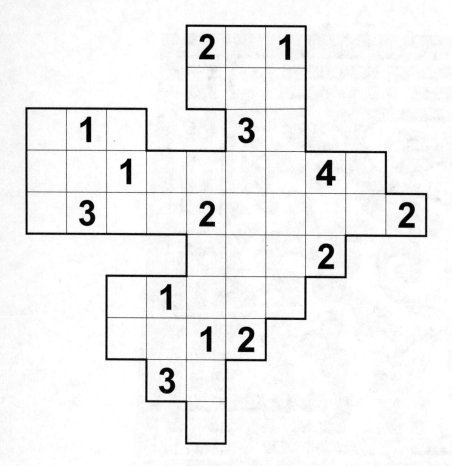

TELEPHONE TRIOS

Using the numbers and letters on a standard telephone, what three seven-letter words or phrases from the same category can be formed from these telephone numbers?

224-5363   _ _ _ _ _ _ _

468-7866   _ _ _ _ _ _ _

582-2625   _ _ _ _ _ _ _

★★ Triad Split Decisions

In this clueless crossword puzzle, each answer consists of two words whose spellings are the same, except for the consecutive letters given. All answers are common words; no phrases or hyphenated or capitalized words are used. Some of the clues may have more than one solution, but there is only one word pair that will correctly link up with all the other word pairs.

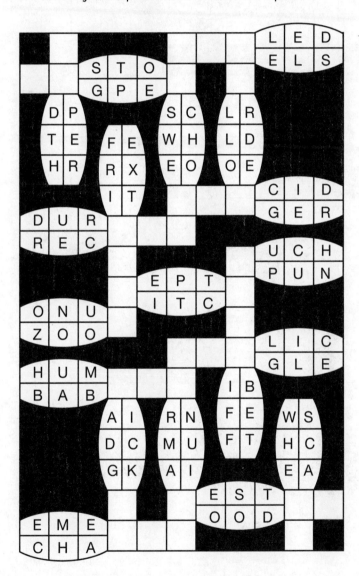

TRANSDELETION

Delete one letter from the word REMEDIAL and rearrange the rest, to get something that might be very valuable.

_____

★★ Go the Distance by Fred Piscop

ACROSS

1 Annoyed with
6 Fish feature
10 "Dancing Queen" group
14 On the double
15 Two-tone cookie
16 Big swig
17 Novice Boy Scout
19 On the briny
20 Road-gripping ability
21 Put on a leash
23 Guffaw syllable
24 African plain
25 Zero of *The Producers*
29 Burger topping
32 Took a trajectory
33 Androcles' extraction
34 Mattress filler
37 "High Hopes" lyricist
38 Congo's former name
39 Make eyes at
40 __-mo replay
41 Line from the heart
42 Bring about
43 Totally preoccupy
45 Darner's need
46 Van Gogh locale
48 __ Na Na
49 Yucatán builders of old
51 Least dense
56 Lendl of tennis
57 Utility measurer
59 St. Philip __
60 Bad to the bone
61 Ham it up
62 Word after "Ye"
63 Titled Brit
64 Dentist's order

DOWN

1 Damon of film
2 Imitative one
3 Comic Carvey
4 Electrical letters
5 Chewed on a ring, perhaps
6 Really like
7 Laundry-room item
8 Summer sign
9 Former Mississippi senator
10 Shooting marbles
11 Second-rate
12 Run in the wash
13 In pieces
18 Mideast money
22 Not lumpy
25 PC alternatives
26 Nonwritten test
27 Place to spend recess
28 Sawbuck
29 Debt markers
30 Circle dance
31 Bard's "before"
33 Does road work
35 Rick's film love
36 Marsh plant
38 Actress Caldwell
39 Galley tool
41 Org.
42 Smooth talker
44 Kid's cap
45 Whaler's adverb
46 __ acid (protein component)
47 "Bolero" composer
48 Be in a bee
50 __'pea (*Popeye* kid)
51 Recipe direction
52 Big rig
53 School on the Thames
54 Prepares, as an alarm
55 Plum or gum
58 Actress Gardner

★★ ABC

Enter the letters A, B, and C into the diagram so that each row and column has exactly one A, one B, and one C. The letters outside the diagram indicate the first letter encountered, moving in the direction of the arrow. Keep in mind that after all the letters have been filled in, there will be two blank boxes in each row and column.

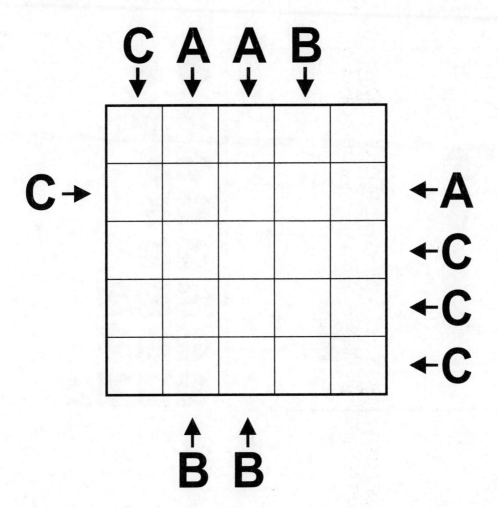

NATIONAL TREASURE

There is only one common uncapitalized five-letter word that can be formed from the letters in FINLAND. What is it?

— — — — —

★★ Find the Ships

Determine the position of the 10 ships listed to the right of the diagram. The ships may be oriented either horizontally or vertically. A square with wavy lines indicates water and will not contain a ship. The numbers at the edge of the diagram indicate how many squares in that row or column contain parts of ships. When all 10 ships are correctly placed in the diagram, no two of them will touch each other, not even diagonally.

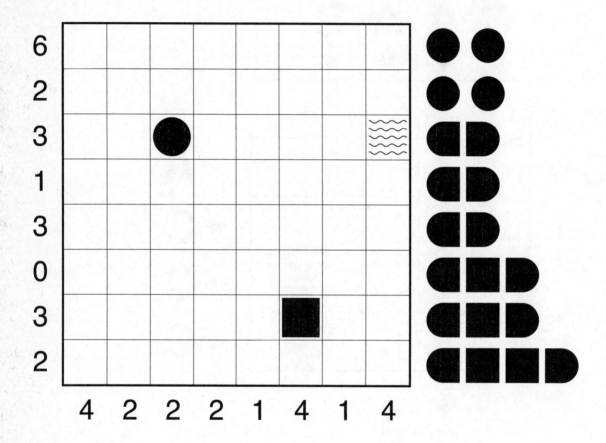

TWO-BY-FOUR

The eight letters in the word QUOTIENT can be rearranged to form a pair of common four-letter words in only one way, if no four-letter word is repeated. Can you find the two words?

— — — —   — — — —

★★ Disappearing Act by Norma Steinberg

ACROSS

1 Texas city
5 Sir __ Guinness
9 Trudge
13 Nuptial vows
14 Courageous
15 Theater section
16 Beatles song subject
18 Small bit of land
19 Invent
20 Pointy-nosed animal
22 Pronoun for a boat
23 Couples
25 Florentine river
26 Part of a hammer head
27 Bring up
30 Exchange
33 New Orleans streetcar
35 Smidgen
36 "Why?"
38 __ and Bradstreet
39 R2-D2 or C-3PO
41 "... man __ mouse?"
42 Cut off, as whiskers
45 Memorial Day race
46 Eventful journey
48 Mexican food
50 Author Sheehy
51 Middle Eastern sandwich
52 Faux __
55 Columbus' patron
58 Yuletide door decor
60 Maggie Smith's title
61 Love-letter words
63 More than
64 Colorado resort
65 Bloke
66 Not as much
67 *Atlantis* org.
68 Witnesses

DOWN

1 Hoisting machine
2 Put on a pedestal
3 Cringe
4 Workplace safety org.
5 "__ we there yet?"
6 Buddhist priests
7 Author Hunter
8 Mythical horse/man
9 Malleable
10 Missed, as an opportunity
11 Stare at
12 Roebuck, e.g.
14 Made beer

17 Feminine suffix
21 Made a goof
24 Eventually
26 Second ltr. addenda
27 Four score and ten
28 Sudden attack
29 Whirlpool
30 "Beat it!"
31 Part of a phrase
32 Part of a team's schedule
34 Soccer mom's vehicle
37 Actor Davis
40 Bolivian river

43 *The Little Foxes* playwright
44 Evolution theorist
47 Fencing swords
49 Trite humor
51 Sudden inhalations
52 Name on a check
53 Observe Yom Kippur
54 Closes
55 Role model
56 Put in the bank
57 Bart Simpson's sister
59 Omelet ingredient
62 Ross or Red

★★ **Meet Your Match**

From the pictures and comments below, match each of the four fellows with his blind date.

Barry — My blind date has short hair

Gary — NO COMMENT

Harry — NO COMMENT

Larry — My blind date always wears earrings

Deena — My blind date has glasses

Lena — NO COMMENT

Mina — NO COMMENT

Zena — My blind date has a mustache

BETWEENER

What four-letter word belongs between the word at left and the word at right, so that the first and second word, and the second and third word, each form a common compound word?

CARE __ __ __ __ WAY

★★ Sudoku

Fill in the blank boxes so that every row, column, and 3x3 box contains all of the numbers 1 to 9.

		8		4				
			6	1	5			
2						5		
	1			2			9	
6	4		5	9	7		2	8
	5			8			6	
		6						2
			3	6	8			
				5		4		

MIXAGRAMS

Each line contains a five-letter word and a four-letter word that have been mixed together (the order of the letters in each word has not been changed). Unmix the two words on each line and write them in the spaces provided. When you're done, find a two-part answer to the clue by reading down the letter columns in the answers.

CLUE: Western name

Z A Z U I N R E G   =   _ _ _ _ _   +   _ _ _ _

S C A B P U R A L   =   _ _ _ _ _   +   _ _ _ _

S N A L O O R E T   =   _ _ _ _ _   +   _ _ _ _

L E B U R V E R Y   =   _ _ _ _ _   +   _ _ _ _

★★ Fences

Connect the dots with vertical or horizontal lines, so that a single loop is formed with no crossings or branches. Each number indicates how many lines surround it; squares with no number may be surrounded by any number of lines.

```
·   ·   ·   ·   ·   ·   ·   ·   ·
  2       2               2
· ·   · ·   ·   ·   ·   · ·   ·
  1       2               1
· ·   · ·   ·   ·   · ·   ·
  3 2       3             1
· · · ·   · ·   ·   ·   · ·   ·
          3
              0
· ·   ·   · ·   ·   ·   ·   ·
  3       3           2 2
· ·   ·   · ·   ·   ·   · ·   ·
  3               0       1
· ·   ·   ·   ·   ·   · ·   ·
  2               3       2
· ·   ·   ·   ·   ·   ·   · ·
```

ADDITION SWITCH

Switch the positions of two of the digits in the incorrect sum at right, to get a correct sum.

$$\begin{array}{r} 8\,3\,5 \\ +\,2\,9\,1 \\ \hline 5\,2\,6 \end{array}$$

★★ At the Salon by Daniel R. Stark

ACROSS

1 Hit hard
5 Coffee holders
9 Castaways' creations
14 Glom __ (take possession of)
15 Publicize loudly
16 TV host Winfrey
17 Winter precipitation
18 Sicilian active volcano
19 007 after Connery
20 Show disdain
23 Fitness center
24 Icy downpours
25 Not slouching
27 German river
30 Mud bricks
33 Kindergarten trio
36 Dice throw
38 South American capital
39 More gloomy
41 Publicize
42 Smooth fabric
43 Refreshments
44 First-aid device
46 Bard's "before"
47 California peak
49 Open contempt
51 Statesman of India
53 Meditative exercise
57 Scoundrel
59 Washer functions
62 Prefix for physicist
64 Brit's blackjack
65 Attila's subjects
66 Madonna role
67 Stringed instrument
68 Hosiery shade
69 Check endorser
70 Notable times
71 Type of terrier

DOWN

1 Pear varieties
2 Cancel
3 Mall unit
4 Funny mistake
5 Fork or spoon
6 By __ (from memory)
7 Habit wearers
8 Not fresh
9 Had a good frolic
10 Soldier's addr.
11 Winter hazard
12 Furniture cover
13 Mets' former home

21 Additional
22 Rug exporter
26 Drink with a burger
28 Tide type
29 Nefarious deeds
31 Eastern potentate
32 Well-thought-out
33 Fortas and Burrows
34 Ho-hum
35 Carpenter's technique
37 Guitarist Clapton
40 To be, to Brutus

42 Wander off
44 Madras garment
45 Arrow parts
48 King's place
50 Spots for statues
52 Dad's brother
54 Henhouse sound
55 Actor Fonda
56 Campaign topic
57 Daisy Mae creator
58 Away from shore
60 Lemony
61 "¿Cómo __ usted?"
63 Canapé topper

★★ Number-Out

Shade squares so that no number appears in any row or column more than once. Shaded squares may not touch each other horizontally or vertically, and all unshaded squares must form a single continuous area.

5	1	2	6	6	6
3	6	1	1	4	5
3	2	1	5	5	5
3	4	1	5	3	1
1	5	4	6	3	2
2	3	5	3	2	6

OPPOSITE ATTRACTION

Unscramble the letters in the phrase BIKER FAX to form two common words that are opposites of each other.

_____   _____

★★ Hyper-Sudoku

Fill in the blank boxes so that every row, column, 3x3 box, *and* each of the four 3x3 gray regions contains all of the numbers 1 to 9.

		1			5			8
7						6		
				8				1
9			8	7			2	
	3	2			9			
	1		3				6	
1			3				4	
8			7				3	
	4	5		9				

CENTURY MARKS

Inserting plus signs and minus signs, as many as necessary, in between the nine digits below, create a series of additions and subtractions whose final answer is 100. Any digits without a sign between them are to be grouped together as a single number.

$$2 \quad 4 \quad 6 \quad 8 \quad 1 \quad 6 \quad 3 \quad 1 \quad 8 \quad = \quad 100$$

★★ Dogging It by Fred Piscop

ACROSS

1 DC figures
5 Chuckleheads
9 All the time
14 Keep __ (persist)
15 Nabisco brand
16 Ice-skate feature
17 "Don't go away!"
19 Saturn feature
20 Huck's buddy
21 Resting on
22 List of candidates
23 Playwright Burrows
24 "A mouse!"
25 Plead for mercy
33 Popeye's foe
34 Foreboding
35 Séance sounds
37 Shopping channel
38 Mimic's skill
39 4:00 social
40 Clock ticks, for short
42 Mom's mom
43 Playground apparatus
45 Fail to act
48 YOU __ HERE
49 Fork over
50 Gives the willies to
53 Clumsy one
55 Sense of self
58 Wretched digs
59 Hurry
61 Signs of spoilage
62 Gad about
63 Fact fudger
64 All wound up
65 Reach across
66 Cut back

DOWN

1 Time gone by
2 Director Preminger
3 Actor Neeson
4 Porker's pad
5 1990 Supreme Court appointment
6 Florence's river
7 Chick sound
8 Groundskeeper's buy
9 Leno follower
10 Burn like a candle
11 Vehicle with a turret
12 Barely beat
13 Hatchling's home
18 Forbidden
22 Pint-sized
23 Toward the rear
25 Cookouts, for short
26 Polar drudges
27 Handbag name
28 Leave the amateur ranks
29 "In other words ..."
30 Creator of the *Nautilus*
31 Gown material
32 Lay out
36 Loses firmness
38 Choreographer de Mille
41 Givers of the evil eye
43 Elm offering
44 "__ cool!"
46 Threat ender
47 Uttered
50 Mixologist's measure
51 Spy's writing
52 Stratford's river
53 Martial-arts blow
54 Kilauea outflow
55 Director Kazan
56 Shifter's selection
57 Cruel dude
59 AARP members
60 Matterhorn, e.g.

★ Spend Your Dollars

Find these worldwide locales where dollars are legal tender, that are hidden in the diagram, either across, down, or diagonally. (The individual words of multi-word answers are hidden separately.) There's one additional six-letter locale in the category, not listed below, that's also hidden in the diagram. What's that place?

```
D S E T A T S T U V A L U B T
N A F E F B J I G R E N A D A
A D I W N A R A N P A L A U N
L A J B M E I U U G F I J E T
A N P A J B W S N K A D L S I
E A I B I M V T I E W P O E G
Z C E M A N I R U S I D O C U
A A A I Y W I A H A A S Z R A
B N C Z T B A L Q B T D E I E
F A I I A R N I R S E N N S U
I Y H T N A M A R S H A L L N
J U I A U I B I Y E W L N A I
X G B R M K M G J I B S E N T
A D U B R A B O A I A I N D E
E Z I L E B S T D O F T L D D
```

ANTIGUA
AUSTRALIA
BAHAMAS
BARBADOS
BARBUDA
BELIZE
BRUNEI
DOMINICA
FIJI
GRENADA
GUYANA
JAMAICA
KIRIBATI
LIBERIA
MARSHALL ISLANDS
NAMIBIA
NAURU
NEW ZEALAND
PALAU
SINGAPORE
SURINAME
TAIWAN
TUVALU
UNITED STATES
ZIMBABWE

INITIAL REACTION

Identify the well-known proverb from the first letters in each of its words.

A. R. S. G. N. M. _____

★★ Dicey

Group the dice into sets of two or more whose sums equal seven or less.
The dice in each set must be connected to each other by a common horizontal
or vertical side.

SAY IT AGAIN

What five-letter word for a type of building, when pronounced differently, is a person who works
with automobiles?

— — — — —

★★ 747 Seating by Fred Piscop

ACROSS

1 Reindeer herders
6 Hotfooted it
10 Melville's whaler
14 Everglades wader
15 Gymnast Korbut
16 Scale down
17 Where to find TV dinners
20 One of the Smothers Brothers
21 Miniature-golf shot
22 Roofing pro
23 Buffalo Bill __
24 Weightlifter's exercise
25 Head over heels
28 Young girl
31 Sheer fabric
32 Actress Winslet
33 Tanning-lotion letters
36 Place to find bargains
40 Sweetie
41 Be abundant
42 Stiller's mate
43 Disreputable nightspots
45 Army radioman's nickname
46 Long-eared equines
49 X marks it
50 Italian city
52 Abbr. on a phone
53 Bullring cry
56 Fast-food restaurant feature
59 Fall tool
60 Abba of Israel
61 Grammarian's concern
62 Singletons
63 All-work, no-play student
64 City leader

DOWN

1 Took off
2 "Farming" starter
3 Year-end formal
4 Dispenser candy
5 Avoid, in a way
6 Easy mark
7 Whodunit's essence
8 Freudian concern
9 Most scoutmasters
10 Beehive's locale
11 Waste maker, maybe
12 Van Gogh locale
13 Brewpub lineup
18 Hosiery shade
19 Mont Blanc's range
23 Fountain offering
25 Allergy symptom
26 __ contendere
27 Creditor's claim
28 Ceremonial staffs
29 Tabloids couple
30 Dry, on wine labels
32 Patella's place
33 Have top billing
34 Exec's extra
35 Become threadbare
37 Off-road goer, briefly
38 Marketplace
39 In order
43 Digs deeply
44 "Understood"
45 Cast out
46 "Male" word form
47 Clear wrap
48 Sports-shoe feature
49 Gumption
51 Hobo fare
52 Algerian port
53 Jazz singer Anita
54 Letterhead symbol
55 Fancy jug
57 *The Sopranos* network
58 Code-cracking org.

★★ One-Way Streets

The diagram represents a pattern of streets. P's are parking spaces, and the black squares are stores. Find the route that starts at a parking space, passes through all stores exactly once, and ends at the other parking space. Arrows indicate one-way traffic for that block only. No block or intersection may be entered more than once.

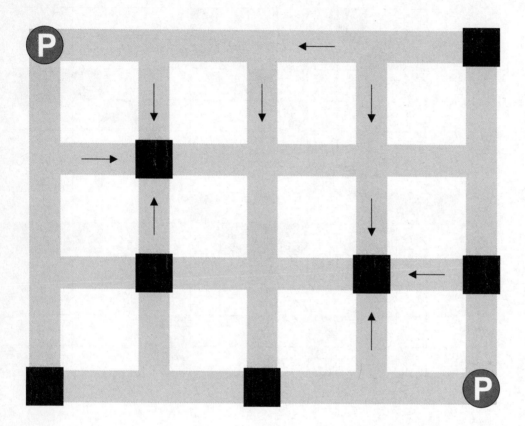

SOUND THINKING

There are two common uncapitalized words whose only consonant sounds are R, K, and L, in that order, and don't start with an R. One of the words is the hyphenated AIR-COOL. The other word isn't hyphenated. What is it?

_____

★★ 123

Fill in the diagram so that each rectangular piece has one each of the numbers 1, 2, and 3, under these rules: 1) No two adjacent squares, horizontally or vertically, can have the same number. 2) Each completed row and column of the diagram will have an equal number of 1s, 2s, and 3s.

SUDOKU SUM

Without repeating any digits, complete the sum at right, by filling one digit in each of the five blanks.

```
    3 8 _
+   _ _ 5
    _ _ 1
```

★★★ Line Drawing

Draw four straight lines, each from one edge of the square to another edge, so that each of the six regions has an odd number of coins and totals an odd number of cents.

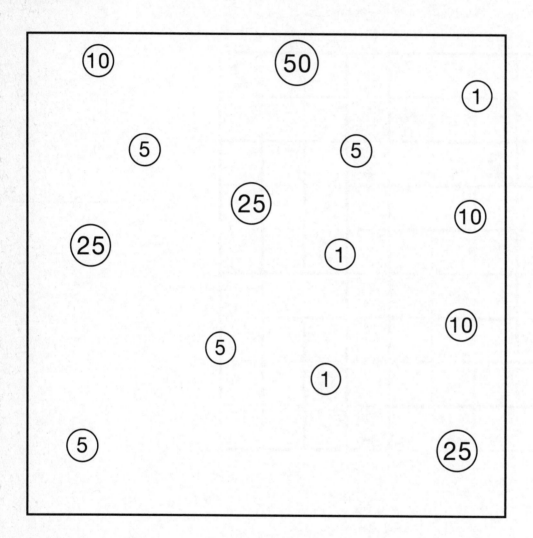

THREE OF A KIND

Find the three hidden words in the sentence that, read in order, go together in some way.

When in despair, who faces reality?

★★ Working It Out by Shirley Soloway

ACROSS

1 Shoe part
5 Restaurant chain: Abbr.
9 Tasty
14 Related by blood
15 Lion hair
16 Run off together
17 Sloop pole
18 Legal claim
19 Get extra mileage out of
20 Somehow
23 Agreement
24 Ill-intentioned
25 Vietnamese holiday
27 __ *Rides Again* (James Stewart film)
32 Do a tailor's job
36 Parka attachment
39 *Fidelio* feature
40 Somehow
43 Moran of *Happy Days*
44 Proof word
45 Talks wildly
46 Stretching muscle
48 Female sheep
50 Seafood selection
53 Texas city
58 Somehow
63 Orient Express terminus
64 Major defeat
65 Catering establishment
66 English-class topic
67 Bell sound
68 Women's magazine
69 Impertinent
70 Chorus member
71 Subtraction word

DOWN

1 Latin dance
2 Gives approval for
3 Shoppers' compilations
4 __ nous (confidentially)
5 White Rabbit's cry
6 Signal, as a taxi
7 Night owl's time
8 Type of pasta
9 Unruffled
10 Oriole or Angel
11 Rain cats and dogs
12 __ facto
13 Antelope's playmate
21 Emcee's text
22 __ Warbucks
26 Norse thunder god
28 Poet Teasdale
29 Disney sci-fi film
30 Mob scene
31 Talks and talks and talks and ...
32 Help feloniously
33 Harp relative
34 Tissuelike
35 Major time periods
37 Nonprofit's URL suffix
38 Orchestral reed
41 County in Ireland
42 Statement of belief
47 Irish playwright
49 Refuses to leave
51 Main artery
52 One way to cook
54 Lucy's landlady
55 Oil source
56 Does business in
57 French city
58 Literary work
59 Shuttle org.
60 Major time periods
61 *La Cage aux Folles* props
62 Reunion attendee

★★ Star Search

Find the stars that are hidden in some of the blank squares. The numbered squares indicate how many stars are hidden in the squares adjacent to them (including diagonally). There is never more than one star in any square.

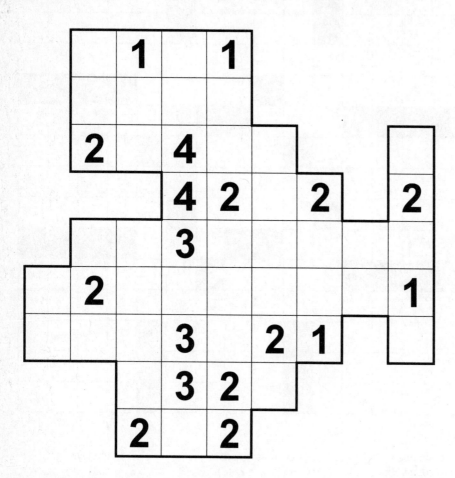

TELEPHONE TRIOS

1	ABC **2**	DEF **3**
GHI **4**	JKL **5**	MNO **6**
PRS **7**	TUV **8**	WXY **9**
*	**0**	**#**

Using the numbers and letters on a standard telephone, what three seven-letter words or phrases from the same category can be formed from these telephone numbers?

266-6933   _ _ _ _ _ _ _

476-8249   _ _ _ _ _ _ _

733-8474   _ _ _ _ _ _ _

★★ Pair o' Dots

Draw nine straight lines that connect two dots of the same color, so that none of the lines touch another line.

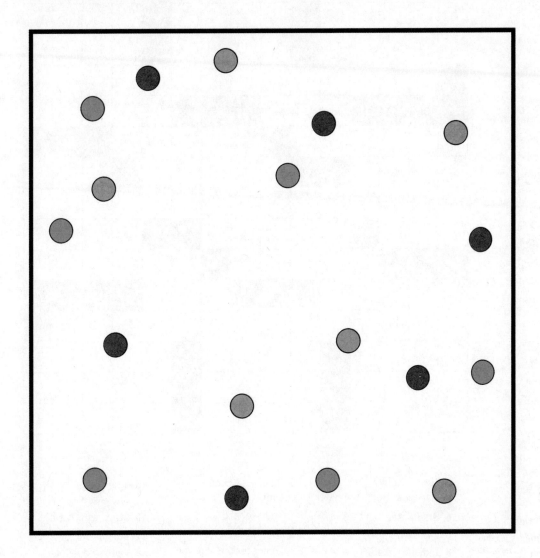

THREE AT A RHYME

Rearrange these letters to form three one-syllable words that rhyme.

A C D D D D O O Q U

_____   _____   _____

★★ Precious Few by Fred Piscop

ACROSS

1 Move stealthily
6 Invigorates, with "up"
10 Common rhyme scheme
14 Grand __ National Park
15 Earth Day subj.
16 Detective's job
17 Battleship blast
18 Twistable cookie
19 HS math course
20 Light hair color
23 Take a stab at
24 Map within a map
25 Wee-hours flight
29 Argentina neighbor
32 Clickable picture
33 Pension-legislation acronym
34 Smidgen
37 Executive perk
41 Industrious bug
42 Pass off
43 Black, to bards
44 Get rid of
45 Like saunas
47 Be of use
50 Prankster's ammo
51 Seniors' workout program
58 "Merry old" king
59 School on the Thames
60 Cuts and pastes
62 Brewpub offerings
63 Night sight
64 Fully anesthetized
65 Respire, as a Rottweiler
66 Grand Ole __
67 Elbows or ziti

DOWN

1 Holy ones: Abbr.
2 Clear a hurdle
3 "__ never fly!"
4 Bright star
5 Like some pines
6 Indiana's state flower
7 Hosiery shade
8 Limerick, e.g.
9 Mess maker
10 Play opener
11 Farm structures
12 In reserve
13 Sire, biblically
21 Ill temper
22 Purple shade
25 Latvia's capital
26 Business-school subj.
27 Knucklehead
28 Wrap up
29 Computer mishap
30 Trumpeter Al
31 "This __ test"
33 Long tale
34 Hefty horn
35 Electron's locale
36 Declare false
38 Cyber-send to the IRS
39 Part of NIMBY
40 Bray starter
44 Sell off
45 Where the buoys are
46 Start, as a hobby
47 Composers' org.
48 Cello's cousin
49 Burns partner
50 Postal-card cost, once
52 San __, Italy
53 Where to get off
54 Former queen of Jordan
55 Author Ferber
56 Frees (of)
57 "Leave it in"
61 Mexican Mrs.

★★ Hyper-Sudoku

Fill in the blank boxes so that every row, column, 3x3 box, *and* each of the four 3x3 gray regions contains all of the numbers 1 to 9.

		4	2			5	
						4	6
			7	6		9	
				2			
1	5	8	3		6		
	2		4	1			
	9	8				2	
	4	5	7				
8				9	4		

MIXAGRAMS

Each line contains a five-letter word and a four-letter word that have been mixed together (the order of the letters in each word has not been changed). Unmix the two words on each line and write them in the spaces provided. When you're done, find a two-part answer to the clue by reading down the letter columns in the answers.

CLUE: Iron, for one

M A C G O L I A L = _ _ _ _ _ + _ _ _ _

L O U Z O N L E L = _ _ _ _ _ + _ _ _ _

U R G E L I L T Y = _ _ _ _ _ + _ _ _ _

B U R N A F I N T = _ _ _ _ _ + _ _ _ _

★★ ABC

Enter the letters A, B, and C into the diagram so that each row and column has exactly one A, one B, and one C. The letters outside the diagram indicate the first letter encountered, moving in the direction of the arrow. Keep in mind that after all the letters have been filled in, there will be two blank boxes in each row and column.

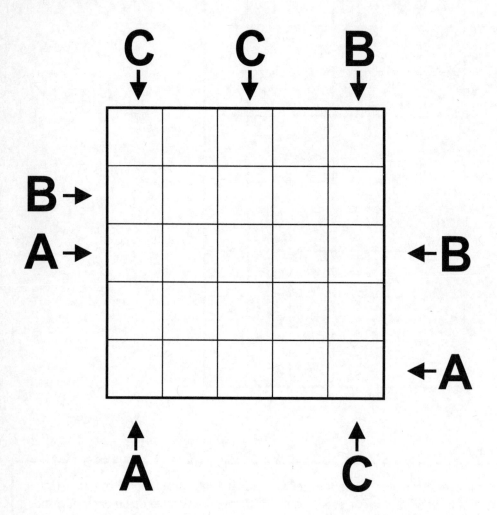

NATIONAL TREASURE

Find two common uncapitalized five-letter words that can be formed from the letters in ECUADOR, that both start with vowels and are anagrams of each other.

— — — — —   — — — — —

★★ Build-Ups by Fred Piscop

ACROSS

1 Mends
6 Morning haze
10 Salary max
13 T-man Ness
14 Plane measure
15 Sandbox toy
16 Chevy Chase film of '80
18 "Inner" word form
19 Thumbs-up
20 Big name in pianos
22 Hurler's stat.
24 Goes limp
25 Lamb dish
29 __ gratia artis
31 Work the aisles, informally
32 Subtle glow
33 Little, in Lille
35 Boot from office
39 Condo division
40 '70s war zone
41 Netmen's org.
42 Sprinter's assignment
43 Corday's victim
45 Tailor's line
46 Frat-house letter
48 Sense of self
49 Neaten, as a lawn
50 Annual foursome
54 Coll. major
56 Thanksgiving prize
58 Very shortly
63 Garfield's foil
64 Rio beach
66 Comic Foxx
67 Hi's comics mate
68 Inflexibility
69 Poetic palindrome
70 Work with acid
71 Most trivial

DOWN

1 Penta- doubled
2 "Sad to say ..."
3 Disencumbers
4 Junction point
5 Composer Jule
6 __-jongg
7 Nest eggs, briefly
8 Religious factions
9 Meals in cardboard containers
10 "Is it OK?"
11 Actor Quinn
12 Artful dodges
15 Ritzy digs
17 Sandal part
21 Uncertainties
23 Fight venue
25 Author Bellow
26 Melt ingredient
27 "__ go bragh"
28 Turning point
30 Glassy look
34 Publicist's concern
36 Pre-owned
37 Without a date
38 Easy to manage
43 Mr. Peanut accessory
44 Gin partner
47 Goblin starter
50 Took an oath
51 Down source
52 Stage whisper
53 Schnozzola
55 Twist out of shape
57 Long story
59 Irish Rose's man
60 Long story
61 Grandson of Eve
62 Links vehicle
65 Bat wood

★★ Wheels and Cogs

When the caveman turns the handle on the cog, will the pointer move toward the green or purple dinosaur?

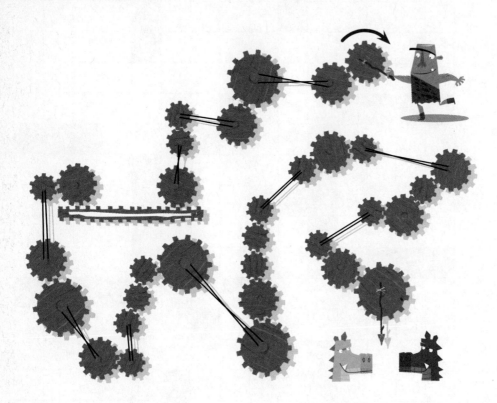

BETWEENER

What four-letter word belongs between the word at left and the word at right, so that the first and second word, and the second and third word, each form a common compound word?

STEAM __ __ __ __ WRECK

★★ Find the Ships

Determine the position of the 10 ships listed to the right of the diagram. The ships may be oriented either horizontally or vertically. A square with wavy lines indicates water and will not contain a ship. The numbers at the edge of the diagram indicate how many squares in that row or column contain parts of ships. When all 10 ships are correctly placed in the diagram, no two of them will touch each other, not even diagonally.

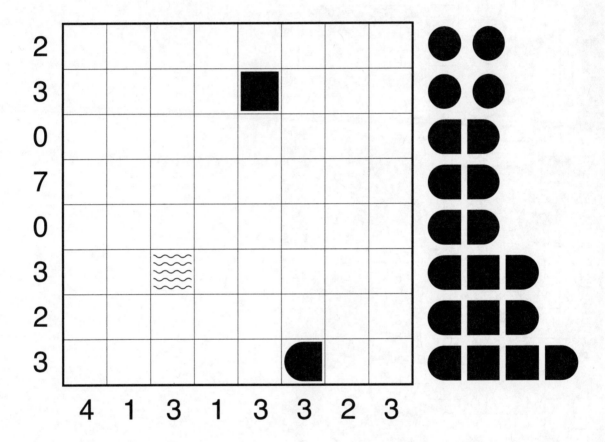

TWO-BY-FOUR

The eight letters in the word RICOCHET can be rearranged to form a pair of common four-letter words in three different ways, if no four letter word is repeated. Can you find all three pairs of words?

___ ___ ___ ___   ___ ___ ___ ___   ___ ___ ___ ___   ___ ___ ___ ___

___ ___ ___ ___   ___ ___ ___ ___

★★ Triad Split Decisions

In this clueless crossword puzzle, each answer consists of two words whose spellings are the same, except for the consecutive letters given. All answers are common words; no phrases or hyphenated or capitalized words are used. Some of the clues may have more than one solution, but there is only one word pair that will correctly link up with all the other word pairs.

TRANSDELETION

Delete one letter from the word OUTCLASS and rearrange the rest, to get something sharp.

_____

★★ Uncle by Shirley Soloway

ACROSS

1 Ashen
5 Prescriptions, briefly
9 Airplane chair-backs
14 Trebek of TV
15 Jai __
16 Event's locale
17 Winter wear
18 Criminal band
19 Length of time
20 Resigned
23 Part of AD
24 Italian erupter
25 Some turkeys
28 Give a soaking to
33 That woman
36 Something to read on a PDA
39 Pip
40 Resigned
44 "Excuse me!"
45 Political tactic
46 They ran at 33⅓ rpm
47 Galactic distance
50 Beef cut
52 Resigned
55 Salad veggie
58 Resigned
65 Video-game name
66 Had on
67 Little snack
68 Razor sharpener
69 Memo abbr.
70 Singer Laine
71 Large quantity
72 Be out of
73 Model Macpherson

DOWN

1 Negotiated agreement
2 Kona greeting
3 Become aware of
4 Scope
5 Biblical trio
6 Oomph
7 *Divine Comedy* author
8 Tourist attraction
9 Prime-time celeb
10 Bank's take-back
11 From the top
12 Christmas season
13 Have in the catalogue
21 Tried to win over
22 Last stage
26 Wharton deg.
27 She-pigs
29 Magical being
30 Void partner
31 Sound of thunder
32 What "000" might mean
33 Even trade
34 Comedy-club sound
35 Even once
37 Resistance unit
38 German port
41 Printer's measures
42 Chinese belief
43 Author Segal
48 Rigs out
49 Trophy, at times
51 Subtlety
53 Someone from Cedar Rapids
54 Fixed-income investment
56 Rounded hill
57 '50s Ford
58 Breakfast order
59 Kitchen suffix
60 Zhivago's love
61 Let go of
62 Art Deco artist
63 Ship out
64 Something to tie

★★ 123

Fill in the diagram so that each rectangular piece has one each of the numbers
1, 2, and 3, under these rules: 1) No two adjacent squares, horizontally or
vertically, can have the same number. 2) Each completed row and column of the
diagram will have an equal number of 1s, 2s, and 3s.

		1						
				2			**1**	
	1				**2**			
								2
					1			
			1				**1**	
3								
		2			**3**			
								1

SUDOKU SUM

Without repeating any digits, complete the sum at right,
by filling one digit in each of the five blanks.

$$\begin{array}{r} \_\ \_\ 3 \\ +\ 4\ 1\ 5 \\ \hline \_\ \_\ \_ \end{array}$$

★★ Fences

Connect the dots with vertical or horizontal lines, so that a single loop is formed with no crossings or branches. Each number indicates how many lines surround it; squares with no number may be surrounded by any number of lines.

```
3               0

3     1  3  0

      1        1  3

3              3     2

3     1              1

   3  2        3

      2  2  1     3

   2              3
```

ADDITION SWITCH

Switch the positions of two of the digits in the incorrect sum at right, to get a correct sum.

```
  6 9 4
+ 3 8 2
-------
  5 7 1
```

★★ 3 on 66 by Fred Piscop

ACROSS

1 Cornfield cries
5 Transplant, as a plant
10 Grabbed the tab
14 Oater challenge
15 Bring a smile to
16 Bumpkin
17 Paddock parent
18 Moon valley
19 Oscar role for Julia
20 City on Route 66
23 Assign stars to
24 Farm food
25 Messy place
28 Fighter pilots
30 Many MDs
33 Art sch. class
34 Be wild about
35 Gullible sort
36 City on Route 66
40 Business card abbr.
41 Slow critter
42 Greet the day
43 Start of MGM's motto
44 *NFL Live* network
45 Like some aspirin
47 Ante- kin
48 Oodles
49 City on Route 66
55 Ardor
56 Thick carpets
57 Actress Downey
59 Gymnast Korbut
60 In first place
61 Computer-screen image
62 Ran in the wash
63 Yule tunes
64 Gumbo veggie

DOWN

1 DJ's stack
2 *Rigoletto* solo
3 Close, in hide and seek
4 Declares true
5 It hardly ever happens
6 Writer Zola
7 Door sign
8 Scandinavian capital
9 Ring chewers
10 Veep's superior
11 Subtle glow
12 Hieroglyphics bird
13 Cozy room
21 Squealer
22 Lets up
25 Rice alternative
26 ICBM part
27 Exasperates
28 Mgmt.
29 Phone-cord shape
30 Astronaut's garb
31 Analyze grammatically
32 Emulated moles
34 "Make it fast!"
37 Tech support callers
38 Available now
39 *Messiah*, for one
45 Necklace fasteners
46 Cry of delight
47 Argue (for)
48 Computer language
49 Use a plow
50 Prod on
51 "This can't be!"
52 Actress Winslet
53 __ turtle soup
54 Cupid alias
55 Watch pocket
58 Santa __, CA

★★ Sets of Three

Group all the symbols into sets of three, with each set having either all the same shape and three different colors or all the same color and three different shapes. The symbols in each set must all be connected to each other by a common horizontal or vertical side.

SAY IT AGAIN

What five-letter term for a type of Winter Olympics athlete, when pronounced differently and capitalized, is also a type of weapon?

— — — — —

bRain BREaTHER
TUBULAR: GREAT USES FOR CARDBOARD TUBES

Every household has empty cardboard tubes—from small toilet paper tubes to medium paper towel tubes to long mailing or gift wrap tubes. The next time you're about to throw one out, consider the many ways it can be recycled:

Make boot trees
To keep the tops of long, flexible boots from flopping over and developing ugly creases in the closet, insert cardboard mailing tubes into them to help them hold their shape.

Keep linens crease-free
Wrap tablecloths and napkins around cardboard tubes after laundering to avoid the creases they would get if they were folded. Use long tubes for tablecloths and paper towel or toilet paper tubes for napkins. To guard against stains, cover the tubes with plastic wrap first.

Make a kazoo
Got a bunch of bored kids driving you crazy on a rainy day? Cut three small holes in the middle of a paper towel tube. Then cover one end of the tube with wax paper secured with a strong rubber band. Now hum into the other end, while using your fingers to plug one, two, or all three holes to vary the pitch. Make one for each kid. They may still drive you crazy, but they'll have a ball doing it!

Carpet tubes
Carpet stores will probably be glad to give you the long, thick cardboard tubes that they ordinarily discard; just ask. Because the tubes can be up to 12 feet long, you might want to ask a store employee to cut one to the size you want before you attempt to cart it away.

Make a hamster toy
Place a couple of paper towel or toilet paper tubes in the hamster (or gerbil) cage. The little critters love running and walking through the tubes, and they like chewing on the cardboard, too. When the tubes start looking ragged, just replace them with fresh ones.

Protect important documents
Before storing diplomas, marriage certificates, and other important documents, roll them tightly and insert them in paper towel tubes. This prevents creases and keeps the documents clean and dry.

Keep Christmas lights tidy
Spending more time untangling your Christmas lights than it takes to put them up? Make yuletide prep easier by wrapping your lights around a cardboard tube and securing them with masking tape. Put small strands of lights or garlands *inside* cardboard tubes, and seal the ends of the tubes with masking tape.

★ Mystery Category

Find the 21 items from a well-known category that are hidden in the diagram, either across, down, or diagonally. Answers include one two-word phrase, whose words are hidden separately.

```
M A S C K E N T U C K U O Y E
I N A O K A N S A I A V E N Q
C O X L U O N A G I H C I M O
H M E O M T G A N U T A Y R E
I R T R N L A R T I M C E G R
S E E A H O O H M N E G C N A
A V V D K F N I S N O C S I W
N M F O I A G R E N K M B M A
E D O L K E N T U C K Y R O L
V T A H O I K S A L A E O Y E
A C P R A R A L A S K A Y W D
D U G M P L I N O S D N O Z F
A I D A H O K D X I E E R O Y
A Y O H A L K O A W S N K J W
```

WHO'S WHAT WHERE

The correct term for a resident of Honolulu, Hawaii, is:

A) Honoluler   B) Honolulite

C) Honolian   D) Honolulan

★★ Hyper-Sudoku

Fill in the blank boxes so that every row, column, 3x3 box, *and* each of the four
3x3 gray regions contains all of the numbers 1 to 9.

		5			2	3	1	4
						7		
				3				
	8	2				1		6
6		4			5			
						2		
4	9	3		5				
						9		2
1	2		9		6		7	

MIXAGRAMS

Each line contains a five-letter word and a four-letter word that have been mixed together (the order of the letters in each word has not been changed). Unmix the two words on each line and write them in the spaces provided. When you're done, find a two-part answer to the clue by reading down the letter columns in the answers.

CLUE: Unknown ladies

J R E E W E A L D	=	_ _ _ _ _	+	_ _ _ _
R E A P D R O O N	=	_ _ _ _ _	+	_ _ _ _
S N A U R I V E E	=	_ _ _ _ _	+	_ _ _ _
E K N E M I S S Y	=	_ _ _ _ _	+	_ _ _ _

★★★ Jam Session by Doug Peterson

ACROSS

1 Moved along a curve
6 ERA or RBI
10 Ring things
14 Jeweler's lens
15 Bohemian
16 Track shape
17 In dire straits
19 Toy-brick brand
20 Board member, briefly
21 Commandment complement
22 Philanthropist Carnegie
24 Med. care option
26 Superman's real name
28 Scale notes
31 In a stressful situation
36 King topper
37 *Ivanhoe* author
38 Subtle atmosphere
39 New-car reading
41 Walks
44 Tag info
45 Scoots along
47 Sylvester, to Tweety
48 Having no options
51 Bashful
52 With 46 Down, *City Slickers* star
53 Alley prowler
55 Spanish dance
58 Barfly
60 Cognizant of
64 State firmly
65 In trouble
68 Handout from a hostess
69 Thailand, formerly
70 Irani religion
71 Busy bugs
72 Hard to hold
73 Icky residue

DOWN

1 Baby-wipes additive
2 Gravy thickener
3 Adorable
4 Period of time
5 Bear lair
6 Shopping event
7 Knickknack
8 Banking convenience
9 *Romeo and Juliet* character
10 Overlaid decoration
11 At any point
12 Conjurer
13 Not too busy

18 "Right now!"
23 OT book
25 Cologne scent
27 Excalibur wielder
28 Roundup rope
29 Last part of *The Crucible*
30 Commandeer
32 Type of fin
33 Sudden winds
34 Heep of literature
35 Dapper
40 Three-headed watchdog of myth
42 *Swan Lake* princess

43 Scandinavian capital
46 See 52 Across
49 Basketball filler
50 Halter, e.g.
54 Principled
55 Crimson Tide, to fans
56 Bakery need
57 Fast season
59 "Good heavens!"
61 Classic soda brand
62 Cardinals or Orioles
63 Steinbeck migrant
66 Flaky dessert
67 *CSI* network

★★ **One-Way Streets**

The diagram represents a pattern of streets. P's are parking spaces, and the black squares are stores. Find the route that starts at a parking space, passes through all stores exactly once, and ends at the other parking space. Arrows indicate one-way traffic for that block only. No block or intersection may be entered more than once.

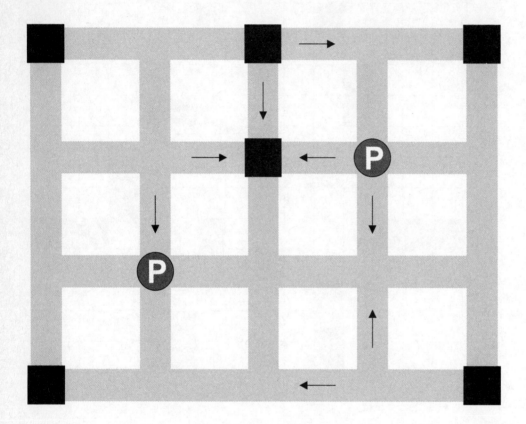

SOUND THINKING

What is the only common word whose only consonant sounds are S, N, T, P and D, in that order?

_____

★★ Star Search

Find the stars that are hidden in some of the blank squares. The numbered squares indicate how many stars are hidden in the squares adjacent to them (including diagonally). There is never more than one star in any square.

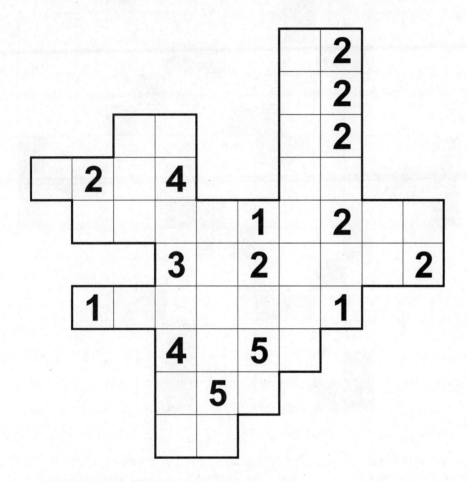

TELEPHONE TRIOS

Using the numbers and letters on a standard telephone, what three seven-letter words or phrases from the same category can be formed from these telephone numbers?

266-3873 _ _ _ _ _ _ _

358-7837 _ _ _ _ _ _ _

697-8439 _ _ _ _ _ _ _

★★★ Vowel Shift by Fred Piscop

ACROSS

1 Parsley unit
6 "Finished" rm.
10 Printer's widths
13 Coeur d'__, ID
14 Sales on the Net
16 Daisy __ Yokum
17 Safe place
18 Kind of pen
20 "Am __ believe ..."
21 __ Perignon
22 Nursery rhyme dieter
23 Salad ingredient
28 Wise one
29 *Mad* genre
30 Place to graze
32 Shirt with a slogan
33 West Point sch.
34 Improper act
36 Microsoft cofounder
39 Cow catchers
41 Stash
44 Draft dispenser
45 Poetic nighttime
46 Audiophile's rig
48 Commotions
50 Cotton eater
53 Leaves in a hurry
55 Align the cross hairs
56 Tick off
57 Teddy Roosevelt, in 1912
60 Meir of Israel
62 Environmental word form
63 Still for rent
64 Thumb twiddler
65 __ Moines
66 Poi source
67 Suspicious

DOWN

1 Sirs of old India
2 Tableland
3 Stages a coup
4 Suffix meaning "imitation"
5 __-Xers (boomers' kids)
6 Gillespie's music
7 Notary's need
8 __ de mer
9 Up to, briefly
10 Bahrain, for one
11 Ran the team
12 Small sofa
15 Collectible vinyl
19 Co-__ (some apartments)
21 Poor grade
24 An arm and a leg
25 Pat on the back
26 Director Kazan
27 Take a break
31 "__ Fideles"
34 British sports cars
35 Lauder of cosmetics
37 Leopold's co-defendant
38 Lantern-jawed TV host
39 Epithet for Irma
40 Handsome men
42 Wright guy
43 More off-the-wall
44 Indented, perhaps
46 Personal ad abbr.
47 Legendary cow owner
49 Cardinal cap logo
51 Surgeon's beam
52 Deceive
54 Dallas sch.
58 Toronto's prov.
59 Slangy suffix
60 Hodges of baseball
61 "To a ..." work

★★ Indian Archer

Enter the maze at top left, pass through all the stars exactly once, and then exit at right. You may not retrace your path.

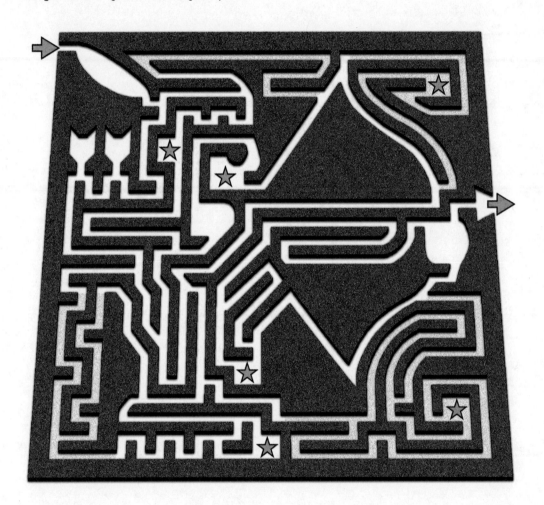

THREE AT A RHYME

Rearrange these letters to form three one-syllable words that rhyme.

B B L D D D M O O U U

_____   _____   _____

★★ Sudoku

Fill in the blank boxes so that every row, column, and 3x3 box contains all of the numbers 1 to 9.

		1	5			7		
	5				7		1	
8		4				5		6
	2			6				4
1				2			3	
3		5				6		8
	9		7				4	
		6			1	9		

CENTURY MARKS

Inserting plus signs and minus signs, as many as necessary, in between the nine digits below, create a series of additions and subtractions whose final answer is 100. Any digits without a sign between them are to be grouped together as a single number.

3   3   9   1   5   9   4   7   5   =   100

★★★ Split Pea by Fred Piscop

ACROSS

1 Take potshots
6 Come up short
10 Sign holder
14 Softened, with "down"
15 Beans partner
16 No more than
17 Park section
19 Salty drop
20 Quick __ wink
21 The inevitable
22 Like rosebushes
24 Alley game
26 Ten C-notes
27 "Outer" word form
28 Comparatively comely
32 Frequent Stallone costar
35 Carson predecessor
36 Ran like heck
37 Vacuum feature
38 Brownish yellow
39 "Come __!"
40 Java vessels
41 Gets 100 on
42 Something desirable
43 In shreds
45 Chart shape
46 Criminal charges
47 Mexican munchies
51 Kind of cat
54 *Exodus* author
55 Bond yield: Abbr.
56 Actress Hatcher
57 *Easy Rider* actor
60 "How are you?" reply
61 Olympics blade
62 Less fresh
63 Forum wear
64 Criticizes
65 Leafs through

DOWN

1 Mar. 17 honoree
2 Urban pollution
3 Ancient Peruvian
4 Pig's digs
5 Imposing building
6 Places to pledge
7 Leeds' river
8 Sprain treatment
9 Like cowhide
10 Shove off
11 Letters near "0"
12 Musial of baseball
13 Conservative Brit
18 Quitter's word
23 In vogue
25 '80s Soviet policy
26 __-fatty acids
28 Handled clumsily
29 Charged particles
30 Sal's canal
31 $50 Boardwalk outlay
32 Boarded up
33 Bar mitzvah dance
34 "__ it a pity?"
35 Duelers' distances
38 Roofing material
42 Tries to hit
44 Musical talent
45 Pants purchase
47 Alder and elder
48 Singer Ronstadt
49 Wound up
50 Marquee toppers
51 Keep __ (persist)
52 Disney clown fish
53 Pirate's quaff
54 Lone Star sch.
58 Prefix with log
59 Flamenco shout

★★ Split Decisions

In this clueless crossword puzzle, each answer consists of two words whose spellings are the same, except for the consecutive letters given. All answers are common words; no phrases or hyphenated or capitalized words are used. Some of the clues may have more than one solution, but there is only one word pair that will correctly link up with all the other word pairs.

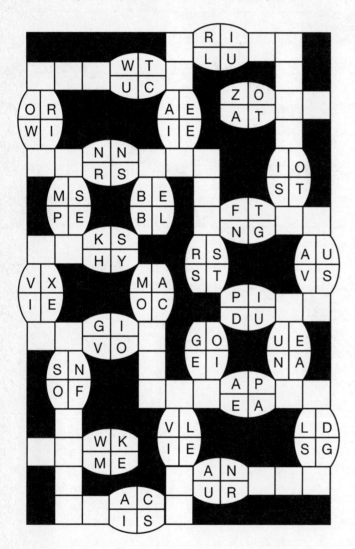

TRANSDELETION

Delete one letter from the word OUTBURST and rearrange the rest, to get a two-word travel term.

_____

★★ Number-Out

Shade squares so that no number appears in any row or column more than once. Shaded squares may not touch each other horizontally or vertically, and all unshaded squares must form a single continuous area.

3	1	1	6	4	2
1	4	5	1	3	1
2	2	6	4	3	3
5	2	3	3	6	5
4	2	2	3	5	1
6	5	4	3	2	3

OPPOSITE ATTRACTION

Unscramble the letters in the phrase SWEAT SET to form two common words that are opposites of each other.

_____   _____

★★★ Spooked by Doug Peterson

ACROSS

1 Johnny Reb's color
5 Mental vagueness
9 Song of David
14 Run the show
15 Patron
16 Foil maker
17 Jazz singer ___ James
18 Tiny bit
19 Flushed
20 Slight possibility
23 Street sealer
24 Celery serving
25 Slumber-party duds
28 Rival of Skippy
30 Popeye's girlfriend
31 Protrude
34 Feedbag morsels
36 German coal region
38 Ornamental wood
40 Newsworthy craft of '27
43 Permanent place
44 Fr. holy women
45 In the matter of
46 Adjective suffix
47 Pouch
49 Yank hard
51 Lacrosse team count
52 Wall Street figures
54 ___ de guerre
56 Hitchcock film of '43
62 5% of a ream
63 Economist Smith
64 *Lion King* villain
65 Tour de France participant
66 Pasta, in brand names
67 French pronoun
68 Holds back
69 Makes a sharp turn
70 Connecticut campus

DOWN

1 Diver Louganis
2 Teammate of Gehrig
3 Palo ___
4 Baker's supply
5 Twain, for one
6 "In your dreams!"
7 Greek consonants
8 Kid's construction kit
9 Line of latitude
10 Moved warily
11 Like some appliances
12 Prospector's bonanza
13 Wall-calendar page
21 ___ Mahal
22 Bale material
25 Riders after rustlers
26 Godzilla's stomping grounds
27 Winged wader
29 Upscale toy store
31 Take part in a tilt
32 Join forces
33 Actress Cicely
35 Overflow letters
37 Toward the rudder
39 Feathery wrap
41 Behind-the-scenes group
42 Devastating waves
48 In the past
50 Thor or Odin
52 Muslim palace area
53 Words of agreement
55 Walk slowly
56 Diamonds, for example
57 Raise
58 Viper tooth
59 Golden State sch.
60 Musket projectile
61 Bring to bay
62 NFL VIPs

★★ ABC

Enter the letters A, B, and C into the diagram so that each row and column has exactly one A, one B, and one C. The letters outside the diagram indicate the first letter encountered, moving in the direction of the arrow. Keep in mind that after all the letters have been filled in, there will be two blank boxes in each row and column.

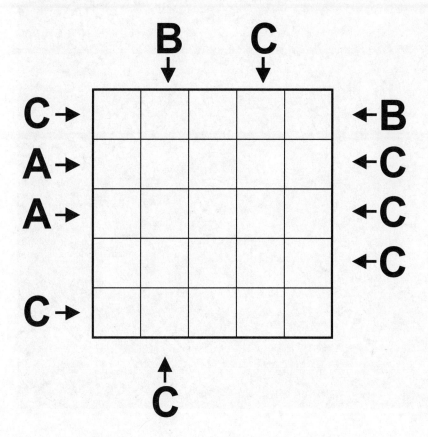

CLUELESS CROSSWORD

Complete the crossword with common uncapitalized seven-letter words, based entirely on the letters already filled in for you.

★★ For Openers

Which of the 12 keys will fit in each of the locks?

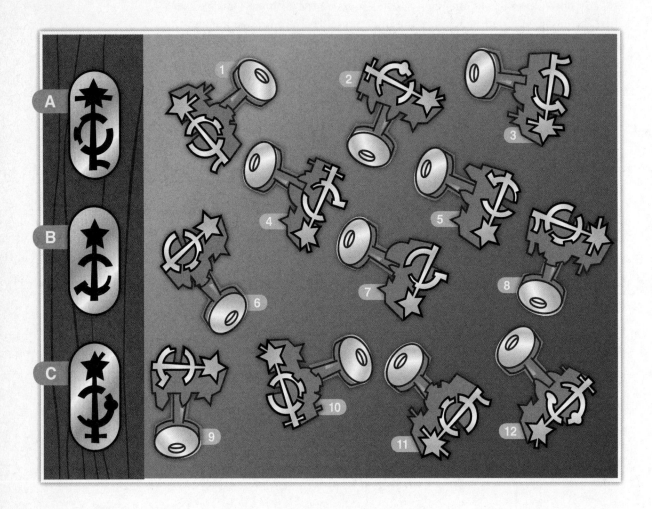

BETWEENER

What four-letter word belongs between the word at left and the word at right, so that the first and second word, and the second and third word, each form a common compound word?

SIDE __ __ __ __ BACKER

★★★ Line Drawing

Draw four straight lines, each from one edge of the square to another edge, so that the words in each of the five regions have something in common.

CRITICAL

QUIZ

OX

RITZ

ZOO

CROQUET

ZEBRA

KAYAK

AQUA

QUARTZ

NIX

SQUEEZE

THREE OF A KIND

Find the three hidden words in the sentence that, read in order, go together in some way.

Impatient, he exclaimed, "I want another banknote!"

★★★ Dew Lines by Randall J. Hartman

ACROSS

1 Old saying
6 Patton, for Scott
10 "Huh?"
14 Wanderer
15 A fan of
16 Bzzz-y place
17 Charles Goren's specialty
20 Lots of mos.
21 *Name That* __
22 Moves slowly
23 Minuteman container
24 Beauty preceder
25 "In the Still of the Night," for one
29 Allergic reaction
33 *Interiors* director
34 Actor Stephen
35 Nobelist Wiesel
36 Plow the field
37 Large shrimp
39 Tribal knowledge
40 No-good
41 Have a meal
42 Had a meal
43 Goes out with
44 Legal right
47 OPEC commodity
48 Hankerings
49 Immature
52 With 53 Across, emphatic denial
53 See 52 Across
56 Spike Lee film
59 "Peculiar" word form
60 Switch ender
61 Refrain for Old MacDonald
62 Moonshine ingredient
63 Make money
64 Fender flaws

DOWN

1 Capp of comics
2 Gloomy
3 Concert equipment
4 Guy's companion
5 Book printing
6 Parlor pieces
7 Start a pot
8 Hwy.
9 Winter ride
10 Expert
11 Keep a low profile
12 Batting stats.
13 Shirt shape
18 *I Spy* star
19 Fish eggs
23 Big waves
24 Once more
25 Goes out with
26 Martini garnish
27 Stan's partner
28 Take to the pulpit
29 Souvenirs
30 Unrivaled
31 Royal addresses
32 Pays attention to
37 Family tree
38 Actor Julia
42 Gave
45 Long squeezer
46 Take five
47 Free-throw score
49 Luke's teacher
50 Singer Redding
51 Phrase of apprehension
52 Inventor Sikorsky
53 It may be put on a house
54 Monogram unit: Abbr.
55 They can be fragile
56 Not too bright
57 401(k) alternative
58 Hurry

★★ Find the Ships

Determine the position of the 10 ships listed to the right of the diagram. The ships may be oriented either horizontally or vertically. A square with wavy lines indicates water and will not contain a ship. The numbers at the edge of the diagram indicate how many squares in that row or column contain parts of ships. When all 10 ships are correctly placed in the diagram, no two of them will touch each other, not even diagonally.

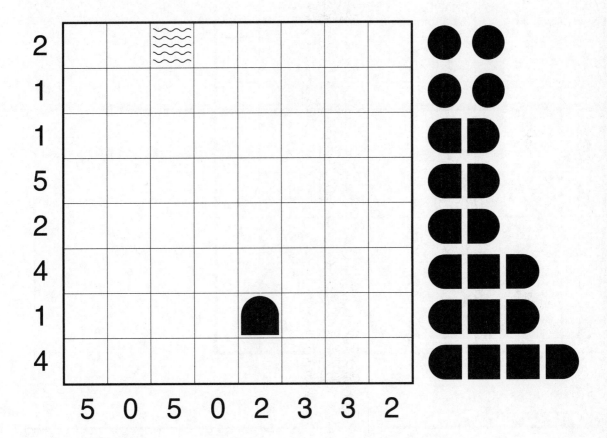

TWO-BY-FOUR

The eight letters in the word TACITURN can be rearranged to form a pair of common four-letter words in two different ways. Can you find both pairs of words?

_ _ _ _   _ _ _ _

_ _ _ _   _ _ _ _

★★★ Hyper-Sudoku

Fill in the blank boxes so that every row, column, 3x3 box, *and* each of the four 3x3 gray regions contains all of the numbers 1 to 9.

			2		7			
		1	5	8	9			
							8	
9			3		6		2	
6	4			7	5			
				9				
				5		6		
8	7	6		4			5	

MIXAGRAMS

Each line contains a five-letter word and a four-letter word that have been mixed together (the order of the letters in each word has not been changed). Unmix the two words on each line and write them in the spaces provided. When you're done, find a two-part answer to the clue by reading down the letter columns in the answers.

CLUE: Act One author

T Y R E A U M P H   =   _ _ _ _ _   +   _ _ _ _

C A P R A P O A M   =   _ _ _ _ _   +   _ _ _ _

R I P E N S A R E   =   _ _ _ _ _   +   _ _ _ _

H O P R U T S E T   =   _ _ _ _ _   +   _ _ _ _

★★★ Noisemakers by Doug Peterson

ACROSS

1 Moved sneakily
6 Emulates Johnny Appleseed
10 Stressed out
14 Painter Rousseau
15 Go cold turkey
16 Despicable
17 On the highest shelf
18 Cold War inits.
19 Faces the pitcher
20 Exit memorably
23 Saloon swingers
24 Vocal inflection
25 *Mal de __*
28 Ambulance attendant, briefly
29 Part of a guffaw
30 Singer Sumac
33 Slender instrument
35 Farming word form
37 Cruise stopovers
39 Baffler
42 Kingdom near Fiji
43 Clown fish of film
44 Long ago
45 Authorized
46 CD forerunners
48 Speakers' hesitations
50 Family man
51 Sitarist Shankar
53 Pet rescue org.
55 Handed down punishment
60 Timber wolf
61 *The West Wing* actor
62 Marilyn's birth name
63 Actor Estrada
64 Trucker, often
65 The Academy Awards, e.g.
66 DNA carrier
67 Football-field division
68 Freight haulers

DOWN

1 Guzzle
2 Seized auto
3 Opposite of ecto-
4 Full of hubris
5 Walk gingerly
6 Weapons for Junior
7 Sends packing
8 Genie's bestowal
9 Shale layers
10 French spa
11 Anaheim attraction
12 Pouring sound
13 "You got it!"
21 Smith College graduate
22 Antiseptic acid
25 "Be prepared," for one
26 Hi-tech reading material
27 Tournament type
29 Condiment with a kick
31 Much-visited place
32 Sought answers
34 Silly Putty holder
36 I-80, for one
38 Sellout letters
40 Divide evenly
41 Vitality
47 Buccaneers' business
49 Script sections
52 Responded to reveille
53 Venomous reptile
54 Superior to
55 Folk stories
56 Island off Tuscany
57 Utah city
58 Bus starter
59 Yoga accessories
60 Relay segment

★★★ Fences

Connect the dots with vertical or horizontal lines, so that a single loop is formed with no crossings or branches. Each number indicates how many lines surround it; squares with no number may be surrounded by any number of lines.

```
2   2     0     2   1
                        1
  1   3     3
        3       1
    3       2
        3       2   1
  1
    0 2   1   0 1
```

ADDITION SWITCH

Switch the positions of two of the digits in the incorrect sum at right, to get a correct sum.

```
  382
+ 118
-----
  950
```

★★★ No Three in a Row

Enter the maze at top left, pass through all the squares exactly once, and then exit, all without retracing your path. You may not pass through three squares of the same color consecutively.

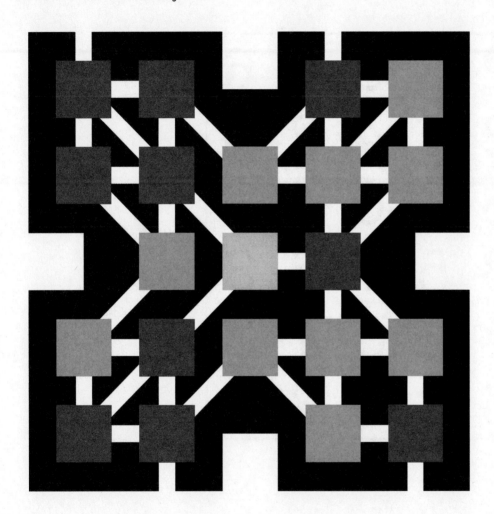

SAY IT AGAIN

What six-letter word meaning "majestic," when pronounced differently and capitalized, is also a word seen on calendars?

— — — — — —

★★ Number-Out

Shade squares so that no number appears in any row or column more than once. Shaded squares may not touch each other horizontally or vertically, and all unshaded squares must form a single continuous area.

6	2	4	3	5	6
3	3	1	4	2	4
5	3	6	6	4	3
1	3	5	1	6	3
2	4	2	5	1	3
4	6	6	1	3	5

OPPOSITE ATTRACTION

Unscramble the letters in the phrase DEFER INFO to form two common words that are opposites of each other.

_____   _____

★★★ Fancy Footwork by Shirley Soloway

ACROSS

1 Outline
6 Upper edge
10 Nile biters
14 Spoof
15 Uncommon
16 Former National League stadium
17 "Moving right __ ..."
18 Airport-counter name
19 Right away
20 Doesn't deal with
23 Looks good (with)
24 Affected, in a way
25 Polecat relatives
29 Perseverance
31 Online bidding mecca
32 Chimney coating
33 Granola bit
36 "It's not only my fault!"
41 Compass pt.
42 Like a D.C. office
43 Commits a hockey infraction
44 *The Longest Day* author
45 Without a goal
48 "Farewell, François"
51 Besides
52 Making short work of
59 Others: Lat.
60 Have the courage
61 Pie fruit
62 Burn the surface of
63 All finished
64 Didn't reveal
65 Stevenson character
66 Drain cleaners
67 Hits the brakes

DOWN

1 Mild tiff
2 Luau dance
3 On
4 *On Golden __*
5 Interlock, as gears
6 Orthodontist's offering
7 Great reviews
8 Eye part
9 Flat land formation
10 Distribute by type
11 Rallying cry
12 Unskilled laborers
13 Annie's dog
21 Statement reverser
22 Blues singer Bonnie
25 Fancy party
26 Israeli diplomat
27 Gardener's tool
28 Deli bread
29 Came down with
30 Milne creation
32 Costa del __
33 Fairy-tale starter
34 Iron and Stone
35 Prepare the salad
37 Soviet spacecraft
38 New Deal power pgm.
39 Ashen
40 Be under the weather
44 Hit the hay
45 Makes changes in
46 -oid relative
47 Marshy ground
48 Covered with water
49 Chicago mayor
50 Greek epic
51 See eye to eye
53 Revered one
54 Annapolis athletes
55 October birthstone
56 Until
57 Aura
58 Coop residents

★★★ 123

Fill in the diagram so that each rectangular piece has one each of the numbers 1, 2, and 3, under these rules: 1) No two adjacent squares, horizontally or vertically, can have the same number. 2) Each completed row and column of the diagram will have an equal number of 1s, 2s, and 3s.

SUDOKU SUM

Without repeating any digits, complete the sum at right, by filling one digit in each of the five blanks.

```
    3 0 8
+  _ 5 _
  _ _ _
```

★★★ Find the Ships

Determine the position of the 10 ships listed to the right of the diagram. The ships may be oriented either horizontally or vertically. A square with wavy lines indicates water and will not contain a ship. The numbers at the edge of the diagram indicate how many squares in that row or column contain parts of ships. When all 10 ships are correctly placed in the diagram, no two of them will touch each other, not even diagonally.

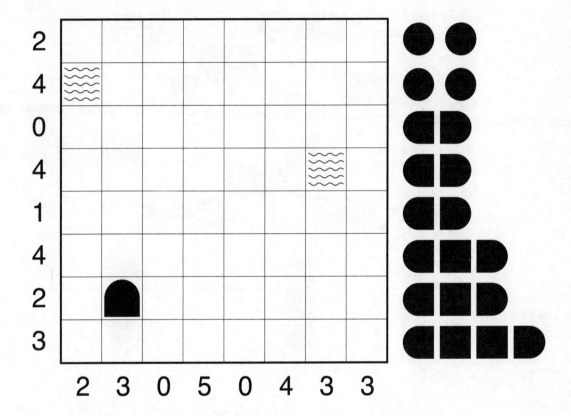

TWO-BY-FOUR

The eight letters in the word UPHEAVAL can be rearranged to form a pair of common four-letter words in only one way, if no four-letter word is repeated. Can you find the two words?

___ ___ ___ ___   ___ ___ ___ ___

★★★ Learning Experience by Randall J. Hartman

ACROSS

1 __ tai
4 Declares
9 Tokyo cartoon
14 Javelin's path
15 Fragrant shrub
16 Divas' vehicles
17 Dundee denial
18 *A Bell for __*
19 Spreadsheet entries
20 Kid's riding aid
23 Shakespearean bad guy
24 Nationality suffix
25 "Equal" start
27 One of Washington's generals
31 Jeff Gordon org.
34 *Les __-Unis*
37 Junior's transport, briefly
38 Michael Caine film of '83
42 Walk stealthily
43 Muscat resident
44 Fake drakes
46 Cautious
51 "That's disgusting!"
52 Psi preceder
55 Architect Saarinen
56 Certain graduate student
62 About
63 English estate
64 Diesel of *XXX*
65 Keats and Yeats
66 TV studio sign
67 *The Name of the Rose* author
68 Actress MacDowell
69 Doles out
70 Karate ranking

DOWN

1 Long-legged insect
2 Genesis landing place
3 Big chill of long ago
4 Ben's predecessor at the Fed
5 Second of a Caesarean trio
6 Joie de vivre
7 Statistical measure
8 Flat-bottomed vessels
9 "I cannot tell __"
10 Half of a golf course
11 Hinted at
12 Entrée with eggplant
13 Hartford hrs.
21 Chit
22 Roost resident
26 Galena or bauxite
28 Tom Sawyer's girlfriend
29 SFO stat
30 Alliance headquartered in Brussels
32 Some courtyards
33 __ Lanka
35 Director Burton
36 Slowdown
38 Board-choosing activity
39 Horse-traded
40 Card game
41 African antelope
42 Star Wars inits.
45 MIT, e.g.
47 Bro or sis
48 Investigated, with "into"
49 Beethoven's Third
50 Hostile to
53 TV greeting
54 Foolish
57 Start of a play
58 Laptop holder
59 Black fly
60 Pâté de __ gras
61 Blows it
62 Schedule C expert

★ Operetta Pair

Find these titles and terms associated with Gilbert and Sullivan that are hidden in the diagram, either across, down, or diagonally. The individual words of all multiple-word titles are hidden separately. Ignore words contained within parentheses.

```
L U P J B E Y P I W I K E J K W O E O E Y
P I U I R H C G Q O P N O Q X S G T V T E
I R B T O B F N L D U E H G R A N D R R I
Y O E R K H G A E E B D N Z H Y D M O A S
N E M O E Y N N F I F M A Z S F O F R C L
R P D J N T W A R G T V V D A D A K C J E
P O O D H I T V C L H A I B Y N I L Z X L
A O S E N B F I M V T S P E I E C T L I M
I N E D L O G L S Y K O V P U D A E M E V
X C O F N L H L E T A R T H U R G I V W N
Q W A L S I P U E C U C K D K Y T P K I S
H C L B X W W S E T Y E J D U E L T A C N
Q T A X X A A S Y Y X R U Y D K W Y L K I
P R I N C E S S Y C S E Y S G D E H O E E
L Y R D E K P C Q N E R O G I D D U R D M
O B T V N O D O L E G O N D O L I E R S D
R L W T T E X I S L C H T A W H V U Z L K
T R E B L I G C W L O M W H D E R Q A W V
G K N H B H V E F E M U N S E E S R B I R
W K V W T O L R L C P A I Z W A E O F V L
M U S I C A L A D X O P Q Q U M T K R E P
M U F E A U N X P E S R R X E T W R P S H
G C C R I T Z I P E E Y N A P M O C E E T
J M E H I R F A H V R W A N A F C P A H B
X P M O R J I T Z B M Q Q N O T N R I F Q
O E C R Y F Q A N S A N C D S T T V L A O
H H O N T M E G F E R O P E R S I A A D J
M I D L R O W S I T C U N S P A V M A S S
O E Q Y A Z N Z I A A R M S G C U K P I Z
J G R Z M E J T X R D H K I J R I G B H U
Y I C R R G N O S I I S M U D M H A P P Y
B N Y W Y L O G L P A T J M S Z Z U J R L
```

ARTHUR SULLIVAN
BROKEN HEARTS
COMPOSER
D'OYLY CARTE OPERA COMPANY
(The) EMERALD ISLE
FALLEN FAIRIES
(W S) GILBERT
(The) GOLDEN LEGEND
(The) GONDOLIERS
(The) GRAND DUKE
HAPPY ARCADIA
HIS EXCELLENCY
HMS PINAFORE
IOLANTHE
IVANHOE
LIBRETTIST
(The) LIGHT (of the) WORLD
(The) MARTYR (of) ANTIOCH
(The) MERRY WIVES (of) WINDSOR

(The) MIKADO
MUSICAL THEATRE
PATIENCE
(The) PIRATES (of) PENZANCE
PRINCESS (Ida)
(The) ROSE (of) PERSIA
RUDDIGORE
(The) SONG (of the) WRENS
(The) SORCERER
THESPIS
TOPSYTURVEYDOM
TRIAL (by) JURY
UTOPIA, LIMITED
(The) WICKED (World)
(The) WINDOW
(The) YEOMEN (of the) GUARD

IN OTHER WORDS

There is only one common uncapitalized word that contains the consecutive letters RMC. What is it?

_____

★★★ Go With the Flow

Entering the maze where indicated, pass through all the yellow circles exactly once, and then exit. You must go with the flow, making no sharp turns, and you may use paths more than once.

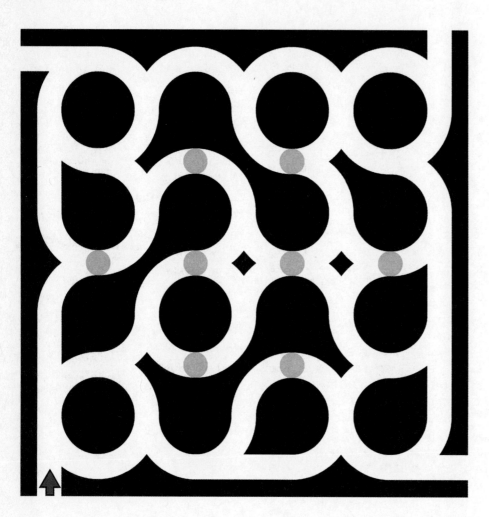

THREE AT A RHYME

Rearrange these letters to form three one-syllable words that rhyme.

A D E E G L M M M N O O O

_____   _____   _____

★★★ Star Search

Find the stars that are hidden in some of the blank squares. The numbered squares indicate how many stars are hidden in the squares adjacent to them (including diagonally). There is never more than one star in any square.

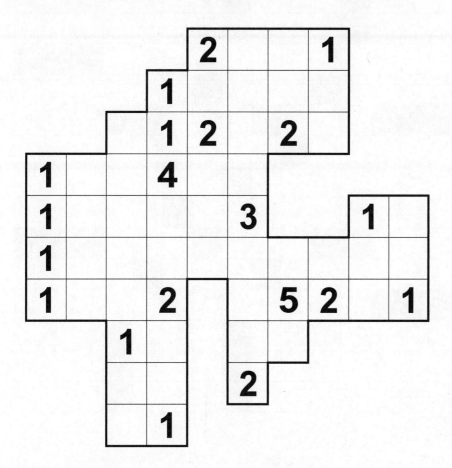

TELEPHONE TRIOS

Using the numbers and letters on a standard telephone, what three seven-letter words or phrases from the same category can be formed from these telephone numbers?

394-2878   _ _ _ _ _ _ _

328-4483   _ _ _ _ _ _ _

847-3688   _ _ _ _ _ _ _

★★★ Burning Issue by Alison Donald

ACROSS

1 Netflix delivery
4 George's brother
7 Big bashes
14 Brazilian hot spot
15 Cycle prefix
16 Unbinds
17 Words at the altar
18 Roof goo
19 Programming language
20 Dating-service goal
23 Slugger Sammy
24 Calendar abbr.
25 ___ Pieces (candy)
29 Pkg. deliverer
31 Bull Run general
33 Bronze, for one
34 Boy Scout rank
37 Truce
40 Type of racehorse
42 Put off the inevitable
43 Cry of surprise
45 Out of practice
46 Singer Sumac
47 Govt. air monitor
48 TV alien
49 Cavalryman
52 Bull Run soldier
54 Fortune partner
58 McCourt memoir
61 Uses a spyhole
64 Prom wear
65 USNA grad
66 Dazzle
67 "We ___ the World"
68 Enzyme ending
69 Sailor's asset
70 NFL scores
71 Forrest Gump's lieutenant

DOWN

1 Sink-stain source
2 Part of 1 Across
3 Let's Make a Deal choices
4 Rope fiber
5 Makes into law
6 Blessed event
7 ___ Romeo
8 Ottoman
9 Jedi's power
10 ___ World Turns
11 Cash or cloth ender
12 Genetic letters
13 Item on an IRS form
21 Defective
22 Backless slipper
26 Leaves port
27 Snowy heron
28 Run-down
30 Clipping candidates
32 Comfort
34 Gas additive
35 Lunchroom lure
36 ___ Heights, Israel
37 Do photo editing
38 Noble title
39 Makes light and airy
41 Coming out
44 Actor Malden
48 "Ridiculous!"
50 Seasonal song
51 Follow
53 Really bother
55 Out in front
56 High-IQ group
57 Ruhr River city
59 Comes to a halt
60 Graph lines
61 Dads
62 Pilot's hdg.
63 Greek letter

★★★ Sudoku

Fill in the blank boxes so that every row, column, and 3x3 box contains all of the numbers 1 to 9.

	7						6	
9				6	8			1
		3	2			8		
	8					1		
	9			5			7	
		6					9	
		5			7	3		
6			9	3				2
	4						1	

MIXAGRAMS

Each line contains a five-letter word and a four-letter word that have been mixed together (the order of the letters in each word has not been changed). Unmix the two words on each line and write them in the spaces provided. When you're done, find a two-part answer to the clue by reading down the letter columns in the answers.

CLUE: New Year's Day event

B A S I I O B R F N = _ _ _ _ _ + _ _ _ _

S A R L O G O W N = _ _ _ _ _ + _ _ _ _

L E A D S A W E N = _ _ _ _ _ + _ _ _ _

T I H S R E L E W = _ _ _ _ _ + _ _ _ _

★★★ One-Way Streets

The diagram represents a pattern of streets. A and B are parking spaces, and the black squares are stores. Find the route that starts at A, passes through all stores exactly once, and ends at B. Arrows indicate one-way traffic for that block only. No block or intersection may be entered more than once.

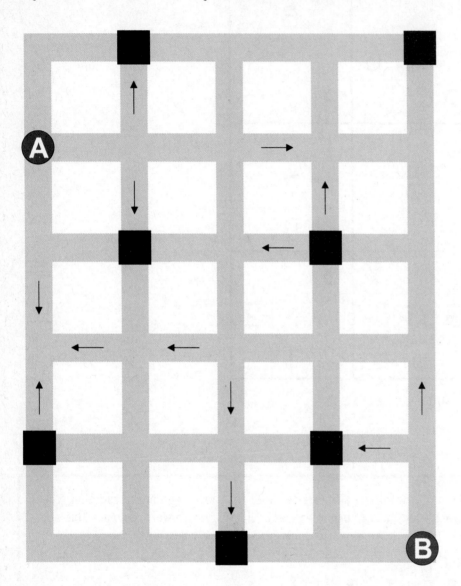

SOUND THINKING

There are only two common uncapitalized words whose only consonant sounds are D, L, and J, in that order. One of them is DELUGE. The other word has five syllables. What is it?

_____

★★★ ABC

Enter the letters A, B, and C into the diagram so that each row and column has exactly one A, one B, and one C. The letters outside the diagram indicate the first letter encountered, moving in the direction of the arrow. Keep in mind that after all the letters have been filled in, there will be two blank boxes in each row and column.

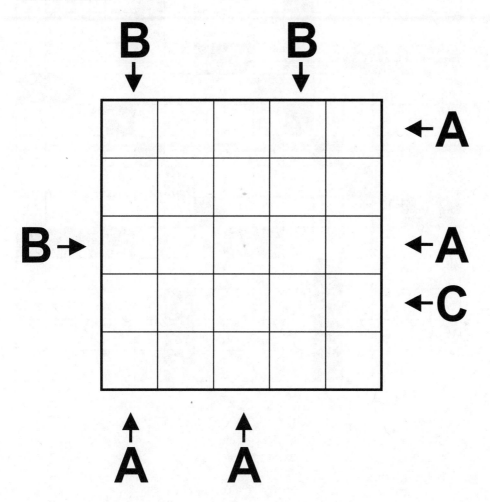

NATIONAL TREASURE

Using the letters in COSTA RICA, we were able to form only one common uncapitalized eight-letter word. If it's a type of puzzle, what's the word?

— — — — — — — —

★★★ Clock Work by Richard Silvestri and Jay Martin

ACROSS

1 Goes out with
6 Like lightning
10 Glasgow girl
14 Residence
15 Ratio words
16 At the peak of
17 All charged up
18 Bibliography abbr.
19 Soccer legend
20 German refusal when the workday starts?
22 Humorist Barry
23 Little bit
24 Yelled from the bleachers
26 Annoy
30 Use plastic
32 Homeric work
33 Jalopy
34 Oddjob's creator
37 Diplomatic agreement
38 Wall Street unit
39 Gawk at
40 Yellowstone beast
41 Make amends
42 Cowboy's "Yippee!"
43 Skateboarding mishap
45 Fasten securely
46 Paint basecoat
48 Caught onto
49 High, in combinations
50 Fairway warning in the afternoon?
57 Trick
58 Something to pump
59 Left the depths
60 Score after deuce
61 Rig on the road
62 Looked a long time
63 Adjacent
64 Be optimistic
65 Onlookers

DOWN

1 Daybreak
2 Anne Nichols character
3 Singer Amos
4 Perfect place
5 Calmed down
6 Mr. Hyde, for one
7 Piedmont province
8 Ollie's partner
9 Put up with
10 Peke, e.g.
11 Had a late supper?
12 Puzzle out
13 Running back's asset

21 Pit contents
25 Substance for smelting
26 Old King Cole request
27 Holy Land airline
28 Orders to attack in the evening?
29 Sylvester, to Tweety Bird
30 Stretch one's neck
31 Hounds' quarry
33 Karate maneuver
35 Shampoo ingredient
36 Element #10
38 Sea urchin's cousin
39 Feedbag morsel

41 Verb for you
42 Power rating
44 Customer
45 Big snake
46 Wrap material
47 Avoid adroitly
48 Bottle dweller
51 Black-and-white snack
52 Win going away
53 Ravel
54 Move like the Blob
55 Software buyer
56 National League team

★★★ What's Next?

Which one of the numbered squares should replace the question mark, to follow the logical pattern in each of these three sequences?

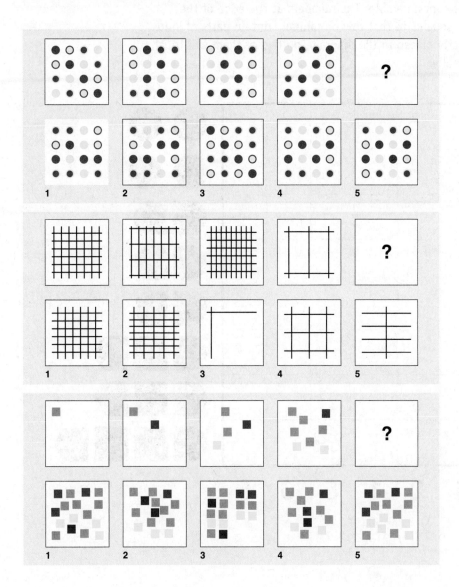

BETWEENER

What four-letter word belongs between the word at left and the word at right, so that the first and second word, and the second and third word, each form a common compound word?

WATCH __ __ __ __ LEADER

★★★ Find the Ships

Determine the position of the 10 ships listed to the right of the diagram. The ships may be oriented either horizontally or vertically. A square with wavy lines indicates water and will not contain a ship. The numbers at the edge of the diagram indicate how many squares in that row or column contain parts of ships. When all 10 ships are correctly placed in the diagram, no two of them will touch each other, not even diagonally.

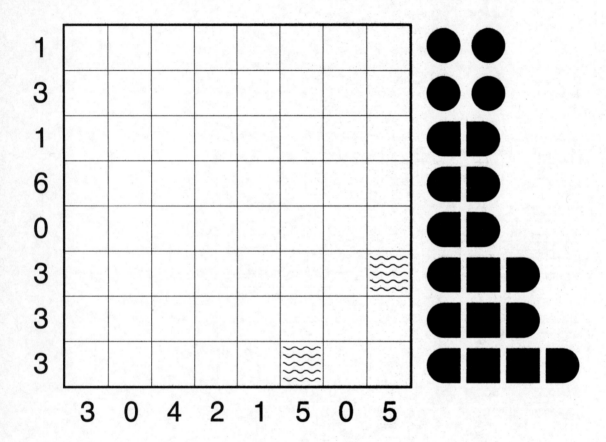

TWO-BY-FOUR

The eight letters in the word VERMOUTH can be rearranged to form a pair of common four-letter words in only one way, if no four-letter word is repeated. Can you find the two words?

— — — —   — — — —

★★★ 123

Fill in the diagram so that each rectangular piece has one each of the numbers 1, 2, and 3, under these rules: 1) No two adjacent squares, horizontally or vertically, can have the same number. 2) Each completed row and column of the diagram will have an equal number of 1s, 2s, and 3s.

SUDOKU SUM

Without repeating any digits, complete the sum at right, by filling one digit in each of the five blanks.

```
  _ 5 _
+ 7 _ 3
_____
  _ _ 1
```

bRain BREATHER
INSIGHTS FROM THE SUPREME COURT

When you throw on a robe and preside over the nation's top court day in and day out, year after year, you're bound to develop pretty good insight into the human condition. Here are some observations from Supreme Court justices past and present. Timeless thoughts? You be the judge.

THE COURTROOMS OF AMERICA TOO OFTEN HAVE PIPER CUB ADVOCATES TRYING TO HANDLE THE CONTROLS OF BOEING 747 LITIGATION.

—WARREN E. BURGER, CHIEF JUSTICE (1969–86)

Everything I did in my life that was worthwhile, I caught hell for.

—EARL WARREN, CHIEF JUSTICE (1953–69)

Swift justice demands more than just swiftness.

—POTTER STEWART, JUSTICE (1958–81)

Lawyers spend a great deal of their time shoveling smoke.

—OLIVER WENDELL HOLMES, JUSTICE (1902–32)

If Columbus had an advisory committee, he would probably still be at the dock.

—ARTHUR J. GOLDBERG, JUSTICE (1962–65)

When I was 40, my doctor advised me that a man in his 40s shouldn't play tennis. I heeded his advice carefully and could hardly wait until I reached 50 to start again.

—HUGO BLACK, JUSTICE (1937–71)

Having family responsibilities and concerns just has to make you a more understanding person.

—SANDRA DAY O'CONNOR, JUSTICE (1981–2006)

When we lose the right to be different, we lose the privilege to be free.

—CHARLES EVANS HUGHES, JUSTICE (1910–16) AND CHIEF JUSTICE (1930–41)

★★★★ Lots Will Be Lost by Donna Levin

ACROSS

1 Word on an invoice
6 Naval noncoms
10 Stitch
13 Rod Stewart ex
14 Cardiologist's concern
15 Islet
16 Miller's imprecation?
18 TNT alternative
19 Orient
20 Odds' counterpart
21 Do an accessory's job
22 Drastic diet in Duluth?
26 Straight up
28 "Caro __" (*Rigoletto* aria)
29 Soup scoop
30 Massive power quantity
34 __ Lanka
35 Grand Canyon transportation
37 Card game
38 Deserts
41 Violin stroke
43 Sow sound
44 Antennae
46 Landscape with care?
50 Sweet debut of 1912
51 "It's __ here!" (baseball announcer's cry)
52 In shape
55 Topper
56 Help from Hopalong?
59 Take advantage of
60 Altercation
61 *Daily Planet* reporter
62 *La Méditerranée*, e.g.
63 Seine tributary
64 Beasts of burden

DOWN

1 Libertine
2 Essayist's alias
3 Newspapers + radio + television
4 Impart
5 Soft 55 Across
6 Ties that bind
7 Captive
8 NBA periods
9 Was in session
10 Breathing aid
11 Palliates
12 *Father Knows Best* mom
14 Choreographer de Mille

17 Hankerings
21 Some
23 Society column word
24 Benin neighbor
25 Doc bloc
26 Rick's inamorata
27 Something counted by dieters
30 Kay Miniver's title
31 Encumbrance, so to speak
32 Something exploited
33 Pulls along
35 Pro __
36 X and Y, in algebra
39 Scrubbed, as a mission

40 It's cast at a casino
41 Press finish
42 Duel weapons
44 __ Martin (car)
45 Cyberauction site
46 Boring
47 Wipe out
48 Discourage
49 Jazzman Blake
53 Words of comprehension
54 Chain components, for short
56 __-Magnon
57 Avignon assent
58 Feathered wrap

★★★ Fences

Connect the dots with vertical or horizontal lines, so that a single loop is formed with no crossings or branches. Each number indicates how many lines surround it; squares with no number may be surrounded by any number of lines.

```
3 1 2   2 1   2
              2
2           3
  1 2         3
1       3 2
  2           3
2
1   2 3   3 3 2
```

ADDITION SWITCH

Switch the positions of two of the digits in the incorrect sum at right, to get a correct sum.

```
  375
+ 209
─────
  881
```

★★★ Number-Out

Shade squares so that no number appears in any row or column more than once. Shaded squares may not touch each other horizontally or vertically, and all unshaded squares must form a single continuous area.

1	1	5	6	3	6
4	5	3	1	3	6
3	5	4	6	6	2
3	3	3	4	5	4
5	6	2	2	1	4
1	6	6	3	2	4

OPPOSITE ATTRACTION

Unscramble the letters in the phrase UNCUT LANE to form two common words that are opposites of each other.

_____   _____

★★★★ No Monkeying Around by Merle Baker

ACROSS

1 Like a clear path
5 Clears out
11 Amount of money
14 Skywalker mentor
15 Former Mideast leader born in Jerusalem
16 Lao-__
17 "Ape" man's study
19 Middle muscles
20 Bombshell
21 Jim Jordan radio role
23 Daisy starter
24 Internet access points
25 Button stuff
28 Some tourist destinations
30 Prefix with skeleton
31 Sputnik stat
34 Former CBS anchor
38 *The Ape Man*
41 Bed board
42 *West Side Story* Oscar winner
43 And the rest
44 "Good grief!"
46 Urban open space
48 Heathens
51 Capital of Samoa
53 Calliope's sister
54 Total
59 __-headed (blond)
60 Ape man, maybe
62 Sound of disapproval
63 Art-class objects
64 This, in Tijuana
65 "All right"
66 Grandstander
67 Vintage cars

DOWN

1 Word with blood or bold
2 *Gilmore Girls* girl
3 Comics-page dog
4 "Chanson __" (song of '58)
5 More than fills
6 Cohort
7 Breathing sound
8 Get an __ effort
9 *GQ*, e.g.
10 Block
11 Wapiti fighters
12 Turkic language
13 Sources of inspiration
18 Idol's attribute
22 *Seinfeld* friend Kramer
24 Big name in fashion
25 Bills
26 Rink maneuver
27 Fountain order
28 Sikorsky and Stravinsky
29 Zaire's Mobutu __ Seko
32 Big cats
33 Start of many hymns
35 Pupil's locale
36 Airhead
37 Geometry prefix
39 Wore away
40 Downcast
45 Fairy-tale figures
47 Soup kitchen volunteer
48 Insignificant
49 Sprang up
50 Stares densely
51 Not on the level
52 Johnny-jump-up
54 Greek peak
55 Manipulative sort
56 Seine tributary
57 Biblical preposition
58 Boxing stats
61 "__ the Walrus"

★★★ Solitaire Poker

Group the 40 cards into eight poker hands of five cards each, so that each hand contains two pairs or better. The cards in each hand must be connected to each other by a common horizontal or vertical side.

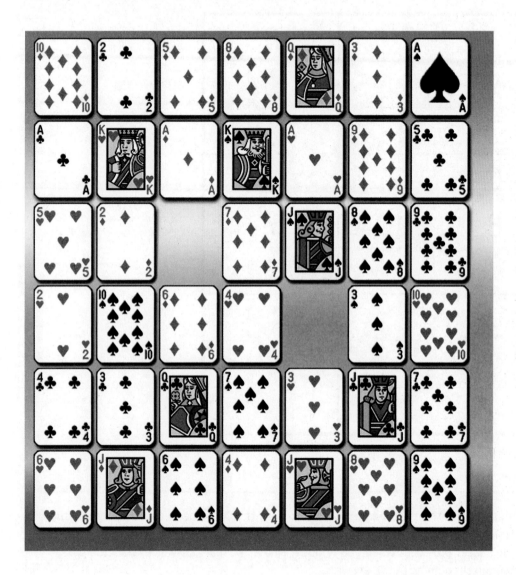

★★★ Hyper-Sudoku

Fill in the blank boxes so that every row, column, 3x3 box, *and* each of the four
3x3 gray regions contains all of the numbers 1 to 9.

				7			8	
9			4	1	5		3	
	3	7		2				
		6						
		8		9	4		7	
	4			3			5	
			1					
	6	3						1
4								

MIXAGRAMS

Each line contains a five-letter word and a four-letter word that have been mixed together (the order of the letters in each word has not been changed). Unmix the two words on each line and write them in the spaces provided. When you're done, find a two-part answer to the clue by reading down the letter columns in the answers.

CLUE: Egg order

O G A M U T E E R =	_ _ _ _ _ + _ _ _ _
V I P T U A M A L =	_ _ _ _ _ + _ _ _ _
P L E A U S S E L =	_ _ _ _ _ + _ _ _ _
P R O B R E O T Y =	_ _ _ _ _ + _ _ _ _

★★★ Film Trail

Beginning with GUYS AND DOLLS, then moving up, down, left or right, one letter at a time, trace a path of these famous films.

AN AMERICAN IN PARIS	LEAVING LAS VEGAS	ROXANNE
BRIEF ENCOUNTER	LOVE STORY	SABRINA
BRINGING UP BABY	MY FAIR LADY	STAGE DOOR
DR ZHIVAGO	NINOTCHKA	THE AFRICAN QUEEN
FROM HERE TO ETERNITY	NOTTING HILL	THE APARTMENT
GIGI	ON GOLDEN POND	THE AWFUL TRUTH
~~GUYS AND DOLLS~~	OUT OF AFRICA	THE KING AND I
HIS GIRL FRIDAY	PILLOW TALK	THE PHILADELPHIA STORY
IT HAPPENED ONE NIGHT	PRIDE AND PREJUDICE	TITANIC
JANE EYRE	ROMAN HOLIDAY	TRULY MADLY DEEPLY
LADY AND THE TRAMP	ROMEO AND JULIET	WORKING GIRL

```
G U T H E K I O N E G H T P I L W T K G
S Y T N E M N D E N I E I J D L O A L I
A D O L L T G A N E J T L U N A M O R G
N D R I S R A N D P A N E F A O E R Y I
A S L G H A P I I P R Y E Y I R L O T B
B Y F S I E H T A E B R M E C A E S R
R A R W F Y T P U I G N I U D I D V O I
I D I A U B A B G N P R E J V A Y S L E
N T H E L T R U T N D I R P I E L A G F
A A C I R F O R H A E D L Y N G L A E E
O U T O F A X Y M A D L P E L I H S V N
A D I L N A A L T Y R Y D E L O G N I C
Y H E O H M N U R T O L I O P N G O T O
A T T M P O N I A S D A H N N E D L T U
N D R A T R E H P L E E P D W K A N O N
A N A Y H E A F R L T H N I O H O N E T
M L A D Z R D C I R I G G K R C T I R T
E O V I H I S A N Q T O E T E G E N R I
R G A I N R N E E U E R I N R A D O O T
I C A N P A F R O M H E T Y S T C I N A
```

INITIAL REACTION

Identify the well-known proverb from the first letters in each of its words.

B. I. I. T. E. O. T. B. _____

★★★★ Wife's Tale by Doug Peterson

ACROSS

1 Catches red-handed
6 Light disperser
11 Bunch of bills
14 Host with a book club
15 Twain contemporary
16 Step on it
17 Start of a quote
19 Sportscaster Cross
20 Divine archer
21 Spanish pianist
23 Like streets in Dickens novels
26 Shot, for short
28 Box-spring supporter
29 Middle of quote
32 Picked out of a lineup
33 Move like honey
34 Ball
35 __ Paese cheese
36 Crumb toter
37 Inspiration for Keats
39 Laid up
42 Right-angle shape
44 Getaway spot
46 Cookie with a 1¾" diameter
47 End of quote
51 "__ off?"
52 Turn down
53 Actually existing
54 Rattle a saber at
56 Pinking-shears sound
57 LPGA star Se Ri __
58 Source of quote
64 Enzyme ending
65 Tony contender
66 Tigger's creator
67 "You there!"
68 Caramel-filled candies
69 Bohemian

DOWN

1 Japanese drama
2 The Simpsons clerk
3 Returns org.
4 Bearing a tag
5 Omar of filmdom
6 Advanced degs.
7 __ Tafari (Haile Selassie)
8 George's lyricist
9 Hard-and-fast
10 Running event
11 Copters
12 Collision cushioner
13 Hoffa director
18 Fanciful idea
22 PC operator
23 Fast-talking
24 Classroom assistant
25 Universal opener
26 Candy in a dispenser
27 Tristram's beloved
30 Corkscrew pasta
31 Sweetie
36 Landon of Kansas
38 Eye part
40 Cask sediment
41 Rich vein
43 Money in Malta
45 Novelist Rohmer
46 Hold 'em holding
47 Tuba sound
48 Tension
49 Worldwide cultural org.
50 Baffler
55 Industry magnate
56 Bygone polit. entities
59 Natl. League city
60 San Diego attraction
61 Layered sandwich
62 Come-__ (inducements)
63 King of Spain

★★ Triad Split Decisions

In this clueless crossword puzzle, each answer consists of two words whose spellings are the same, except for the consecutive letters given. All answers are common words; no phrases or hyphenated or capitalized words are used. Some of the clues may have more than one solution, but there is only one word pair that will correctly link up with all the other word pairs.

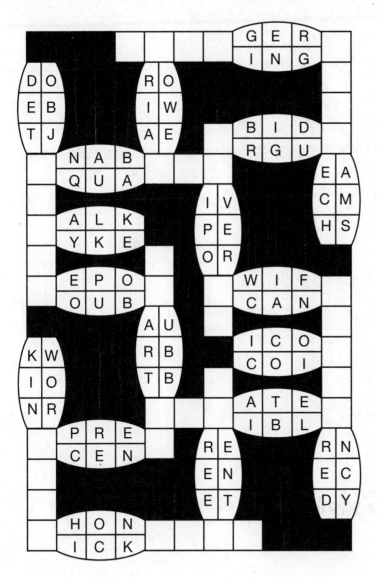

TRANSDELETION

Delete one letter from the word SELECTING and rearrange the rest, to get a type of science.

_____

★★★ One-Way Streets

The diagram represents a pattern of streets. A and B are parking spaces, and the black squares are stores. Find the route that starts at A, passes through all stores exactly once, and ends at B. Arrows indicate one-way traffic for that block only. No block or intersection may be entered more than once.

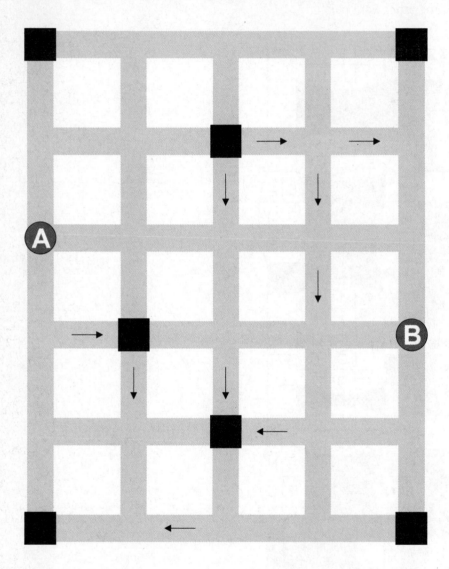

SOUND THINKING

The only common uncapitalized word whose only consonant sounds are F, B, L, and T, in that order, has five syllables. What is it?

_____

★★★★ Take a Good Look by Merle Baker

ACROSS

1 First name in country
5 They may be tested
10 Did the crawl
14 1994 NL Manager of the Year
15 Liqueur flavoring
16 Charter
17 Word-processing command
18 Something to let off
19 Word-processing command
20 Hoity-toity
23 Compass reading
24 Word with hat or hand
25 Used a fork, perhaps
27 Radiation band
32 Smack ender
33 Mauna __
34 Anklebone
36 Tyrolean tune
39 Belgrade native
41 Glaze of egg white
43 "Well done!"
44 With respect to
46 Appropriate, in a way
48 Period
49 Writer Ambler
51 Put by
53 Visibly moved
56 It fell in March 2001
57 Tie __
58 Back-burner
64 Big Apple gallery district
66 Toon coyote
67 Françoise's friend
68 Straw in the wind
69 Sporting blades
70 O'Hara abode
71 Puts on
72 Sold, with "in"
73 Graph lines

DOWN

1 Too quick
2 *The Time Machine* race
3 Winner of five consecutive Wimbledons
4 Write
5 Taxed one's patience
6 Worldwide: Abbr.
7 In __ of
8 Exams for would-be attys.
9 Mideast native
10 Boat pronoun
11 Like some jets
12 Spring up
13 Parceled (out)
21 Black key, at times
22 Not any
26 Blessing
27 Rick's love
28 Thumbs-down votes
29 Strained
30 First name in seal
31 Wrestling meets
35 Bank deposit of a sort
37 Neutral tone
38 Bound
40 Gun-barrel diameter
42 Superlatively commodious
45 Mideast coin
47 Small combo
50 Talked big
52 Book insertion
53 "Don't worry"
54 Singer Judd
55 Card-reader instruction
59 Court statement
60 Film segment
61 Film format
62 Ersatz swing
63 Thumbs-up votes
65 Switch positions

★★★ Straight Ahead

Entering the grid where indicated, pass through all of the blue squares, and then exit. You must travel horizontally or vertically in a straight line, and turn only to avoid passing through a black square. It is okay to retrace your path.

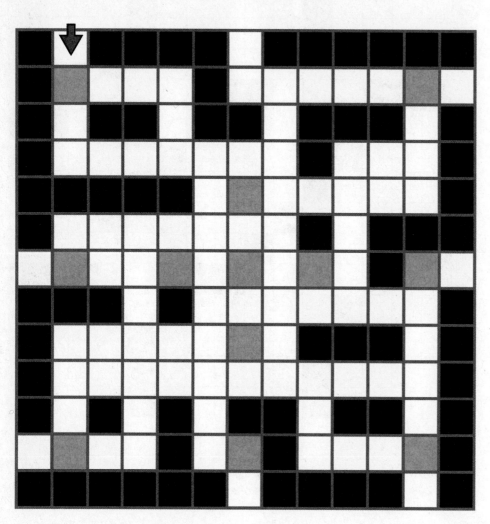

SAY IT AGAIN

What six-letter word for a type of meal, when pronounced differently, is also a verb meaning "hit"?

— — — — — —

★★★ Star Search

Find the stars that are hidden in some of the blank squares. The numbered squares indicate how many stars are hidden in the squares adjacent to them (including diagonally). There is never more than one star in any square.

		1		3			
	2		3	6		4	
							1
	3			4			
		3				3	1
	4			1			
	1	1	1	1	1		

TELEPHONE TRIOS

1	ABC 2	DEF 3
GHI 4	JKL 5	MNO 6
PRS 7	TUV 8	WXY 9
*	0	#

Using the numbers and letters on a standard telephone, what three seven-letter words or phrases from the same category can be formed from these telephone numbers?

546-4746   _ _ _ _ _ _ _

626-2437   _ _ _ _ _ _ _

754-7737   _ _ _ _ _ _ _

★★★ Sudoku

Fill in the blank boxes so that every row, column, and 3x3 box contains all of the numbers 1 to 9.

				8	5	3		
	1		2				8	
2		8				6		
1							7	
6				7				2
	8							5
	4					9		1
	9				8		3	
		3	9	5				

CENTURY MARKS

Inserting plus signs and minus signs, as many as necessary, in between the nine digits below, create a series of additions and subtractions whose final answer is 100. Any digits without a sign between them are to be grouped together as a single number.

5　4　6　1　1　8　7　2　7　=　100

★★★★ Terse Comment by Ann W. Masten

ACROSS

1 Game quests
8 Wimbledon winner in '55
15 About 2.5 centimeters
16 Toast recipient
17 Start of an observation
19 Not included: Abbr.
20 Phillips of CNN
21 Lowdown
22 Ringmaster, e.g.
25 Biblical pronoun
27 Bit of encouragement
30 Daughter of Hyperion
31 Pay no attention to
35 Kind of camera
36 Catch
38 Wainwright product
39 Middle of observation
42 Chutzpah
43 Auto debut of '57
44 Favorite
45 Nag's activity
47 CDLXXV doubled
48 QB stat
49 Polished off
50 Cannes cup
52 Persian poet
55 Discontinuities
57 Leave the ground
61 End of observation
65 Alliance
66 Came into
67 Summer pest
68 Scotch cocktails

DOWN

1 Tofu source
2 "And giving __, up ..."
3 Squabble
4 Narrow path
5 "Messenger" compound
6 Cool
7 Hops to
8 B.C. character
9 Make alternations
10 Far East airline
11 2000 Best Song Oscar winner
12 Suffix for smash
13 Take a second tour
14 Nantes noggin
18 Bleaching agent
23 GI accessory
24 Volcanic shape
26 Coiner of "atomic bomb"
27 Intimidate, with "out"
28 Parting word
29 Comparatively correct
31 Anchor, for one
32 Where Memphis is
33 Murmured
34 Bolt fasteners
37 Erstwhile post-office abbr.
40 Banter
41 Doesn't commit
46 Undo
50 Toll rd.
51 Howdy Doody's original name
52 Metrical tributes
53 Bebop pioneer
54 Latin preposition
56 Angel or Oriole
58 Franc replacer
59 __-deucey
60 Many profs.
62 NASCAR race airer
63 Lennon's middle name
64 Wagering locale

★★★ ABC

Enter the letters A, B, and C into the diagram so that each row and column has exactly one A, one B, and one C. The letters outside the diagram indicate the first letter encountered, moving in the direction of the arrow. Keep in mind that after all the letters have been filled in, there will be two blank boxes in each row and column.

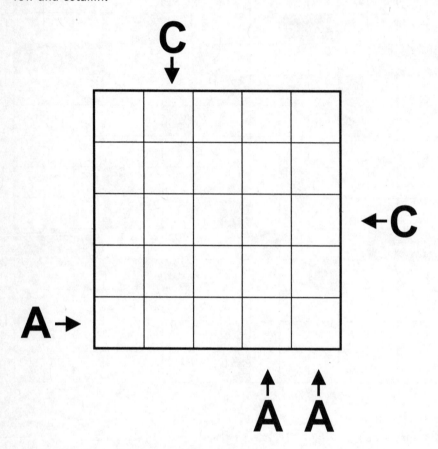

CLUELESS CROSSWORD

Complete the crossword with common uncapitalized seven-letter words, based entirely on the letters already filled in for you.

B	O	B	S	W	E	P
A	■		■			■
Z					U	
Z	■		■		■	
A		B		I		G
R	■		■	Z	■	N
S		R	K			

★★★ Find the Ships

Determine the position of the 10 ships listed to the right of the diagram. The ships may be oriented either horizontally or vertically. A square with wavy lines indicates water and will not contain a ship. The numbers at the edge of the diagram indicate how many squares in that row or column contain parts of ships. When all 10 ships are correctly placed in the diagram, no two of them will touch each other, not even diagonally.

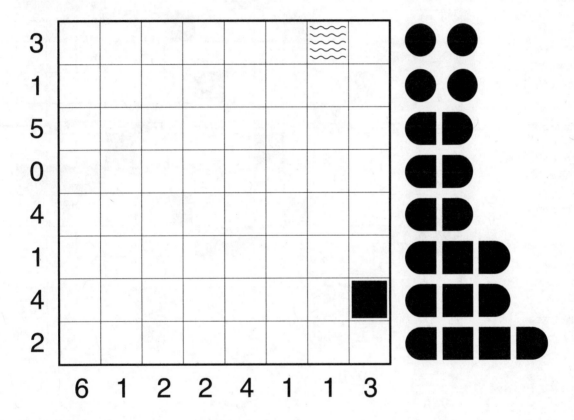

TWO-BY-FOUR

The eight letters in the word WAYFARER can be rearranged to form a pair of common four-letter words in two different ways, if no four-letter word is repeated. Can you find both pairs of words?

READ   DEAR
FARE   REAF

★★★★ It's Only a Movie by Merle Baker

ACROSS

1 Not fully closed
5 Last of a series
10 Old Testament book
14 "No problem!"
15 Voting places
16 Delete
17 Movie disclaimer word
19 Frost product
20 Vast quantities
21 Slanted type: Abbr.
23 Made over
24 Taxpayer's ID
26 List separator
30 Movie disclaimer phrase
33 Davis' org.
36 Office helper
37 Rib
38 "___ and Away"
40 Food and water
42 Construction area
43 Celestial belt
45 Sleep symbols
47 Saturn or Mercury
48 Movie disclaimer word
51 *What's Up, Doc?* star
52 Publishing execs.
53 Sherpa's land
57 Tempest in a teapot
59 Audiophile's purchase
60 *Time* 2005 Person of the Year
63 Movie disclaimer word
66 Maintain
67 Lunch preceder, perhaps
68 Author Ferber
69 Pen entrance
70 Lukewarm
71 Start a hand

DOWN

1 Concerning
2 Energy, so to speak
3 Moved in a curved path
4 Full price
5 Makes a choice
6 Miss Piggy's query
7 "Evil Woman" group
8 Bonding
9 Mgr.'s helper
10 Goes off
11 Madhouse
12 Wish undone
13 Twenties source
18 Mumbai's land
22 Lot measurement
24 Dish or street preceder
25 Expelled, in a way
27 *M*A*S*H* extra
28 Spot near Sicily
29 "Doe, ___ ..."
31 Leonardo's hometown
32 Beginning
33 Capital of the Inca empire
34 Stirrer
35 WWII hero Murphy
39 *Little House on the Prairie* garment
41 Family rooms
44 Rights org.
46 Father Christmas
49 Crave
50 Looked impolitely
54 Roaring group
55 Prudential competitor
56 True-blue
58 USAF NCO
59 Iditarod vehicle
60 Sack
61 Caesar's eggs
62 Final amount
64 Plan, with "out"
65 Here, in Martinique

★★ Arm Art

Which of the 10 transfers produced the temporary tattoo?

THREE AT A RHYME

Rearrange these letters to form three one-syllable words that rhyme.

E E E E G G G M R R R S U U

_____ _____ _____

★★★ 123

Fill in the diagram so that each rectangular piece has one each of the numbers 1, 2, and 3, under these rules: 1) No two adjacent squares, horizontally or vertically, can have the same number. 2) Each completed row and column of the diagram will have an equal number of 1s, 2s, and 3s.

SUDOKU SUM

Without repeating any digits, complete the sum at right, by filling one digit in each of the five blanks.

```
    _ 2 7
  + 6 _ _
  _ 4 _
```

★★★ Fences

Connect the dots with vertical or horizontal lines, so that a single loop is formed with no crossings or branches. Each number indicates how many lines surround it; squares with no number may be surrounded by any number of lines.

```
3  2    3  1       2

      3               1

3            2  1  3

2                     2

3                     3

   3  2  3            1

0                 1

1          2  2    1  1
```

★★★★ Ark-Ana by Richard Silvestri

ACROSS

1 Matures, as wine
5 Chanel of fashion
9 Tonsorial tool
14 Draw in
15 Have a premiere
16 Informed
17 Ontario neighbor
18 Soccer legend
19 Israeli desert
20 Lewis' foolish partner?
23 Dallas sch.
24 Back biters
28 Maze runner
31 Speck
34 Sniff out
36 At full force
38 Tin Pan Alley topic
40 Naval greeting
41 Hybrid songbird?
44 Eventful times
45 Exact
46 Beast of Borden
47 Gimel follower
49 First-class
51 Isn't out of
52 Poe woman
54 Part of TGIF
56 Dogfish roe?
62 Distant
66 Software buyer
67 Russian Everyman
68 *Boom Town* star
69 A-line creator
70 Muse count
71 Nitrous __ (laughing gas)
72 Allay
73 Upper hand

DOWN

1 Composer Wilder
2 Spiritual guide
3 Norse explorer
4 Hunts for
5 Pretext
6 Crude group
7 Battery unit
8 Wee hour
9 Irritate
10 Blow away
11 Half a crooked course
12 Comstock output
13 Hit the accelerator
21 Muscat native
22 Calgary Stampede, for one
25 In any way
26 Same old discussion
27 Smelting refuse
28 Competed at Indy
29 Ethically neutral
30 Mexicali munchie
32 Patron saint of Norway
33 Sacred part-song
35 Little ones
37 *Peer Gynt* playwright
39 Chianti, e.g.
42 '60s jacket
43 Egg containers
48 Chewy candy
50 Conductor Boulez
53 Piano piece
55 Excel
57 VOA agcy.
58 Model T contemporaries
59 Gung-ho
60 Pealed
61 Proposer's prop
62 In the past
63 Not rigid
64 Kabuki accessory
65 Dated

★★★ Hyper-Sudoku

Fill in the blank boxes so that every row, column, 3x3 box, *and* each of the four 3x3 gray regions contains all of the numbers 1 to 9.

	1			8	2	4		
6								2
3			9	7				
	2	4		1		3		
						9	5	
	6		5				8	
			2		3			
	3	7			5			

MIXAGRAMS

Each line contains a five-letter word and a four-letter word that have been mixed together (the order of the letters in each word has not been changed). Unmix the two words on each line and write them in the spaces provided. When you're done, find a two-part answer to the clue by reading down the letter columns in the answers.

CLUE: Gleason character

S A P O U R P A L = _ _ _ _ _ + _ _ _ _

C O O K U P E R A = _ _ _ _ _ + _ _ _ _

F O U R G R E T E = _ _ _ _ _ + _ _ _ _

A L O R G U G E O = _ _ _ _ _ + _ _ _ _

★★ Split Decisions

In this clueless crossword puzzle, each answer consists of two words whose spellings are the same, except for the consecutive letters given. All answers are common words; no phrases or hyphenated or capitalized words are used. Some of the clues may have more than one solution, but there is only one word pair that will correctly link up with all the other word pairs.

TRANSDELETION

Delete one letter from the word TRIPLANE and rearrange the rest, to get an occupation.

_____

★★★★ Mixed Media by Ed Stein

ACROSS

1 Enliven
5 European duck
9 Short breaths
14 "Miracle Mets" outfielder
15 Intl. relief org.
16 Hawkeye
17 With 56 Down, famous "pair"
20 __ soda
21 Warm
22 Unit of energy
23 Insect stage
24 High bond rating
26 With 58 Down, famous "pair"
34 Call off, as a launch
35 Where the Wabash R. flows
36 Pudding ingredient
37 Abbr. on dumbbells
38 Least original
42 Family dog
43 Subtraction word
45 Unified
46 Arm bones
48 With 61 Down, famous "pair"
52 '60s First Lady
53 Deadly sin
54 Hack follower
57 Dom of comedy
60 "Gotcha!"
63 Alternate title for this puzzle
66 Came up
67 *Star Trek: Deep Space Nine* character
68 Rock-song affirmative
69 At present
70 Deadlocked
71 Mini-maelstrom

DOWN

1 Binges
2 Indian tourist stop
3 Fervor
4 Enlightenment movement
5 Shrimp dish
6 Song from *Flashdance*
7 *Das Rheingold* role
8 "Up, Up and Away" composer
9 Balm of __ (fragrant resin)
10 Gmail competitor
11 __'pea
12 '60s TV host
13 Tight
18 Rides hard
19 They have twisted horns
23 __ *favor*
25 Slow equine
26 __ d'Aosta (Italian region)
27 Declined
28 Martini partner
29 Had the flu
30 Chemical suffix
31 Magoo's nephew
32 Twice
33 "Pass"
39 Just so
40 Shakers founder Lee
41 Newspaper section
44 NASCAR sponsor
47 "Once in Love With __"
49 South __, MA (Mount Holyoke locale)
50 Hall of *Days of Our Lives*
51 Yoke up a team
54 Shoe covering
55 Sol preceder
56 See 17 Across
58 See 26 Across
59 State sch.
60 Got a hole in one
61 See 48 Across
62 Pale as a ghost
64 Charitable TV spot
65 Ensign's affirmative

★★★ Color Paths

Find the shortest path through the maze from the bottom to the center, by using paths in this color order: red, blue, yellow, red, blue, etc. Change path colors through the white squares. It is okay to retrace your path.

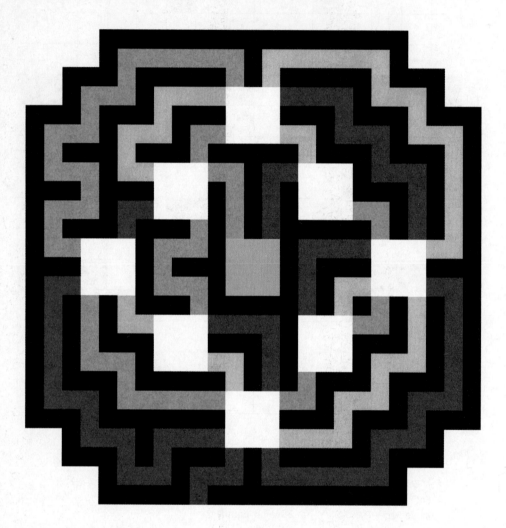

BETWEENER

What five-letter word belongs between the word at left and the word at right, so that the first and second word, and the second and third word, each form a common compound word?

BITTER __ __ __ __ __ HEART

★★★ Number-Out

Shade squares so that no number appears in any row or column more than once. Shaded squares may not touch each other horizontally or vertically, and all unshaded squares must form a single continuous area.

4	4	1	5	2	2
3	2	2	6	4	5
2	4	5	3	1	6
2	1	1	3	6	5
5	6	6	3	3	4
6	3	4	1	2	5

OPPOSITE ATTRACTION

Unscramble the letters in the phrase IRE EXTENT to form two common words that are opposites of each other.

_____   _____

★★★ One-Way Streets

The diagram represents a pattern of streets. A and B are parking spaces, and the black squares are stores. Find the route that starts at A, passes through all stores exactly once, and ends at B. Arrows indicate one-way traffic for that block only. No block or intersection may be entered more than once.

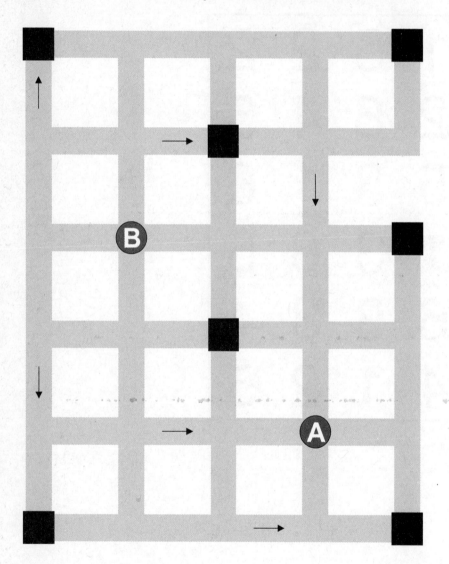

SOUND THINKING

There are only two common uncapitalized words whose only consonant sounds are H, D, N, and T, in that order. One of them is HADN'T. The other word has no apostrophe. What is it?

_____

★★★★ Say Cheese! by Doug Peterson

ACROSS

1 Peloponnesian city
6 Australian rock band
10 USAF rank
14 Intimidate
15 Erstwhile Big Apple stadium
16 Mimicked
17 French farewell
18 Concert souvenirs
20 Subject of the quote
22 *Uno + due*
23 Gabor of *Green Acres*
24 WWII females
26 Start of a quote
30 Atomized
33 Paid players
34 Nosh
36 Raw materials
37 Middle of quote
39 WWII battle site
40 Limbo prop
41 *Fargo* director
42 Detail-oriented
43 End of quote
47 Growth: Abbr.
48 Movers' vehicle
49 Mex. neighbor
52 Speaker of the quote
57 Foggy
59 Trapper John in *M*A*S*H*
60 Against
61 Nitwit
62 Hit the road
63 Cookbook instruction
64 Skirt feature
65 French females

DOWN

1 Roll with the punches
2 Speeder spotter
3 Semblance
4 Till fillers
5 Baffle
6 Of the stars
7 Guitarist Atkins
8 Profound
9 ATM output
10 Tropical cocktail
11 Ten-speed components
12 Catch on to
13 Scoring plays, for short
19 Wolf calls
21 "Egg" starter
25 Makes waterproof
26 Tag players
27 Think out loud
28 Hosp. sites
29 Garden-pond fish
30 Wild bunch
31 Qom resident
32 Olduvai Gorge locale
35 Happy Meal bonus
37 Little one
38 Chuckle sound
39 Have a bite
41 Data holder
42 Get by trickery
44 Patisserie product
45 Commercial
46 Not refined
49 Run-of-the-mill
50 Work out
51 Much of Chile
53 Some checkers
54 Adored star
55 BMW competitor
56 Holiday number
57 Airline to Stockholm
58 Explosive letters

★★★ Sudoku

Fill in the blank boxes so that every row, column, and 3x3 box contains all of the numbers 1 to 9.

		9				3	6	
					5			
	3				8	4	5	
			4					
	5		8	3	6		7	
			2					
	8	1	7				4	
			2					
	9	4				1		

MIXAGRAMS

Each line contains a five-letter word and a four-letter word that have been mixed together (the order of the letters in each word has not been changed). Unmix the two words on each line and write them in the spaces provided. When you're done, find a two-part answer to the clue by reading down the letter columns in the answers.

CLUE: Hi-fi accessory

T O D U R A T C H = _ _ _ _ _ + _ _ _ _

A N E V I N O L Y = _ _ _ _ _ + _ _ _ _

C O P E R I K L Y = _ _ _ _ _ + _ _ _ _

K E A N O T B E N = _ _ _ _ _ + _ _ _ _

★★★ Star Search

Find the stars that are hidden in some of the blank squares. The numbered squares indicate how many stars are hidden in the squares adjacent to them (including diagonally). There is never more than one star in any square.

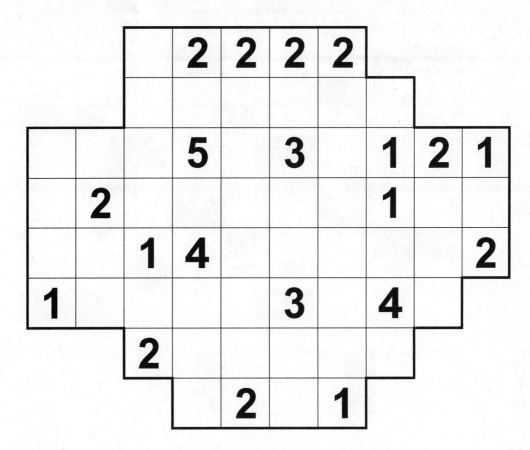

TELEPHONE TRIOS

1	ABC 2	DEF 3
GHI 4	JKL 5	MNO 6
PRS 7	TUV 8	WXY 9
*	o	#

Using the numbers and letters on a standard telephone, what three seven-letter words or phrases from the same category can be formed from these telephone numbers?

227-4825   _ _ _ _ _ _ _

637-8344   _ _ _ _ _ _ _

728-4647   _ _ _ _ _ _ _

★★★★ Arf! Arf! by Randall J. Hartman

ACROSS

1 Syrup sources
7 Tiny time unit: Abbr.
11 Shade tree
14 Make an impression on
15 Casual agreement
16 Kung __ chicken
17 Start of a quip
20 Tick off
21 Mother-of-pearl
22 Hit the brakes
25 Part 2 of quip
28 His work was often sketchy
30 They might be pale
31 Goes along with
32 "__ you kidding?"
33 New England soda fountain
36 La-la lead-in
37 Part 3 of quip
41 Engineer's spot
42 __ Ramon, CA
43 Water-temperature tester
44 NATO member
46 Hawaiian island
48 Sonora shawls
50 Part 4 of quip
54 Pop pianist Alicia
55 Knight's weapon
56 Nouveau __
58 End of quip
64 Sigma follower
65 Ltr. on a handkerchief
66 Plaza Hotel girl of fiction
67 "Lucky Lady in the fifth," e.g.
68 Something to crack
69 Out of breath

DOWN

1 Day or night starter
2 French friend
3 Not COD
4 Retail purchase plan
5 Samuelson's field: Abbr.
6 Publicity ploys
7 "No way!"
8 Vast body
9 Pitcher part
10 Purse contents
11 Memorable time
12 Dern of film
13 A cappella composition
18 Santa's chuckle
19 Carlsbad Caverns denizens
22 Sticky wickets
23 October sign
24 Role for Clooney
26 Scoot
27 Bread spread
29 Compass reading
32 Had something
33 Scenic word ender
34 CBS founder
35 Deep gulf
38 Needle case
39 Film __
40 Broadcast
45 Brings aboard
46 Ramsgate raincoats
47 Vinegary
48 Be good for
49 Avoid
50 Country guitarist Lester
51 Neighbor of 46 Across
52 Finish
53 Land of the Minoans
57 Copter prefix
59 Lennon's mate
60 Box top
61 Tucked out of sight
62 Verb ending
63 Got hitched

★★★ Turn Maze

Entering at the bottom and exiting at the top, find the shortest path through the maze, following these turn rules: You must turn right on red squares, turn left on blue squares, and go straight through yellow squares. Your path may retrace itself and cross at intersections, but you may not reverse your direction at any point.

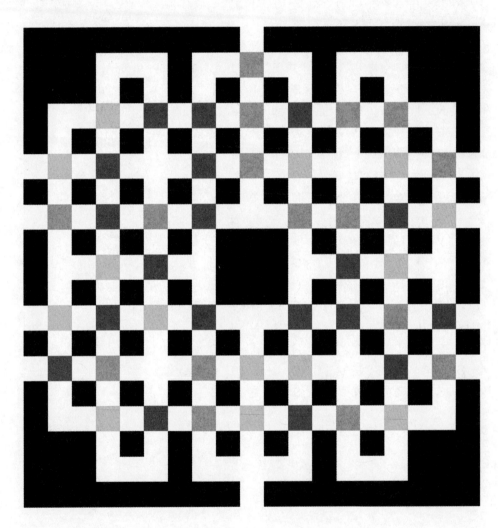

SAY IT AGAIN

What six-letter word meaning "leave behind," when pronounced differently, is also a type of geographic region?

— — — — — —

★★ Jolly Good

Find these seven-letter J words that are hidden in identical J-shapes in the diagram. One answer is shown to get you started.

```
V  E  L  I  N  A  W  J  E  W  E  L  Z  I  W  A  S  G  I  S
W  R  A  B  J  I  A  E  J  A  Y  C  I  Z  Z  I  J  P  E  W
J  Y  N  E  A  N  D  L  A  X  R  J  N  Z  A  W  E  B  O  A
E  T  R  S  W  G  K  L  S  I  E  U  S  U  M  I  R  K  C  S
J  B  U  T  B  A  C  A  M  G  N  J  P  C  J  E  K  J  O  G
U  O  E  R  O  C  B  F  J  E  I  R  A  K  S  W  I  A  I  L
B  X  O  N  P  K  I  N  J  O  N  E  J  D  E  N  T  J  Z  I
E  Q  J  I  O  E  J  E  A  W  B  P  O  A  W  J  B  U  Z  U
T  U  A  P  V  X  U  R  C  J  Q  I  U  W  A  I  O  J  U  Q
B  I  C  E  L  O  Z  Z  K  J  U  N  R  J  D  G  X  U  C  J
E  L  K  R  I  B  S  I  A  A  U  O  N  E  K  S  T  B  A  A
S  H  E  J  N  E  T  S  B  S  L  B  J  L  C  A  E  N  T  C
U  T  W  J  Q  K  E  V  M  M  E  W  R  A  P  J  U  K  E  O
K  I  N  S  U  N  K  E  A  I  R  A  J  B  O  A  J  T  U  N
E  J  I  E  I  J  C  S  N  H  Y  J  E  A  N  M  O  S  E  J
B  W  L  Y  L  O  A  A  E  T  J  O  T  N  E  M  R  Y  J  M
O  X  E  S  T  N  J  W  I  N  E  W  T  G  I  I  N  E  A  T
J  E  V  N  H  Q  G  S  H  I  S  B  I  T  N  B  A  S  C  A
G  A  P  L  V  U  H  J  M  C  T  E  A  S  S  J  L  R  K  T
J  U  J  B  I  T  E  S  A  K  E  N  I  M  S  A  E  J  E  R
```

JACINTH
JACKASS
JACKDAW
JACKETS
JACONET
JACUZZI
JAMMING
JASMINE
JAVELIN
JAWBONE
JELLABA
JERKINS
JERSEYS
JETTIES
JIGSAWS
JOINERY
JONQUIL
~~JOURNAL~~
JUJUBES
JUKEBOX
JUNIPER

WHO'S WHAT WHERE?

The correct term for a resident of Warsaw, Poland, is:

A) Varsovian   B) Warsawite

C) Warsawer   D) Warsawian

★★★ ABC

Enter the letters A, B, and C into the diagram so that each row and column has exactly one A, one B, and one C. The letters outside the diagram indicate the first letter encountered, moving in the direction of the arrow. Keep in mind that after all the letters have been filled in, there will be two blank boxes in each row and column.

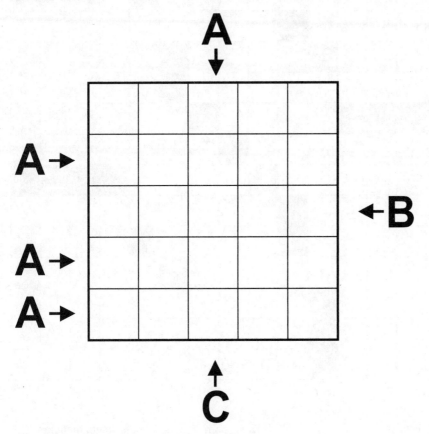

CLUELESS CROSSWORD

Complete the crossword with common uncapitalized seven-letter words, based entirely on the letters already filled in for you.

★★★★★ Themeless Toughie by Merle Baker

ACROSS

1 Mark Twain, for one
11 *Residencia*
15 Begins
16 Time callers
17 Underdog, often
18 Driving-home stat
19 Have a cow
20 Tuscany title
22 "That's __!"
23 Red character
24 Parisian pronoun
25 Not smart
27 Sounds of thunder
28 Makes groovy
29 World's third-largest island
30 Moses and Dorothy
34 Equivoque master
35 Stuck around
36 Mustard family plant
37 Western prowlers
38 Did what was necessary
43 Nip in the bud
44 Sidekick
45 River to the Rhine
46 China/Korea separator
48 Psychic fields
49 It might be pending
50 Bringing in
52 Sept-__, Québec
53 Check
54 Blackjack holdings
55 Think-tank employee

DOWN

1 They have drawing power
2 Gulp down
3 Georgian revolutionary
4 Personalities
5 Heraldic band
6 Run through
7 Shirley Temple feature
8 Admittance
9 They're on the field a lot
10 Norse goddess of fate
11 Rennet and such, for milk
12 Moving about
13 *Clockers* director
14 County official
21 Gives evidence
23 Given evidence
26 Carmaker Maserati
29 Cumbersome
30 Sarawak's locale
31 Mainly
32 Respondent in the Inns of Court
33 Like krypton
34 Where running isn't advisable
36 *Gigi* novelist
38 Experienced
39 Remove slack from
40 Rope for reefing a sail
41 Lippizaner move
42 "Where Have All the Flowers Gone" writer
47 African valley
48 It means "height"
51 Branch

bRain BRᴇᴀTHᴇr
DRUG-FREE HEADACHE RELIEF

Slowly but surely, the medical establishment is embracing naturopathic remedies as an alternative to prescription or over-the-counter drugs. Since virtually everyone has a headache at least once in a while, you'll want to keep these alternative therapies in mind for the next time you feel a headache coming on.

Running hot and cold To cure a tension headache (caused by contractions in the head and neck and brought on by—among other things—stress, anxiety, and lack of sleep), dip a washcloth in hot water, wring it out, and fold it into a compress. Place it on your forehead or the back of your neck to relax tight muscles.

To ease a vascular headache (including migraine and cluster headaches, and stemming from the contraction and expansion of blood vessels in a particular area of the head), follow the same procedure, but use cold water, which constricts the blood vessels and reduces blood flow, taking the pressure off a hurting head.

Wear a headband Tie a scarf, necktie, or bandana tightly around your forehead to reduce the flow of blood to your scalp and, in turn, to throbbing swollen blood vessels.

Sinus headache self-massage Use your middle fingers to massage the points of the face just opposite your nostrils—that is, at the level of the tip of your nose. Massage with clockwise circles for two or three minutes.

A cup o' joe makes the headache go A clinical trial in Illinois found that caffeine, which reduces the swelling of blood vessels, can reduce both the intensity and frequency of headaches. Subjects in one group were given caffeine alone, and 58 percent reported complete relief. Subjects in the other group were given caffeine in combination with ibuprofen, and 70 percent saw their symptoms disappear.

Head-to-toe headache remedy Blood drawn to the lower body will reduce pressure in the blood vessels of the head, and what's lower than your feet? To help soothe a throbbing vascular headache, soak your feet in a small tub filled with hot water mixed with mustard powder. After a half hour or so, hotfoot it to the nearest towel, dry your feet, and feel better!

Sip ginger tea Ginger tea works especially well for migraines. Pour 3 cups of water over 2 tablespoons of freshly grated ginger, let steep 4-5 minutes, and then strain through a small sieve. Ginger tea bags are also available but the tea lacks the punch of fresh gingerroot.

★★★★ Find the Ships

Determine the position of the 10 ships listed to the right of the diagram. The ships may be oriented either horizontally or vertically. A square with wavy lines indicates water and will not contain a ship. The numbers at the edge of the diagram indicate how many squares in that row or column contain parts of ships. When all 10 ships are correctly placed in the diagram, no two of them will touch each other, not even diagonally.

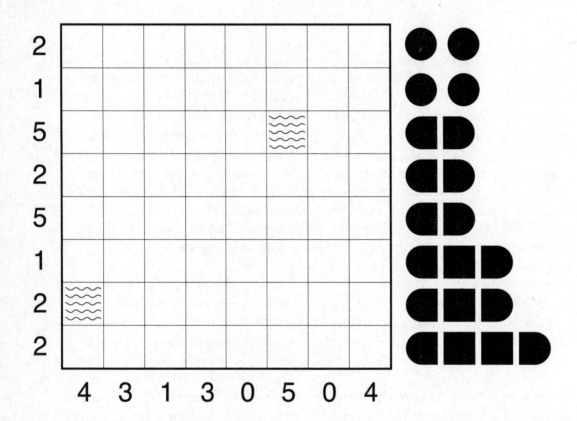

TWO-BY-FOUR

The eight letters in the word AUTUMNAL can be rearranged to form a pair of common four-letter words in only one way, if no four-letter word is repeated. Can you find the two words?

— — — —   — — — —

★★★★ Hyper-Sudoku

Fill in the blank boxes so that every row, column, 3x3 box, *and* each of the four 3x3 gray regions contains all of the numbers 1 to 9.

							3	
	6							
9			1					
	5	3				8	9	
			8				7	
		9	2					
5			4		9			
8	2		1					7
		6						

BETWEENER

What five-letter word belongs between the word at left and the word at right, so that the first and second word, and the second and third word, each form a common compound word?

TOUCH __ __ __ __ __ WALL

★★★★★ Themeless Toughie by Daniel R. Stark

ACROSS

1 Seasoned
8 Cinderella's loss
15 Money-grubbery
16 Certain saver
17 Honors
18 They're out for themselves
19 Range of view
20 *Eve's Diary* writer
22 Something helpful
23 Family member
24 Storm warning
25 Points of convergence
26 *1776* role
27 Faulty
28 Degas contemporary
29 Dregs
31 Hair stuff
32 Called
33 Disagreeable one
34 Reach
37 Like some jobs
41 Dappled horses
42 Traffic blockers
43 Pro __
44 "Hey __" (carny's cry)
45 Pamplona runners
46 Tanless
47 Turkish potentate
48 Juice
49 Type of 48 Across
50 Tell
52 Stemming (from)
54 More noble
55 Distance
56 Regards highly
57 Made lovelier

DOWN

1 Feudal tenants
2 One out
3 Like a hawk
4 Spew
5 Observance
6 Go-to guy
7 Robin's offspring
8 Sewer need
9 Kosher
10 Strong-willed
11 Paste of a sort
12 NBA team

13 Tempts
14 Short break
21 *The Day of the Locust* author
24 Famous last words
25 Geologic fracture
27 Gather together
28 Sheds
30 Peace goddess
31 Bogs down
33 Wide view
34 Work with the flowers

35 Wild felines
36 Night spot
37 Minute opening
38 Sonnet style
39 Hodgepodge
40 Came out
42 Shows fear
45 Alaskan carving
46 Toughie
48 Canapé topper
49 Fodder home
51 Actress Charlotte
53 Unburdened

★★ Crime Scene

Which of the seven sections has the criminal artist painted a white patch over?

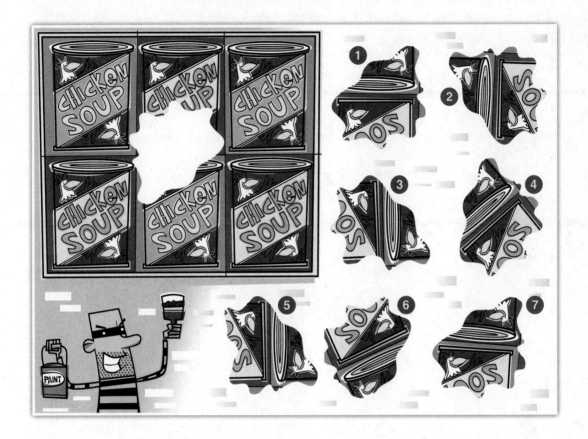

THREE AT A RHYME

Rearrange these letters to form three one-syllable words that rhyme.

A C E E E E I K K L L Q S U

_____ _____ _____

★★★★ Fences

Connect the dots with vertical or horizontal lines, so that a single loop is formed with no crossings or branches. Each number indicates how many lines surround it; squares with no number may be surrounded by any number of lines.

```
·   ·   ·   ·   ·   ·   ·   ·   ·
    3       1           3   3
·   ·   ·   ·   ·   ·   ·   ·   ·
      0
·   ·   ·   ·   ·   ·   ·   ·   ·
                2   3
·   ·   ·   ·   ·   ·   ·   ·   ·
  3       3
·   ·   ·   ·   ·   ·   ·   ·   ·
            2           2
·   ·   ·   ·   ·   ·   ·   ·   ·
      0 3
·   ·   ·   ·   ·   ·   ·   ·   ·
                        3
·   ·   ·   ·   ·   ·   ·   ·   ·
  3 2       3       0
·   ·   ·   ·   ·   ·   ·   ·   ·
```

ADDITION SWITCH

Switch the positions of two of the digits in the incorrect sum at right, to get a correct sum.

```
  790
+ 313
-----
  707
```

★★★★★ Themeless Toughie by Anna Stiga

ACROSS

1 Cry of astonishment
8 Warplane crewman, at times
15 Great accomplishment, in business slang
16 Fragrant blossom
17 Finished
18 Aces
19 Kisses, for instance
20 Amend or abridge
22 Satirical piece
23 Isn't serious
24 Anytown, USA address
26 One in the first generation
27 Sp. title
28 Where gutters are
29 Cash
31 Type of tie
32 Approach
33 Place to relax
36 Literary pseudonym
37 Symbol of royalty, in China
38 Estimates, with "up"
39 Informal farewell
40 Tailor's concern
41 Tubes
44 Serpent's tail
45 Southeastern tree
47 To whom our "millions" are "billions"
48 Usual
50 All the __
51 Calculator key
52 Kiev's river
54 Emmy-winning role of '72, '75, '76 and '90
56 Hams
57 Double
58 Bump back
59 Release

DOWN

1 Resounding blows
2 Bluster
3 Name meaning "beloved"
4 Cares for
5 Low card
6 Fifth-century marauder
7 Try
8 Draft orders
9 Libretti
10 Grammy category
11 Father of Romulus
12 Permanently
13 Take a summer rental, perhaps
14 Was supported by
21 Try to take off
24 Endangered rain-forest resident
25 Rib-eye relatives
28 Go along with
30 Isn't proud of
31 Fit
32 Thingy
33 Edison recording medium
34 Morgan Freeman film of '89
35 Beneath the surface
36 Advanced language study
38 Look
40 Spread out
41 Small shake
42 Not out of the question
43 Went boldly
46 Manual readers
47 Steep-faced hill
49 Word form for "beyond"
51 Cluster
53 Canada's densest prov.
55 Be short

★★★★ 123

Fill in the diagram so that each rectangular piece has one each of the numbers 1, 2, and 3, under these rules: 1) No two adjacent squares, horizontally or vertically, can have the same number. 2) Each completed row and column of the diagram will have an equal number of 1s, 2s, and 3s.

			2				**3**	
3				**1**				
		2				**1**		
2								
	3							**1**

SUDOKU SUM

Without repeating any digits, complete the sum at right, by filling one digit in each of the five blanks.

$$
\begin{array}{r}
\_\ \_\ 9 \\
+\ 5\ 2\ \_ \\
\hline
8\ \_\ \_ \\
\end{array}
$$

★★★ Number-Out

Shade squares so that no number appears in any row or column more than once. Shaded squares may not touch each other horizontally or vertically, and all unshaded squares must form a single continuous area.

2	1	4	6	6	2
1	2	6	4	5	3
6	5	3	4	1	6
5	3	1	4	2	6
6	4	4	2	1	5
3	1	5	1	6	4

OPPOSITE ATTRACTION

Unscramble the letters in the phrase MODEST FELON to form two common words that are opposites of each other.

_____   _____

★★★★★ Themeless Toughie by Daniel R. Stark

ACROSS

1 Funnel-shaped flower
8 Betrayed boredom, perhaps
15 Taconite, e.g.
16 Free
17 Squad car
18 Rummy variety
19 Menu
20 Grill, maybe
22 Bachelor's last stop
23 Elevator guy
24 Didn't move
26 Surfer's stop
27 Fleur-de-___
28 Sinister
30 Brown of renown
31 Tile shapes
33 Least experienced
35 Tough march
36 Work with apples
37 Prestige
40 Space shots
44 Airline to Tokyo
45 Tel Aviv coins
47 It makes ma mad
48 Warns, with "off"
50 Metamorphic rock
51 Select the best
52 Discharges
54 Reply to a skipper
55 Central
56 Drumming sound
58 Do a voice-over
60 Whatnot
61 Place for a letter
62 Struck out
63 Perpetual

DOWN

1 Literally, "small"
2 Unpredictable
3 Camera toter
4 Knots and cords
5 Scent finder
6 Ill temper
7 Gassing up?
8 Foolish
9 ___ diet
10 Arm bone
11 Ends
12 Enemy soldier
13 Newport realty
14 Honey
21 Sequel to *The Good Earth*
24 Makes easier
25 Tough
28 Gawks at
29 Sleeveless garments
32 Fire product
34 Sprinkle
36 False show
37 Supplied the spread
38 Spark
39 Venture need
40 Adequate
41 Train
42 Is germane
43 eBay principals
46 Tickled
49 Put on
51 Shade of pink
53 Galley notation
55 *Good Night, and Good Luck* role
57 Equal
59 Cereal bristle

★★★ Tennis Pro Jigsaw

Find the names of these tennis pros that are arranged in jigsaw puzzle shapes in the diagram. One piece is shown to get you started.

```
M A R A M C H R R O G E A L T M M Y C O
A P I R T I N I S E V R T A H I D N A N
N E A B U E A N A V E R T Y E J R R O N
G T E S A N R N B R N R O L A J E S S S
E L A M M O O M O A O S B I G A A G A I
R T R O P B J A R T I L E B D R O S U E
E I S A R B R U G A M O R K E N A L N L
K M E R R O E A G R A V G E Y S F A A S
C E B S I N E R G V O O R N N T E V M A
N A T N O C T E N E N S R E B O R D R N
S A S N U O C K I V N E F D P E E Y O T
M R T O R T A N B I E W A L L R M A N A
I L H L L Y E P U R G O O L H R E R S O
T D U R A E J A S G I N I A E Y W I L N
H N O J S I C T T E A W A G L E N S L S
L E H E H L A S L R D G N O R E K T E F
N N N B I L E H E M E R A M M N R A B F
A E W C O M B H W O T T N E C H O D E I
V I O J N N A O A D R F R E J O N S U G
S E N E L L O T S D E E O G D U B F A R
```

ALTHEA GIBSON
ANDRE AGASSI
ANGELA MORTIMER
ANN JONES
ARTHUR ASHE
BILLIE JEAN KING
BJORN BORG
BORIS BECKER
BUSTER MOTTRAM
CHRIS EVERT
DON BUDGE
EVONNE
  GOOLAGONG
FRED PERRY
FRED STOLLE
HELEN WILLS
IVAN LENDL
JAROSLAV DROBNY
JIMMY CONNORS
JOHN MCENROE

JOHN NEWCOMBE
KEN ROSEWALL
LEW HOAD
MANUEL SANTANA
MARGARET COURT
MARIA BUENO
MARTINA
  NAVRATILOVA
MAUREEN
  CONNOLLY
PAT CASH
PETE SAMPRAS
ROGER TAYLOR
ROY EMERSON
STAN SMITH
STEFAN EDBERG
STEFFI GRAF
SUE BARKER
VIRGINIA WADE

IN OTHER WORDS

There is only one common uncapitalized word that contains the consecutive letters YFR. What is it?

_____

★★★ The Sphinx

Enter the maze at bottom left, pass through all the stars exactly once, then end in the rectangle at bottom center. You may not retrace your path.

SAY IT AGAIN

What seven-letter word for a time of day, when pronounced differently, is also a verb?

— — — — — — —

★★★★★ Themeless Toughie by Doug Peterson

ACROSS

1 "Fine!"
8 Andrew, for one
15 With *The*, Twain book
17 Showcase
18 Flag
19 Is dazed
20 Hypothetical try, for short
21 Gets stuck
22 Hear again
23 Concluded, in Cannes
24 Orrery element
25 Ancient mariner
26 Dispense
27 Pro's opposite
29 Salon application
30 Procter & Gamble brand
31 Use a lot
32 Rite site
35 Paper cone
39 More sound
40 Where to find Java
41 Helping verb
42 *Iliad* character
43 State tree of Texas
45 XXIX times XXI
46 It begins in Mar.
47 Not so hot
48 Rabbit relative
49 Doesn't do a thing
53 Madagascar, to some scientists
54 Quite smart
55 Set to rest

DOWN

1 [I know it's wrong]
2 Not on the ball
3 Unsettled
4 Crossing charges
5 Jazz technique
6 Willie Mays, in '73
7 Appeal
8 Grant player
9 In a glib manner
10 Eastern closers
11 Hit initials
12 Defensive tissues
13 Anthony Quinn et al.
14 Descendant of Esau
16 Cut canines
21 Angelina's dad
22 Not common
23 Hard to predict
25 Senator or King
26 Major line
28 John and Paul
29 San Quentin's county
31 Caltech locale
32 Saturn frame
33 King David, for one
34 With eyes wide open
35 1992 Oscar winner
36 Carriage horse
37 Lover of Theseus
38 Saxophonist Beneke
43 Stays up in the air
44 Extended period
45 Artemis equivalent
47 Actress Collette
48 One of the Everlys
50 __ soda
51 Home of the NFL Rams
52 Pt. of MST

★★★★ ABCD

Enter the letters A, B, C, and D into the diagram so that each row and column has exactly one A, one B, one C, and one D. The letters outside the diagram indicate the first letter encountered, moving in the direction of the arrow. Keep in mind that after all the letters have been filled in, there will be two blank boxes in each row and column.

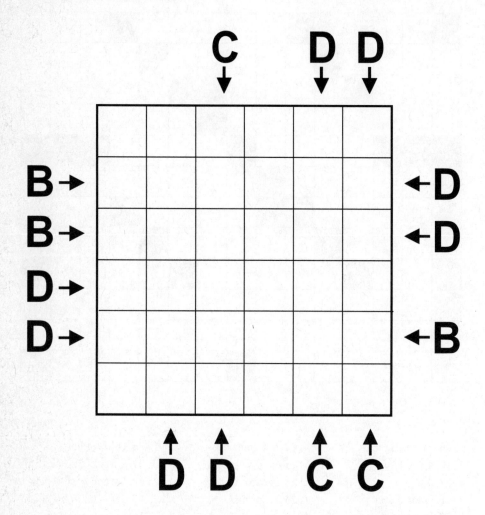

NATIONAL TREASURE

Using the letters in BANGLADESH, we were able to form two common uncapitalized eight-letter words. If they're both plurals, what are they?

_ _ _ _ _ _ _ _   _ _ _ _ _ _ _ _

★★★★ Sudoku

Fill in the blank boxes so that every row, column, and 3x3 box contains all of the numbers 1 to 9.

			7		8			
				5	4			
	6	4				8		
8	7			2				9
5				1			7	2
	9					5	1	
	6	2						
		3		6				

MIXAGRAMS

Each line contains a five-letter word and a four-letter word that have been mixed together (the order of the letters in each word has not been changed). Unmix the two words on each line and write them in the spaces provided. When you're done, find a two-part answer to the clue by reading down the letter columns in the answers.

CLUE: Saw, but not noticed

C H A I V O T E C = _ _ _ _ _ + _ _ _ _

A C R U D O P I T = _ _ _ _ _ + _ _ _ _

N U N E R O S E N = _ _ _ _ _ + _ _ _ _

D O W A R I F L Y = _ _ _ _ _ + _ _ _ _

★★★★★ Themeless Toughie by Daniel R. Stark

ACROSS

1 Reduce, with "down"
8 Franklin tune
15 Easy win
16 Mission figure
17 Fence in
18 Sentimental
19 Compress targets
20 Angry warning
22 Edges
23 Walk-way link
24 America's Cup entrant
26 Fencing gear
27 Certain lobster
28 Noted rubber
30 Family nickname
31 Not straight on
33 Spelling assembly
35 Flits about
36 Polynesian staple
37 Oceania language
39 Toward the right, in a way
43 Comic-book thud
44 Pool accessory?
46 Meet with
47 Winged child
49 Modesto mogul
50 Omen
51 Much more than mere
53 Something to beat
54 Harmful things
55 Kicked in
57 Lennon tune
59 Authorize
60 Sister mag of *American Baby*
61 Sneeze at
62 High point

DOWN

1 Envelop
2 Bent over
3 Moving gradually
4 Yarns
5 Counter's interval, perhaps
6 Scale notes
7 Lens
8 Force through
9 Depot info
10 Remnant
11 Certain army officer
12 Overshadow
13 Say something
14 Freezes up
21 Teased
24 Like some scales
25 Collage introducer
28 Plugged in
29 __ Sea
32 Literally, "I"
34 Assurance
36 Auto part
37 1909 physics Nobelist
38 Sums
39 2004 role for Anne Hathaway
40 Mindless
41 University officials
42 Most mindless
43 Like some moccasins
45 Raise flowers
48 Placid
50 More prudent
52 Musical-work suffix
54 Empty
56 Jodie Foster, circa 1984
58 NBA player

★★★★ One-Way Streets

The diagram represents a pattern of streets. Ps are parking spaces, and the black squares are stores. Find the route that starts at a parking space, passes through all stores exactly once, and ends at the other parking space. Arrows indicate one-way traffic for that block only. No block or intersection may be entered more than once.

SOUND THINKING

There is only one common uncapitalized word whose only consonant sounds are J, B, and N, in that order. What is it?

_____

★★ Split Decisions

In this clueless crossword puzzle, each answer consists of two words whose spellings are the same, except for the consecutive letters given. All answers are common words; no phrases or hyphenated or capitalized words are used. Some of the clues may have more than one solution, but there is only one word pair that will correctly link up with all the other word pairs.

TRANSDELETION

Delete one letter from the word TEENAGERS and rearrange the rest, to get a two-word term for a color.

_____

★★★★★ Themeless Toughie by Anna Stiga

ACROSS

1 Fraction of an inch
5 NYC hub
15 Poetic adverb
16 It has a green-and-white flag
17 Numerical factoid
18 Ship pole
19 Unhealthful
21 Squash, for example
22 R&R provider
23 New England seafood
25 Opposed, in the Ozarks
26 Supplements
29 Word-processor command
31 Quickly and lightly, in music
32 Fuss
33 Sentiment
34 Unhappy spectators, perhaps
38 Lodges
39 Published
40 Pro Football Hall of Fame charter member
43 False front
44 Be suspended
45 Sierra ___ (Mexican range)
46 Ft. Erie's home
47 Seems to be
49 Not seeing straight
53 Bus-seat sharer, perhaps
56 Great-grandson of Marc Antony
57 Midwest region
58 It's saved for a rainy day
59 Ungracious ones
60 Different

DOWN

1 Ago
2 Fond of
3 Push
4 Turning obsolete
5 Fix
6 Causes a start
7 They sound funny
8 Prominent '70s feminist
9 A.J. Soprano portrayer
10 Split up
11 Martina's frequent doubles partner
12 Toy-train scale
13 Isaac Asimov's birthplace
14 Jackson Hole locale
20 Arch
24 Exposition place
25 French toast
26 Many a state name, in D.C.
27 It means "realm"
28 Gossip-column subject
29 Norman athlete
30 Took up
32 New lieutenant general's acquisition
35 A, in Alsace
36 BP takers
37 Femme canonisée, for short
40 Ibsen play
41 Place for a gaucho
42 Pollen holder
43 Sense of taste
45 Secretarial work
47 Baby zebra
48 Stop on the Pony Express
50 Inner fire
51 Stumbles
52 Bozo
54 Written tribute
55 Sinuous shape

★★★★ Looped Path

Draw a continuous, unbroken loop that passes through each of the red, blue, and white squares exactly once. Move from square to square in a straight line or by turning left or right, but never diagonally. You must alternate passing through red and blue squares, with any number of white squares in between.

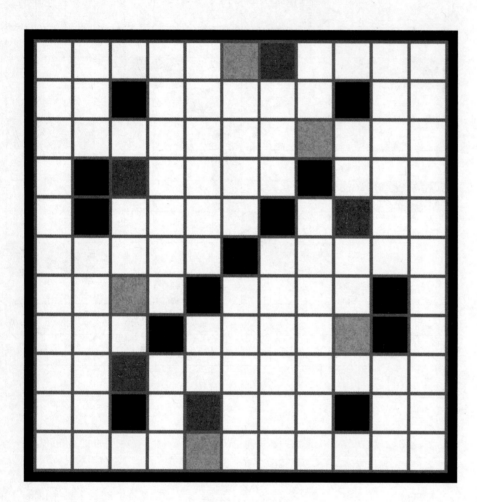

SAY IT AGAIN

What seven-letter word meaning "anger," when pronounced differently, is also something with a fragrance?

— — — — — — —

★★★★ Star Search

Find the stars that are hidden in some of the blank squares. The numbered squares indicate how many stars are hidden in the squares adjacent to them (including diagonally). There is never more than one star in any square.

TELEPHONE TRIOS

Using the numbers and letters on a standard telephone, what three seven-letter words or phrases from the same category can be formed from these telephone numbers?

1	
2	ABC
3	DEF
4	GHI
5	JKL
6	MNO
7	PRS
8	TUV
9	WXY
*	
0	
#	

372-4453   _ _ _ _ _ _ _

274-8853   _ _ _ _ _ _ _

742-5389   _ _ _ _ _ _ _

★★★★★ Themeless Toughie by Doug Peterson

ACROSS

1 Athwart
10 Green stuff
15 Unorthodox
16 Major Joppolo's town
17 Blowtorch gas
18 Soapy minerals
19 Record listing
20 It holds drafts
22 Essence
23 Succeed
24 Bank actions
26 Itty-bitty, in Inverness
27 Proof notation
28 "I'm off!"
30 Tournament game
31 Blaine portrayer
32 Fort Sam Houston locale
37 Legendary landfall
38 Safari sight
39 Bulova watch time?
41 Try to fill a straight
45 Bit of Brooklynese
46 Ames and Russell
47 King Abdullah, for one
48 Sewed up
50 Dallas inst.
51 Chock-full
52 Singer Jones
54 Sorry
56 They're ideal
57 Back to bickering
58 Convertible alternative
59 Combinations

DOWN

1 Is galling
2 Not dated
3 Unspecified alternative
4 Take off
5 "People" person
6 Cunning
7 Crack
8 Flair for improvisation
9 Happy companion
10 Stand in the box
11 First of all
12 Bill booster
13 Away from the public
14 Letter writing and blacksmithing
21 Begin to do
24 San __
25 Puts on the schedule
28 Siesta spots
29 Biographical figure
30 Comb's target
32 Tom treat
33 Exchange preceder
34 Ran on
35 Uris protagonist
36 Lodges
40 Family members
41 Cost, so to speak
42 Syncopated dances
43 Antarctic penguin
44 Adds a lane to
47 Miles of film
49 Garth in *Wayne's World*
51 *Giant* character
53 QVC alternative
55 Wrong

★★★★ Number-Out

Shade squares so that no number appears in any row or column more than once. Shaded squares may not touch each other horizontally or vertically, and all unshaded squares must form a single continuous area.

4	5	6	1	3	1
3	3	4	2	5	5
6	2	6	3	5	1
2	1	1	5	5	4
5	3	1	6	2	1
1	1	5	1	4	6

OPPOSITE ATTRACTION

Unscramble the letters in the phrase FROSTED HENNA to form two common words that are opposites of each other.

_____   _____

★★★★ Line Drawing

Draw five straight lines, each from one edge of the square to another edge, so that one circle has three lines passing through it, one circle has two lines passing through it, one circle has one line passing through it, and the other circles are untouched by lines.

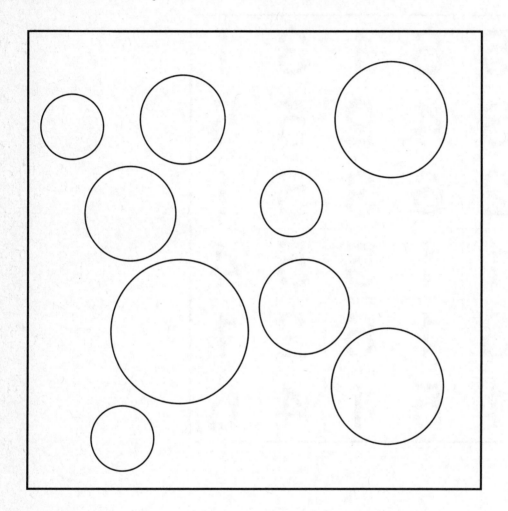

TWO-BY-FOUR

The eight letters in the word BAGUETTE can be rearranged to form a pair of common four-letter words in only one way. Can you find the two words?

— — — —   — — — —

★★★★★ **Themeless Toughie** by Daniel R. Stark

ACROSS

1 Title character of a 1719 novel
7 Dalí or Gris
15 *La Chienne* director
16 Kitchen drain
17 African runner
18 Cure
19 Not aquatic
21 Narrow inlet
22 Solemn agreement
23 Chip handler
24 Stylist's creation
25 Multiple of XIII
26 Jazz guitarist Montgomery
27 Camouflages
28 Get an eyeful
29 Actor on a 1999 US postage stamp
31 Wager
32 Not to be trusted
34 Insect eater
37 Lemon cooler
38 *Bordeaux et Champagne*
39 Legal matter
41 Places for autographs
44 Highly rated
45 Participate, with "in"
46 Conforms (to)
47 Expands while cooking
50 Dundee refusal
51 X to the zero power
52 Have
54 Overlook
56 Mischief maker
57 Freedom
58 Design
59 Imposed, as a payment
60 Doc

DOWN

1 First-night crowd
2 Takes care of
3 Up in the air
4 Be up in the air
5 Slicked up
6 Clean the slate
7 Flagrantly offensive
8 Small liquor glasses
9 Elevated platform
10 Ersatz hook
11 Gary's loc.
12 Dug deeply
13 Call it a night
14 Imagines
20 Yellowish brown
24 Mr. Smith portrayer
27 Unruly bunch
29 Chaps
30 It may be soprano, tenor, or baritone
31 Mug
33 Absorbs, as costs
34 "Gateway of the Americas"
35 Kind of funny
36 Sweater or skirt
38 Jumped over
40 Heinz Field pro
41 Cylindrical cactus
42 Dido's love
43 Athletic attire
44 Refer
47 Sacred
48 Place to rock
49 Drum-set part
52 Stakes
53 Between ports
55 Fight (for)

★★ Triad Split Decisions

In this clueless crossword puzzle, each answer consists of two words whose spellings are the same, except for the consecutive letters given. All answers are common words; no phrases or hyphenated or capitalized words are used. Some of the clues may have more than one solution, but there is only one word pair that will correctly link up with all the other word pairs.

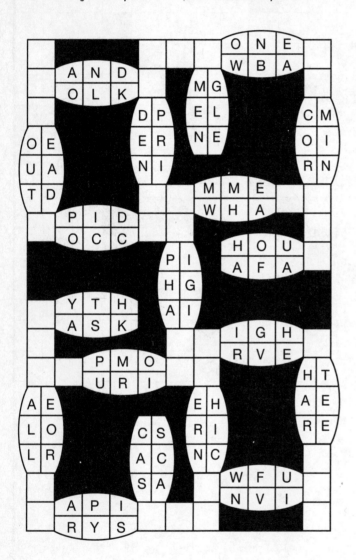

TRANSDELETION

Delete one letter from the word GARRISONED rearrange the rest, to get a two-word term seen on a map of the continental United States.

_____

★★ Wheels and Cogs

When the robot turns the handle on the cog as shown, will the pointer move toward the oil can or the charger?

THREE AT A RHYME

Rearrange these letters to form three one-syllable words that rhyme.

A A A E E G P S S S U U W Z

_____ _____ _____

★★★★★ Themeless Toughie by Merle Baker

ACROSS

1 Skeet device
5 Conformity
15 Greek ally in the Trojan War
16 Blake poem
17 Nutritional figs.
18 Orion follower
19 They make judgment calls
20 Powell successor
21 Speck
22 It has floats and flies
24 Takes the edge off
26 Sierra Nevada attraction
27 High schooler's infraction
29 Garage, e.g.
32 Expected to start on
33 Mall activity
37 Favors
40 Have, as a name
44 Entrance area
45 Inning recap phrase
46 Identical
49 Short shot
50 Prefix with meter
51 Goddess with horns
52 Critical eye
55 Morse clicks
56 Kennedy Center facility
57 Wisteria Lane real-estate agent
58 Like some toads and butterflies
59 Holiday mos.

DOWN

1 Essences
2 Steaks and chops
3 Western Indian
4 Acceptance ensurer
5 African capital
6 Business publishing name
7 Doesn't take anymore
8 Comics dog
9 Literary monogram
10 Brooklynese pronoun
11 *My Life __* (Philip Roth book)
12 Hardly a trifling matter
13 Big bills
14 The right to go out
23 Circular
24 *Too Many Cooks* author
25 Excuses
28 Some alerts
30 Attendees
31 Part of QED
34 Like some DVDs
35 Save
36 Reclusive
38 Squeak by
39 Combs out and does up
40 Mainstay
41 A lack of prospects
42 Waxed
43 Bladed cleaners
47 Uneven
48 Cared for
50 Mark on a map
53 Drain
54 E'en if

PAGE 17
Body Language

```
R O P E ■ ■ R A M ■ P A S T A
A C I D ■ W A G E ■ A S H E N
L A T E ■ A N O N ■ P A I N T
P L A N E F I G U R E ■ P T S
H A S S L E ■ ■ O R B S ■ ■ ■
■ ■ ■ A R O M A S ■ U H O H
S C O O T ■ N A G S ■ T A R A
H O R S E ■ E R A ■ S T P A T
A L D A ■ D A I S ■ H E E L S
W E E K ■ E L A P S E ■ ■ ■
■ ■ ■ R A T S ■ E A G L E S
O A F ■ W I N D O W F R A M E
P R O V E ■ A I D E ■ A B B A
E E R I E ■ P A I D ■ P O E M
N A M E D ■ A L E ■ E R R S
```

PAGE 18
Square Links

CENTURY MARKS
8 + 3 + 29 + 27 + 37 − 4 = 100

PAGE 19
Where to Now?

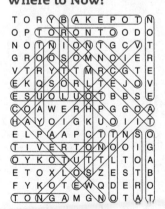

INITIAL REACTION
Talk Is Cheap

PAGE 20
Sudoku

```
8 6 4 9 1 7 3 2 5
9 3 1 5 2 4 6 7 8
2 5 7 3 6 8 1 4 9
4 1 6 7 9 5 2 8 3
5 2 3 6 8 1 7 9 4
7 9 8 4 3 2 5 6 1
3 7 2 8 5 9 4 1 6
6 4 9 1 7 3 8 5 2
1 8 5 2 4 6 9 3 7
```

MIXAGRAMS

A L G A E   S N O B
C O L O N   L A D Y
I N P U T   D O D O
A G A I N   V A S E

PAGE 21
Capital B

```
H O P I ■ M A S H ■ E B B S
O V E N ■ O R E O ■ L U N A R
B A N G K O K T H A I L A N D
O L D E N ■ S U M ■ L I E S
■ ■ ■ S O L O ■ M I F F ■ ■ ■
S O F T W A R E ■ S O R T E D
A G O ■ ■ N A S A ■ A O R T A
B R U S S E L S B E L G I U M
R E N E E ■ S E E P ■ ■ A D E
E S T E E M ■ ■ S T E E P L E S
■ ■ S K I P ■ S E A L ■ ■ ■
A T I T ■ L A S ■ R U L E R
B U D A P E S T H U N G A R Y
S N O R E ■ T E A S ■ U C L A
■ A S S T ■ A M M O ■ P E E N
```

PAGE 22
Fences

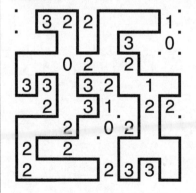

ADDITION SWITCH
2 6 8 + 6 2 5 = 8 9 3

PAGE 23
Line Drawing

IF, ZOO, QUIT, ANNEX

Three of a Kind
THEIR DINERS' CATSUP IS TOO
WATERY, SOME OWNERS CLAIM.

PAGE 24
Piercing

WHO'S WHAT WHERE?
Melburnian

PAGE 25
Meet the Presidents

```
M A R S ■ F I G S ■ S T A S H
O B O E ■ I N I T ■ T A B O O
M I L L A R D F I L L M O R E
S T E E L ■ E T R E ■ E V E R
■ ■ C O A X ■ ■ A I D E ■ ■
M A S T E D ■ V C R S ■ I V E
A C T I ■ D E A L ■ E A T E N
G R O V E R C L E V E L A N D
M I R E D ■ H I F I ■ B L U E
A D E ■ I P O D ■ S E A L E D
■ ■ R U T H ■ N A R C ■ ■
I W O N ■ I A G O ■ L O A D S
T H O M A S J E F F E R S O N
C O M E R ■ A R E A ■ E S S O
H A S T E ■ R E E D ■ S T E W
```

PAGE 26
Number-Out

OPPOSITE ATTRACTION
BUY, SELL

PAGE 27
Straight Ahead

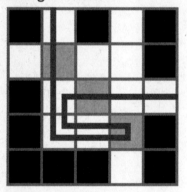

THREE AT A RHYME
LO, OWE, TOE

PAGE 28
Wraparounds

O	M	A	R		L	O	C	A	L		S	C	A	M
D	A	L	E		P	R	O	S	E		C	O	L	A
O	N	E	M	A	N	B	A	N	D		R	T	E	S
R	E	S	I	T		S	T	E	T		E	T	C	H
		S	O	B			R	O	D	E	O			
N	E	W	S	M	E	N			I	N	N	E	R	
A	L	I		T	E	M	P	L	E		B	E	E	
R	I	N		S	T	A	R	L	I	T		E	R	E
C	O	D		P	E	R	S	O	N			L	I	D
S	T	O	N	E			P	E	T	I	T	E	S	
	W	E	D	G	E			R	E	C				
P	E	S	T		A	L	P	S		R	E	A	S	K
L	E	A	P		B	L	U	E	R	I	B	B	O	N
E	L	S	A		L	I	B	R	A		A	L	O	E
A	S	H	Y		E	S	S	A	Y		G	E	N	E

PAGE 29
One-Way Streets

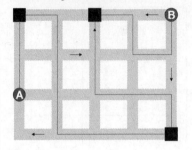

SOUND THINKING
SNOWBIRD

PAGE 30
Split Decisions

TRANSDELETION
RETRIEVER

PAGE 31
Star Search

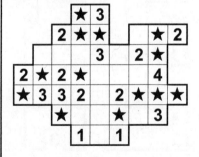

TELEPHONE TRIOS
DEBUSSY, PUCCINI, STRAUSS

PAGE 32
At the Diner

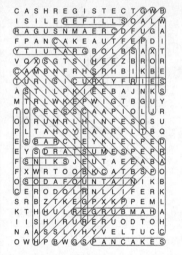

IN OTHER WORDS
NEWTS

PAGE 33
Be Quick

R	U	S	T		R	A	D	A	R		S	E	E	R
A	N	T	I		E	L	U	D	E		H	A	L	O
S	T	A	G		T	A	L	L	S		A	R	I	D
H	I	G	H	T	A	I	L	I	T		K	N	E	E
	L	E	T	U	P			B	I	T	E			
			B	E	L	L			R	O	A	M	E	D
T	A	N	G		D	E	A	L		A	L	A	M	O
A	L	O	O	F		A	D	O		D	E	N	I	M
P	O	S	S	E		S	L	O	W		G	E	R	E
S	T	E	W	E	D		E	P	E	E				
			I	T	E	M			A	R	E	S	O	
W	O	L	F		M	A	K	E	T	R	A	C	K	S
A	L	I	T		U	R	I	A	H		S	A	R	A
R	E	E	L		R	I	N	S	E		E	R	A	S
P	O	S	Y		E	A	G	E	R		L	E	S	S

PAGE 34
Hyper-Sudoku

3	6	1	4	2	8	5	7	9
7	8	4	6	9	5	3	2	1
5	9	2	1	3	7	6	4	8
6	3	5	7	4	9	8	1	2
8	2	7	3	5	1	4	9	6
1	4	9	8	6	2	7	5	3
9	7	3	2	8	4	1	6	5
2	1	6	5	7	3	9	8	4
4	5	8	9	1	6	2	3	7

MIXAGRAMS

E	N	J	O	Y		D	E	B	T
R	E	U	S	E		A	M	O	K
M	A	N	G	O		M	I	N	D
F	A	K	E	R		R	U	D	E

PAGE 35

Close Shave
#9

BETWEENER
ARM

PAGE 36

123

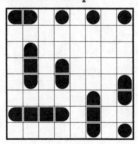

SUDOKU SUM
3 1 9 + 4 0 6 = 7 2 5

PAGE 37

Chophouse

PAGE 38

ABC

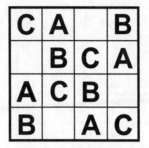

CLUELESS CROSSWORD

PAGE 39

Find the Ships

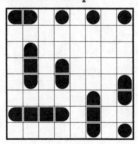

TWO-BY-FOUR
ONCE (or CONE), TURN
(or RUNT); CORN, TUNE;
CURT, NONE (or NEON)

PAGE 40

Taking Up Space

Unlisted word is ROCKET

INITIAL REACTION
Great Minds Think Alike

PAGE 41

Marching Along

PAGE 42

Go With the Flow

THREE AT A RHYME
WE, TEA, FREE

PAGE 43

Fences

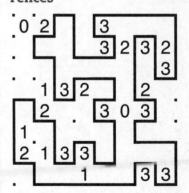

ADDITION SWITCH
6 0 8 + 1 0 9 = 7 1 7

PAGE 44

Outdoor Cooking

Unlisted word is BARBECUE

WHO'S WHAT WHERE?
Swazi

PAGE 45

Washday Woes

L A M S		S A L T		M A R T
E R I E		A S E A		L A S E R
A O N E		T A N S		A R I S E
S M U D G E P O T			S K A T E
H A S S L E		E A S T	
	E N D S		P O W D E R
E R O D E		R A T E		A U D I
M A X I		S A L A D		I N N S
E V E R		A W O L		S N E A K
R E N T A L		N C A A	
	C L E O		L I L A C S
L I T H E		S P O T L I G H T
U S H E R		C U B E		A R I A
C L E A T		A M E R		R E L Y
K E E P		R A Y S		S E E S

PAGE 46

Sudoku

8	3	2	5	4	7	6	9	1
6	4	7	1	9	8	3	2	5
1	5	9	3	2	6	8	4	7
4	9	5	7	3	1	2	8	6
7	2	8	4	6	5	9	1	3
3	1	6	9	8	2	7	5	4
5	7	3	2	1	9	4	6	8
9	6	1	8	7	4	5	3	2
2	8	4	6	5	3	1	7	9

MIXAGRAMS

S W O R D A N O N
V I T A L S W A T
F L O U R O A T H
A D A G E M I S T

PAGE 47

123

2	1	3	1	2	3
3	2	1	2	3	1
1	3	2	1	2	3
3	2	1	3	1	2
2	1	3	2	3	1
1	3	2	3	1	2

SUDOKU SUM
2 0 6 + 1 7 9 = 3 8 5

PAGE 48

Water Carriers

S I T E		M O O S E		E G G S
W O O L		A N I T A		L U L U
A T O M		T I L E R		I T E M
P A N T Y H O S E			V O T E S
	R U I N		P L A T E	
L A B E L S		L E S		R M S
A G R E E		G E N E		B A H
C I A		A M A S S		A P E
E L I		I R I S		H A L L E
D E N		S I S		P E L L E T
	D E E D S		S E A L	
T E R S E		P I P E D R E A M
I R A S		M E D A L		I S L E
E L I A		O L L I E		S P O T
D E N Y		B L E N D		E Y E S

PAGE 49

One-Way Streets

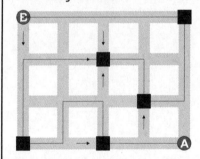

SOUND THINKING
ZUCCHINI

PAGE 50

No Three in a Row

SAY IT AGAIN
ROW

PAGE 51

Star Search

		2		1	
	★	3	★		
			★		2	★	3	★
1		2	★	2			★	2
	★				2		1
	2	★	★		
		★	3		

TELEPHONE TRIOS
DEVOTED, EARNEST, SINCERE

PAGE 52

Easy As Pie

E N D		L P S		M E O W S
R O U S E		E E E		O L D I E
I N T R O		T A C		A L O N E
C O C O N U T C U S T A R D		
A S H		S U E R S		
	A Z T E C		E T S		B R A
A P P E A S E D		S T O L E N
N E P A L		S I R		A V A S T
T E L L O N		N E G L E C T S
E R E		N E T		C L E R K
	M A R I E		B R O
C H O C O L A T E C R E A M
A R U B A		E P A		D I R G E
R U M O R		N I L		L O R E N
E X P E L		T D S		Y D S

PAGE 53
Mythically Speaking

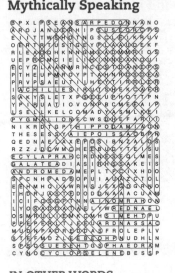

IN OTHER WORDS
PASSKEY

PAGE 55
Line Drawing

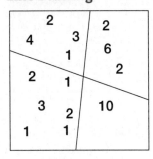

THREE OF A KIND
IN FOOTBALL, OVERTIME WILL EXTEND ERRATIC PLAY.

PAGE 56
ABC

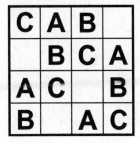

NATIONAL TREASURE
MEG RYAN

PAGE 57
Go West

PAGE 58
Digital Display
A: #9, B: #14, C: #7

BETWEENER
BED

PAGE 59
Far From Forward

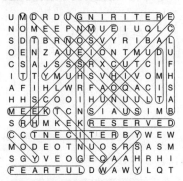

Missing word is SHEEPISH

INITIAL REACTION
There's No Place Like Home

PAGE 60
Find the Ships

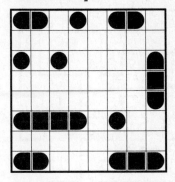

TWO-BY-FOUR
GAZE, IRON; GAIN, ZERO

PAGE 61
Sudoku

4	2	7	3	6	9	5	1	8
3	1	5	8	7	2	6	4	9
9	6	8	1	5	4	2	7	3
8	9	6	5	3	1	7	2	4
2	5	3	4	8	7	9	6	1
1	7	4	9	2	6	8	3	5
6	8	1	2	4	5	3	9	7
7	3	9	6	1	8	4	5	2
5	4	2	7	9	3	1	8	6

MIXAGRAMS

A G I L E   S M U G
B R U I N   L A V A
P A T S Y   A R I A
B Y L A W   R E E F

PAGE 62
Stunning

PAGE 63

Fences

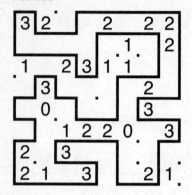

ADDITION SWITCH
3 6 1 + 6 3 1 = 9 9 2

PAGE 64

Triad Split Decisions

TRANSDELETION
PRESIDENT

PAGE 65

123

3	2	1	3	1	2
1	3	2	1	2	3
2	1	3	2	3	1
1	3	2	1	2	3
2	1	3	2	3	1
3	2	1	3	1	2

SUDOKU SUM
4 0 9 + 1 7 3 = 5 8 2

PAGE 66

All Eyes

S	A	S	S		A	D	A	M		R	A	V	E	N
H	U	M	P		D	E	L	I		E	L	I	T	E
A	R	I	A		A	M	E	N		S	P	E	N	T
W	A	T	C	H	P	O	C	K	E	T		W	A	S
	S	H	E	E	T			S	L	U	R	P		
		S	A	T	E	D		S	P	O	O	N		
A	L	L		V	O	W	E	L		B	I	O	S	
L	O	O	S	E		E	P	A		D	E	N	S	E
S	T	O	P		R	O	V	E	R		T	E	A	
	S	K	A	T	E		T	A	X	E	S			
		A	M	A	S	S			P	A	N	E	S	
P	A	L		S	P	O	T	R	E	M	O	V	E	R
O	B	I	T	S		L	O	A	N		R	A	R	E
P	E	K	O	E		I	N	N	S		E	D	G	E
S	T	E	E	L		D	I	K	E		S	E	E	D

PAGE 67

Number-Out

5	4	4	4	3
4	3	5	2	1
1	3	3	3	5
2	1	2	4	5
3	5	2	3	4

OPPOSITE ATTRACTION
WIN, LOSE

PAGE 68

Round and Round

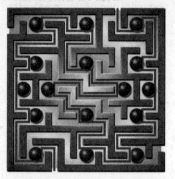

SAY IT AGAIN
BASS

PAGE 69

Fit

WHO'S WHAT WHERE?
Qatari

PAGE 70

Here, Kitty

A	M	E	B	A		N	A	S	H		E	B	A	Y
C	A	M	E	L		I	D	E	A		N	O	N	E
T	R	I	L	L		G	I	L	L		G	A	G	A
S	C	R	A	T	C	H	O	F	F		I	R	I	S
		O	U	T	S			O	N	S	E	T		
B	A	B	B	L	E		P	E	K	E				
L	L	O	Y	D		T	A	I	L	S	P	I	N	S
T	A	R	A		B	O	N	E	S		U	H	O	H
S	N	O	W	B	I	R	D	S		P	R	O	S	E
		H	A	Z	E			H	A	R	P	E	D	
R	O	B	I	N		S	T	A	R					
E	X	E	S		C	L	A	W	H	A	M	M	E	R
B	I	L	K		Z	I	T	I		D	E	A	L	T
I	D	L	E		A	V	I	S		E	M	I	L	E
D	E	E	R		R	E	N	T		S	O	L	E	S

PAGE 71
One-Way Streets

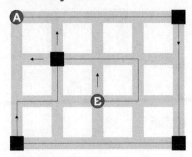

SOUND THINKING
EVASIVE

PAGE 72
Hyper-Sudoku

7	6	9	2	8	5	4	1	3
8	3	1	4	9	6	2	5	7
4	5	2	7	3	1	9	8	6
2	9	8	6	5	4	7	3	1
1	4	5	3	2	7	8	6	9
3	7	6	8	1	9	5	4	2
6	2	3	9	4	8	1	7	5
9	1	4	5	7	3	6	2	8
5	8	7	1	6	2	3	9	4

CENTURY MARKS
24 + 45 + 8 + 9 + 11 + 3 = 100

PAGE 73
Star Search

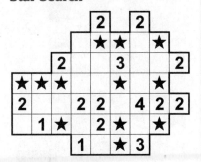

TELEPHONE TRIOS
KETCHUP, MUSTARD, TABASCO

PAGE 74
Sky-High

S	C	A	N		C	H	I	P	S		C	L	E	O
P	O	L	O		A	A	R	O	N		L	O	I	N
A	C	L	U		T	R	A	L	A		O	G	R	E
M	O	O	N	S	H	I	N	E	R		U	S	E	S
	A	T	S	E	A			S	E	N	D			
			W	I	L	D		D	I	N	E	R	S	
E	G	G	S		R	E	A	P		P	I	L	O	T
V	A	L	U	E		E	R	R		S	N	I	D	E
E	M	E	N	D		K	E	E	P			E	A	S	T
S	E	E	F	I	T		S	P	O	T				
			L	E	A	S			S	O	A	R	S	
O	S	L	O		S	T	A	R	S	T	R	U	C	K
A	N	E	W		T	E	H	E	E		I	R	O	N
F	I	N	E		E	V	E	N	S		S	A	N	E
S	P	A	R		D	E	M	O	S		E	L	E	E

PAGE 75
ABC

B	C	A	
A		B	C
C	A		B
	B	C	A

CLUELESS CROSSWORD

S	P	I	N	A	C	H
H		N		V		O
I	N	S	P	E	C	T
V		T		R		S
E	Y	E	L	A	S	H
R		A		G		O
S	A	D	D	E	S	T

PAGE 76
Friendship Chains

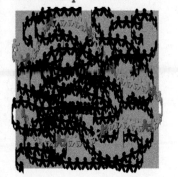

BETWEENER
CAT

PAGE 77
Sudoku

5	7	8	4	2	3	6	9	1
3	1	2	6	9	5	8	4	7
9	4	6	1	8	7	3	5	2
7	9	3	5	6	2	4	1	8
6	8	1	7	4	9	2	3	5
2	5	4	8	3	1	7	6	9
1	3	5	2	7	4	9	8	6
4	6	7	9	1	8	5	2	3
8	2	9	3	5	6	1	7	4

MIXAGRAMS

L E G A L   P O R E
I M B U E   A R M Y
L I L A C   D U E S
Y O D E L   S P O T

PAGE 78
On the Keyboard

G	L	E	N	S		A	C	T	S		M	A	T	H
R	E	B	U	T		S	O	O	T		O	B	E	Y
I	N	A	N	E		S	A	G	A		B	O	N	E
P	A	Y	S	T	H	E	T	A	B		I	R	O	N
			S	A	T			U	L	T	R	A		
S	H	A	D	O	W		L	A	P	S	E			
H	I	T	O	N		G	A	M	E	S	H	O	W	S
A	V	O	N		T	A	M	P	A		O	M	I	T
M	E	M	O	R	I	Z	E	S		A	M	A	N	A
			T	O	N	E	R		C	L	E	R	G	Y
M	O	W	E	D		A	A	A						
I	R	A	N		N	I	G	H	T	S	H	I	F	T
M	A	S	T		A	L	L	Y		K	O	R	E	A
E	T	T	E		B	L	U	E		A	S	I	A	N
S	E	E	R		S	S	T	S		N	E	S	T	S

PAGE 79
Line Drawing

The two words in each region have the same double letters

THREE OF A KIND
WASH A VELVET GLOVE WITH A SMALL BRUSH.

PAGE 80
Find the Ships

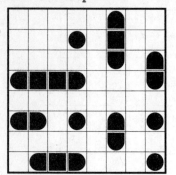

TWO-BY-FOUR
PANG, INTO; PAIN, TONG

PAGE 81
Fences

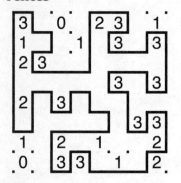

ADDITION SWITCH
2 7 8 + 3 2 6 = 6 0 4

PAGE 82
Somewhat Sassy

P	A	N	S		S	H	I	P		M	A	R	S	H
A	T	O	P		T	A	R	A		A	B	A	T	E
S	O	F	A		A	L	A	N		P	O	K	E	R
S	M	A	R	T	M	O	N	E	Y		L	E	N	O
	S	T	R	A	P			E	D	I	S	O	N	
		O	N	S		C	P	L	U	S				
S	P	E	W			F	L	I	P	C	H	A	R	T
O	R	E		A	G	A	I	N	S	T		B	A	A
B	O	L	D	P	R	I	N	T			L	E	N	D
		A	T	I	L	T			S	E	E			
P	R	A	I	S	E			C	L	A	S	P		
L	O	B	S		F	R	E	S	H	F	R	U	I	T
A	V	O	I	D		I	D	L	E		N	A	P	A
N	E	V	E	R		T	E	A	M		E	V	E	N
T	R	E	S	S		A	N	T	E		D	E	S	K

PAGE 83
Paisley Puzzler
#5

THREE AT A RHYME
HUG, UGH, SMUG

PAGE 84
123

SUDOKU SUM
3 0 9 + 1 7 6 = 4 8 5

PAGE 85
Number-Out

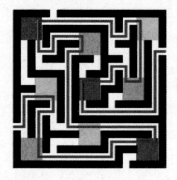

OPPOSITE ATTRACTION
HOT, COLD

PAGE 86
Sweet Talk

PAGE 87
Tri-Color Maze

SAY IT AGAIN
SOWS

PAGE 88
Split Decisions

TRANSDELETION
SURGEON

PAGE 89
Hyper-Sudoku

6	4	3	5	2	7	9	1	8
5	2	8	6	9	1	7	4	3
1	9	7	3	4	8	2	5	6
2	5	4	1	8	3	6	9	7
3	1	6	9	7	2	4	8	5
7	8	9	4	6	5	3	2	1
4	3	1	7	5	9	8	6	2
8	6	5	2	3	4	1	7	9
9	7	2	8	1	6	5	3	4

MIXAGRAMS

TENTH ROOM
POLKA VISA
TROLL EVER
VITAL LURK

PAGE 90
That's Easy

PAGE 91
Where You Live

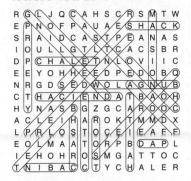

Unlisted word is DWELLING

IN OTHER WORDS
KUMQUAT

PAGE 93
One-Way Streets

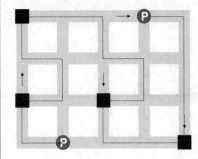

SOUND THINKING
UPBEAT

PAGE 94
Scattered Showers

D	E	C	O	Y		Y	O	R	E		A	P	T	S
A	T	O	N	E		E	W	E	S		I	T	R	Y
S	T	R	E	S	S	A	N	D	S	T	R	A	I	N
H	E	E	D			O	R	S	O		I	T	S	M	E
			G	E	L	S			A	L	S	O		
I	N	K	E	D		A	N	K	A		A	C	H	E
D	O	N			I	A	G	O		N	A	I	L	E	R
E	L	E	C	T	R	O	N	I	C	B	R	A	I	N
A	T	E	A	S	E		O	N	E	A		S	R	I
S	E	L	L		N	E	S	S		L	A	P	S	E
		A	A	A	A		I	L	L	S				
S	E	A	M	Y		R	A	G	E		T	O	T	E
A	G	A	I	N	S	T	T	H	E	G	R	A	I	N
F	O	R	T		S	H	O	T		A	A	H	E	D
E	S	P	Y		T	A	P	S		B	L	U	R	S

PAGE 95
Bully For You

THREE AT A RHYME
DUE, YEW, COUP

PAGE 96
Star Search

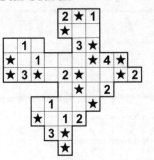

TELEPHONE TRIOS
ABILENE, HOUSTON, LUBBOCK

PAGE 97
Triad Split Decisions

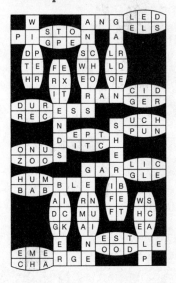

TRANSDELETION
EMERALD

PAGE 98
Go the Distance

M	A	D	A	T		G	I	L	L		A	B	B	A
A	P	A	C	E		O	R	E	O		G	U	L	P
T	E	N	D	E	R	F	O	O	T		A	S	E	A
T	R	A	C	T	I	O	N			T	E	T	H	E	R
			I	A	R		V	E	L	D	T			
M	O	S	T	E	L		C	H	E	E	S	E		
A	R	C	E	D		T	H	O	R	N		A	I	R
C	A	H	N		Z	A	I	R	E		O	G	L	E
S	L	O		A	O	R	T	A		C	A	U	S	E
		O	B	S	E	S	S			T	H	R	E	A	D
A	R	L	E	S			S	H	A					
M	A	Y	A	N	S		S	P	A	R	S	E	S	T
I	V	A	N		W	A	T	E	R	M	E	T	E	R
N	E	R	I		E	V	I	L		E	M	O	T	E
O	L	D	E		E	A	R	L		R	I	N	S	E

PAGE 99

ABC

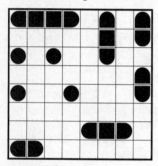

NATIONAL TREASURE
FINAL

PAGE 100

Find the Ships

TWO-BY-FOUR
QUIT, NOTE (or TONE)

PAGE 101

Disappearing Act

W	A	C	O			A	L	E	C		P	L	O	D
I	D	O	S		B	R	A	V	E		L	O	G	E
N	O	W	H	E	R	E	M	A	N		I	S	L	E
C	R	E	A	T	E		A	N	T	E	A	T	E	R
H	E	R		T	W	O	S		A	R	N	O		
		P	E	E	N		N	U	R	T	U	R	E	
S	W	A	P		D	E	S	I	R	E		T	A	D
H	O	W	S	O		D	U	N		D	R	O	I	D
O	R	A		S	H	A	V	E	D		I	N	D	Y
O	D	Y	S	S	E	Y		T	A	C	O			
		G	A	I	L		G	Y	R	O		P	A	S
I	S	A	B	E	L	L	A		W	R	E	A	T	H
D	A	M	E		M	I	S	S	I	N	G	Y	O	U
O	V	E	R		A	S	P	E	N		G	E	N	T
L	E	S	S		N	A	S	A			S	E	E	S

PAGE 102

Meet Your Match
Barry & Lena, Gary & Mina,
Harry & Deena, Larry & Zena

BETWEENER
FREE

PAGE 103

Sudoku

5	9	8	7	4	2	6	1	3
3	7	4	6	1	5	2	8	9
2	6	1	8	3	9	5	4	7
8	1	7	4	2	6	3	9	5
6	4	3	5	9	7	1	2	8
9	5	2	1	8	3	7	6	4
1	3	6	9	7	4	8	5	2
4	2	5	3	6	8	9	7	1
7	8	9	2	5	1	4	3	6

MIXAGRAMS

A	Z	U	R	E		Z	I	N	G
C	A	B	A	L		S	P	U	R
S	N	O	R	T		A	L	O	E
L	E	V	E	R		B	U	R	Y

PAGE 104

Fences

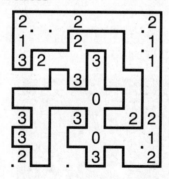

ADDITION SWITCH
$535 + 291 = 826$

PAGE 105

At the Salon

B	A	S	H		U	R	N	S		R	A	F	T	S
O	N	T	O		T	O	U	T		O	P	R	A	H
S	N	O	W		E	T	N	A		M	O	O	R	E
C	U	R	L	O	N	E	S	L	I	P		S	P	A
S	L	E	E	T	S			E	R	E	C	T		
		R	H	I	N	E		A	D	O	B	E	S	
A	B	C		E	L	E	V	E	N		L	I	M	A
B	L	U	E	R		A	I	R		S	A	T	I	N
E	A	T	S		S	P	L	I	N	T		E	R	E
S	H	A	S	T	A		S	C	O	R	N			
		N	E	H	R	U			T	A	I	C	H	I
C	A	D		R	I	N	S	E	C	Y	C	L	E	S
A	S	T	R	O		C	O	S	H		H	U	N	S
P	E	R	O	N		L	U	T	E		E	C	R	U
P	A	Y	E	E		E	R	A	S		S	K	Y	E

PAGE 106

Number-Out

5	1	2	6	6	6
3	6	1	1	4	5
3	2	1	5	5	5
3	4	1	5	3	1
1	5	4	6	3	2
2	3	5	3	2	6

OPPOSITE ATTRACTION
FIX, BREAK

PAGE 107

Hyper-Sudoku

4	6	1	9	2	5	3	7	8
7	8	9	1	4	3	6	5	2
5	3	2	7	6	8	4	9	1
9	5	4	6	8	7	1	2	3
6	7	3	2	1	4	9	8	5
2	1	8	3	5	9	7	6	4
1	9	7	5	3	2	8	4	6
8	2	6	4	7	1	5	3	9
3	4	5	8	9	6	2	1	7

CENTURY MARKS
$2 + 4 + 6 + 8 - 1 + 63 + 18 = 100$

PAGE 108

Dogging It

PAGE 109

Spend Your Dollars

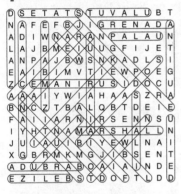

Unlisted answer is CANADA

INITIAL REACTION
A Rolling Stone Gathers
No Moss

PAGE 110

Dicey

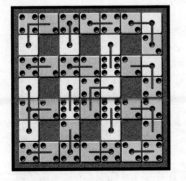

SAY IT AGAIN
TOWER

PAGE 111

747 Seating

PAGE 112

One-Way Streets

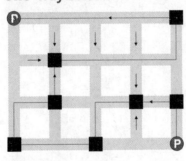

SOUND THINKING
ORACLE

PAGE 113

123

2	3	1	3	2	1	3	1	2
1	2	3	2	1	3	1	2	3
3	1	2	1	3	2	3	1	2
1	2	3	1	2	3	2	3	1
3	1	2	1	3	2	1	2	3
2	3	1	3	2	1	2	3	1
1	2	3	2	1	3	1	2	3
3	1	2	1	3	2	3	1	2
2	3	1	3	2	1	2	3	1

SUDOKU SUM
3 8 6 + 4 0 5 = 7 9 1

PAGE 114

Line Drawing

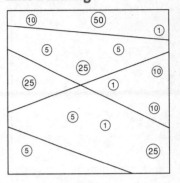

THREE OF A KIND
WHEN IN DESPAIR, WHO FACES
REALITY?

PAGE 115

Working It Out

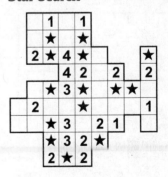

PAGE 116

Star Search

Star Search grid

TELEPHONE TRIOS
ANNOYED, GROUCHY, PEEVISH

244 MIND STRETCHERS

PAGE 117
Pair o' Dots

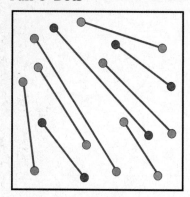

THREE AT A RHYME
ODD, COD, QUAD

PAGE 118
Precious Few

S L I N K		P E P S		A B A B
T E T O N		E C O L		C A S E
S A L V O		O R E O		T R I G
P L A T I N U M B L O N D E				
T R Y			I N S E T	
R E D E Y E		C H I L E		
I C O N		E R I S A		T A D
G O L D E N P A R A C H U T E				
A N T		F O I S T		E B O N
D I T C H		S T E A M Y	
A V A I L			P E A	
S I L V E R S N E A K E R S				
C O L E		E T O N		E D I T S
A L E S		M O O N		U N D E R
P A N T		O P R Y		P A S T A

PAGE 119
Hyper-Sudoku

9	6	1	4	2	8	3	5	7
3	7	2	1	9	5	8	4	6
5	8	4	3	7	6	1	9	2
4	9	6	5	8	7	2	3	1
1	5	8	9	3	2	6	7	4
7	2	3	6	4	1	5	8	9
6	1	9	8	5	4	7	2	3
2	4	5	7	1	3	9	6	8
8	3	7	2	6	9	4	1	5

MIXAGRAMS
```
M A G I C    C O L A
O Z O N E    L U L L
R E L I T    U G L Y
U N F I T    B R A N
```

PAGE 120
ABC

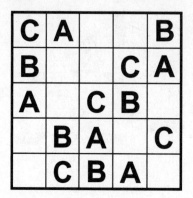

NATIONAL TREASURE
ADORE, OARED

PAGE 121
Build-Ups

D A R N S		M I S T		C A P
E L I O T		A R E A		P A I L
C A D D Y S H A C K			E N D O	
A S S E N T		S T E I N W A Y	
		E R A		S O F T E N S
S T E W		A R S		U S H
A U R A		P E T I T		O U S T
U N I T		N A M		U S T A
L A N E		M A R A T		S E A M
		R H O	E G O		E D G E
S E A S O N S		E N G		
W I S H B O N E		I N A S E C	
O D I E		C O P A C A B A N A	
R E D D		L O I S		R I G O R
E R E		E T C H		L E A S T

PAGE 122
Wheels and Cogs
The purple dinosaur

BETWEENER
SHIP

PAGE 123
Find the Ships

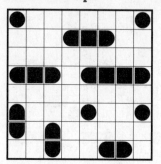

TWO-BY-FOUR
CHIC, ROTE (or TORE); CORE,
CHIT (or ITCH); COTE, RICH

PAGE 124
Triad Split Decisions

TRANSDELETION
CUTLASS

PAGE 125
Uncle

P A L E	M E D S		T R A Y S
A L E X	A L A I		V E N U E
C O A T	G A N G		S P E L L
T H R E W I N T H E T O W E L			
A N N O		E T N A	
	T O M S		D R E N C H
S H E	E B O O K		L U L U
W A V E D A W H I T E F L A G			
A H E M	S M E A R		L P S
P A R S E C		L O I N	
Q U I T		C U K E	
H E L D U P O N E S H A N D S			
A T A R I	W O R E		N O S H
S T R O P	A T T N		C L E O
H E A P S	N E E D		E L L E

PAGE 126

123

3	2	1	3	1	2	1	3	2
2	3	2	1	2	1	3	1	3
3	1	3	2	3	2	1	2	1
1	2	1	3	1	3	2	3	2
2	1	3	2	3	1	3	2	1
1	3	2	1	2	3	2	1	3
3	2	1	3	1	2	1	3	2
1	3	2	1	2	3	2	1	3
2	1	3	2	3	1	3	2	1

SUDOKU SUM
2 9 3 + 4 1 5 = 7 0 8

PAGE 127

Fences

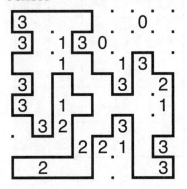

ADDITION SWITCH
1 9 4 + 3 8 2 = 5 7 6

PAGE 128

3 on 66

PAGE 129

Sets of Three

SAY IT AGAIN
LUGER

PAGE 131

Mystery Category

WHO'S WHAT WHERE?
Honolulan

PAGE 132

Hyper-Sudoku

8	7	5	6	9	2	3	1	4
3	6	1	5	4	8	7	2	9
2	4	9	7	1	3	5	6	8
5	8	2	3	7	9	1	4	6
6	3	4	1	2	5	8	9	7
9	1	7	8	6	4	2	5	3
4	9	3	2	5	7	6	8	1
7	5	6	4	8	1	9	3	2
1	2	8	9	3	6	4	7	5

MIXAGRAMS

J	E	W	E	L	READ
A	P	R	O	N	REDO
N	A	I	V	E	SURE
E	N	E	M	Y	KISS

PAGE 133

Jam Session

PAGE 134

One-Way Streets

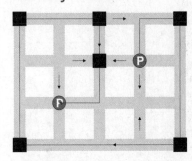

SOUND THINKING
CENTIPEDE

PAGE 135

Star Search

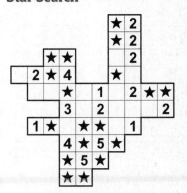

TELEPHONE TRIOS
CONFUSE, FLUSTER, MYSTIFY

PAGE 136
Vowel Shift

S	P	R	I	G		B	S	M	T			E	M	S	
A	L	E	N	E		E	T	A	I	L		M	A	E	
H	A	V	E	N		B	A	L	L	P	O	I	N	T	
I	T	O			D	O	M		S	P	R	A	T		
B	E	L	L	P	E	P	P	E	R		S	A	G	E	
S	A	T	I	R	E			L	E	A		T	E	E	
	U	S	M	A		M	I	S	D	E	E	D			
		B	I	L	L	G	A	T	E	S					
	L	A	S	S	O	E	S			S	T	O	W		
T	A	P		E	E	N		S	T	E	R	E	O		
A	D	O	S		B	O	L	L	W	E	E	V	I	L	
B	O	L	T	S		A	I	M		I	R	E			
B	U	L	L	M	O	O	S	E		G	O	L	D	A	
E	C	O		U	N	L	E	T		I	D	L	E	R	
D	E	S		T	A	R	O		L	E	E	R	Y		

PAGE 137
Indian Archer

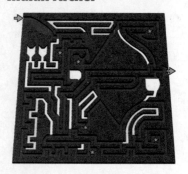

THREE AT A RHYME
BUD, MUD, BLOOD

PAGE 138
Sudoku

6	3	1	5	4	2	7	8	9
9	5	2	6	8	7	4	1	3
8	7	4	9	1	3	5	2	6
5	2	7	3	6	8	1	9	4
4	8	3	1	7	9	2	6	5
1	6	9	4	2	5	8	3	7
3	1	5	2	9	4	6	7	8
2	9	8	7	5	6	3	4	1
7	4	6	8	3	1	9	5	2

CENTURY MARKS
33 + 9 + 15 - 9 + 47 + 5 = 100

PAGE 139
Split Pea

PAGE 140
Split Decisions

TRANSDELETION
TOUR BUS

PAGE 141
Number-Out

3	1	1	6	4	2
1	4	5	1	3	1
2	2	6	4	3	3
5	2	3	3	6	5
4	2	2	3	5	1
6	5	4	3	2	3

OPPOSITE ATTRACTION
EAST, WEST

PAGE 142
Spooked

PAGE 143
ABC

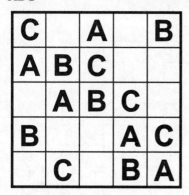

CLUELESS CROSSWORD

D	I	P	L	O	M	A
R		R		U		N
I	N	E	R	T	I	A
Z		S		C		L
Z	O	O	L	O	G	Y
L		R		M		Z
E	X	T	R	E	M	E

PAGE 144
For Openers
A: #11, B: #5, C: #2

BETWEENER
LINE

PAGE 145

Line Drawing

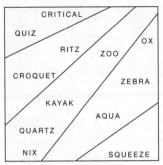

There is one Q and one Z
in each region

THREE OF A KIND
IMPATIENT, HE EXCLAIMED, "I
WANT ANOTHER BANKNOTE!"

PAGE 146

Dew Lines

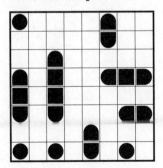

PAGE 147

Find the Ships

TWO-BY-FOUR
CART, UNIT; TACT, RUIN

PAGE 148

Hyper-Sudoku

3	2	9	4	6	1	8	7	5
5	8	4	2	3	7	1	6	9
7	6	1	5	8	9	2	3	4
1	3	7	9	2	4	5	8	6
9	5	8	3	1	6	4	2	7
6	4	2	8	7	5	3	9	1
2	1	5	6	9	8	7	4	3
4	9	3	7	5	2	6	1	8
8	7	6	1	4	3	9	5	2

MIXAGRAMS
TRUMP YEAH
CAROM PAPA
RINSE PEAR
HORSE PUTT

PAGE 149

Noisemakers

C	R	E	P	T		S	O	W	S		E	D	G	Y
H	E	N	R	I		Q	U	I	T		V	I	L	E
U	P	T	O	P		U	S	S	R		I	S	U	P
G	O	O	U	T	W	I	T	H	A	B	A	N	G	
	D	O	O	R	S		T	O	N	E				
M	E	R		E	M	T		H	A	R		Y	M	A
O	B	O	E		A	G	R	O		I	S	L	E	S
T	O	U	G	H	N	U	T	T	O	C	R	A	C	K
T	O	N	G	A		N	E	M	O		O	N	C	E
O	K	D		L	P	S		U	M	S		D	A	D
	R	A	V	I		A	S	P	C	A				
	L	O	W	E	R	E	D	T	H	E	B	O	O	M
L	O	B	O		A	L	D	A		N	O	R	M	A
E	R	I	K		C	B	E	R		E	V	E	N	T
G	E	N	E		Y	A	R	D		S	E	M	I	S

PAGE 150

Fences

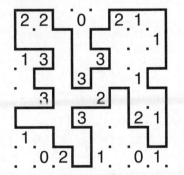

ADDITION SWITCH
$832 + 118 = 950$

PAGE 151

No Three in a Row

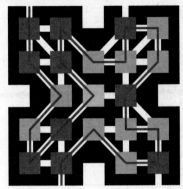

SAY IT AGAIN
AUGUST

PAGE 152

Number-Out

6	2	4	3	5	6
3	3	1	4	2	4
5	3	6	6	4	3
1	3	5	1	6	3
2	4	2	5	1	3
4	6	6	1	3	5

OPPOSITE ATTRACTION
FRIEND, FOE

PAGE 153

Fancy Footwork

S	H	A	P	E		B	R	I	M		A	S	P	S
P	U	T	O	N		R	A	R	E		S	H	E	A
A	L	O	N	G		A	V	I	S		S	O	O	N
T	A	P	D	A	N	C	E	S	A	R	O	U	N	D
			G	O	E	S			A	R	T	S	Y	
F	E	R	R	E	T	S		G	R	I	T			
E	B	A	Y			S	O	O	T		O	A	T	
T	A	K	E	S	T	W	O	T	O	T	A	N	G	O
E	N	E		O	V	A	L			I	C	E	S	
			R	Y	A	N		A	I	M	L	E	S	S
A	D	I	E	U		A	L	S	O					
W	A	L	T	Z	I	N	G	T	H	R	O	U	G	H
A	L	I	I		D	A	R	E		A	P	P	L	E
S	E	A	R		O	V	E	R		S	A	T	O	N
H	Y	D	E		L	Y	E	S		S	L	O	W	S

PAGE 154

123

3	1	2	1	3	2	1	3	2
2	3	1	3	2	1	3	2	1
1	2	3	2	1	3	2	1	3
3	1	2	3	2	1	3	2	1
1	2	3	1	3	2	1	3	2
2	3	1	2	1	3	2	1	3
3	1	2	1	3	2	1	3	2
1	2	3	2	1	3	2	1	3
2	3	1	3	2	1	3	2	1

SUDOKU SUM
3 0 8 + 1 5 9 = 4 6 7

PAGE 155

Find the Ships

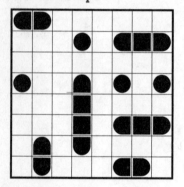

TWO-BY-FOUR
PAVE, HAUL (or HULA)

PAGE 156

Learning Experience

M	A	I		A	V	E	R	S		A	N	I	M	E
A	R	C		L	I	L	A	C		L	I	M	O	S
N	A	E		A	D	A	N	O		I	N	P	U	T
T	R	A	I	N	I	N	G	W	H	E	E	L	S	
I	A	G	O			E	S	E			I	S	O	
S	T	E	U	B	E	N		N	A	S	C	A	R	
		E	T	A	T	S		T	R	I	K	E		
	E	D	U	C	A	T	I	N	G	R	I	T	A	
S	L	I	N	K		O	M	A	N	I				
D	E	C	O	Y	S			G	U	A	R	D	E	D
I	C	K		C	H	I				E	E	R	O	
	T	E	A	C	H	I	N	G	F	E	L	L	O	W
C	I	R	C	A		M	A	N	O	R		V	I	N
P	O	E	T	S		O	N	A	I	R		E	C	O
A	N	D	I	E		M	E	T	E	S		D	A	N

PAGE 157

Operetta Pair

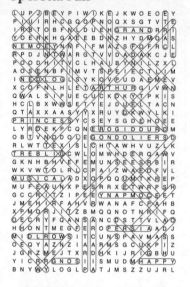

IN OTHER WORDS
ARMCHAIR

PAGE 158

Go With the Flow

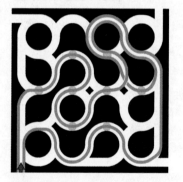

THREE AT A RHYME
DOME, LOAM, GNOME

PAGE 159

Star Search

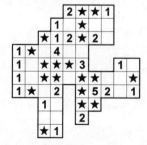

TELEPHONE TRIOS
EXHAUST, FATIGUE, TIRE OUT

PAGE 160

Burning Issue

D	V	D		J	E	B		A	F	F	A	I	R	S
R	I	O		U	N	I		L	O	O	S	E	N	S
I	D	O		T	A	R		F	O	R	T	R	A	N
P	E	R	F	E	C	T	M	A	T	C	H			
S	O	S	A		T	H	U		R	E	E	S	E	S
			U	P	S		L	E	E		A	G	E	
E	A	G	L	E		C	E	A	S	E	F	I	R	E
T	R	O	T	T	E	R		S	T	A	L	L	E	D
H	O	L	Y	S	M	O	K	E		R	U	S	T	Y
Y	M	A		E	P	A		A	L	F				
L	A	N	C	E	R		R	E	B		F	A	M	E
		A	N	G	E	L	A	S	A	S	H	E	S	
P	E	E	R	S	I	N		T	U	X		E	N	S
A	S	T	O	U	N	D		A	R	E		A	S	E
S	E	A	L	E	G	S		T	D	S		D	A	N

PAGE 161

Sudoku

2	7	8	1	4	5	9	6	3
9	5	4	3	6	8	7	2	1
1	6	3	2	7	9	8	5	4
7	8	2	4	9	6	1	3	5
4	9	1	8	5	3	2	7	6
5	3	6	7	2	1	4	9	8
8	2	5	6	1	7	3	4	9
6	1	7	9	3	4	5	8	2
3	4	9	5	8	2	6	1	7

MIXAGRAMS

S H O R N   B A B E
A R G O N   S L O W
L E A S E   D A W N
T H R E W   I S L E

PAGE 162

One-Way Streets

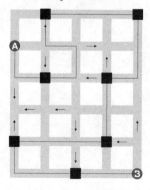

SOUND THINKING
IDEOLOGY

PAGE 163

ABC

B	C			A
C	A		B	
	B	C	A	
A		B		C
		A	C	B

NATIONAL TREASURE
ACROSTIC

PAGE 164

Clock Work

```
D A T E S ■ F A S T ■ L A S S
A B O D E ■ I S T O ■ A T O P
W I R E D ■ E T A L ■ P E L E
N E I N A T N I N E ■ D A V E
■ ■ ■ T A D ■ R O O T E D ■
P E S T E R ■ C H A R G E ■
I L I A D ■ C R A T E ■ I A N
P A C T ■ S H A R E ■ O G L E
E L K ■ A T O N E ■ W A H O O
■ S C R A P E ■ B A T T E N
S E A L E R ■ ■ G O T ■ ■ ■
A L T I ■ F O R E A T F O U R
R U S E ■ I R O N ■ A R O S E
A D I N ■ S E M I ■ G A Z E D
N E X T ■ H O P E ■ E Y E R S
```

PAGE 165

What's Next?

1: Square 4 (every all-yellow spot switches position with the spot one space away clockwise); 2: Square 5 (odd number of vertical lines, even number of horizontal lines); 3: Square 1 (double the number of previous squares, include one square of a new color)

BETWEENER
BAND

PAGE 166

Find the Ships

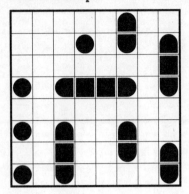

TWO-BY-FOUR
MOVE, HURT (or THRU)

PAGE 167

123

1	2	3	1	2	3	2	1	3
3	1	2	3	1	2	3	2	1
2	3	1	2	3	1	2	1	3
3	1	2	3	1	2	1	3	2
2	3	1	2	3	1	3	2	1
3	1	2	3	1	2	1	3	2
1	2	3	1	2	3	2	1	3
2	3	1	2	3	1	3	2	1
1	2	3	1	2	3	1	3	2

SUDOKU SUM
$258 + 703 = 961$

PAGE 169

Lots Will Be Lost

```
R E M I T ■ ■ C P O S ■ S E W
A L A N A ■ A O R T A ■ C A Y
K I S S M Y G R I S T ■ U S A
E A S T ■ E N D S ■ ■ A B E T
■ ■ M I N N E S O T A F A S T
I C E L E S S ■ N O M E ■ ■ ■
L A D L E ■ M E G A W A T T ■
S R I ■ B U R R O ■ ■ L O O
A B A N D O N S ■ ■ U P B O W
■ ■ O I N K ■ A E R I A L S
H E D G E O N E S B E S T ■ ■
U R E O ■ O U I A ■ I R I M
H A T ■ C O W B O Y B O O S T
U S E ■ R U N I N ■ O L S E N
M E R ■ O I S E ■ A S S E S
```

PAGE 170

Fences

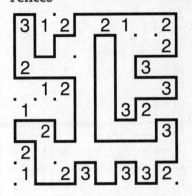

ADDITION SWITCH
$372 + 509 = 881$

PAGE 171

Number-Out

1	1	5	6	3	6
4	5	3	1	3	6
3	5	4	6	6	2
3	3	3	4	5	4
5	6	2	2	1	4
1	6	6	3	2	4

OPPOSITE ATTRACTION
AUNT, UNCLE

PAGE 172

No Monkeying Around

```
T R O D ■ S C R A M S ■ S U M
Y O D A ■ A R A F A T ■ T Z U
P R I M A T O L O G Y ■ A B S
E Y E O P E N E R ■ M C G E E
■ ■ U P S Y ■ ■ K I O S K S
N A C R E ■ ■ I S L E S ■ ■
E X O ■ A P O G E E ■ M U D D
B E L A L U G O S I M O V I E
S L A T ■ M O R E N O ■ E T C
■ ■ E G A D S ■ ■ P L A Z A
P A G A N S ■ ■ A P I A ■ ■
E R A T O ■ O U T A N D O U T
T O W ■ M I S S I N G L I N K
T S K ■ E A S E L S ■ E S T O
Y E S ■ S M A R T Y ■ R E O S
```

PAGE 173
Solitaire Poker

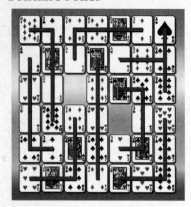

BETWEENER
GLASS

PAGE 174
Hyper-Sudoku

1	5	4	3	7	6	9	8	2
9	8	2	4	1	5	6	3	7
6	3	7	9	2	8	4	1	5
3	1	6	5	8	7	2	9	4
5	2	8	6	9	4	1	7	3
7	4	9	2	3	1	8	5	6
8	7	5	1	4	2	3	6	9
2	6	3	8	5	9	7	4	1
4	9	1	7	6	3	5	2	8

MIXAGRAMS

O U T E R	G A M E
V I T A L	P U M A
E A S E L	P L U S
R O B O T	P R E Y

PAGE 175
Film Trail

INITIAL REACTION
Beauty Is In The Eye Of The Beholder

PAGE 176
Wife's Tale

N	A	I	L	S		P	R	I	S	M		W	A	D
O	P	R	A	H		H	A	R	T	E		H	I	E
H	U	S	B	A	N	D	S	A	R	E		I	R	V
			E	R	O	S		I	T	U	R	B	I	
G	A	S	L	I	T		P	I	C		S	L	A	T
L	I	K	E	F	I	R	E	S	T	H	E	Y	G	O
I	D	E	D		O	O	Z	E		O	R	B		
B	E	L		A	N	T		U	R	N		I	L	L
		E	L	L		I	S	L	E		O	R	E	O
O	U	T	I	F	U	N	A	T	T	E	N	D	E	D
O	N	O	R		N	I	X		I	N	E	S	S	E
M	E	N	A	C	E		S	N	I	P				
P	A	K		Z	S	A	Z	S	A	G	A	B	O	R
A	S	E		A	C	T	O	R		M	I	L	N	E
H	E	Y		R	O	L	O	S		A	R	T	S	Y

PAGE 177
Triad Split Decisions

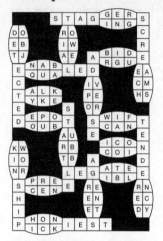

TRANSDELETION
GENETICS

PAGE 178
One-Way Streets

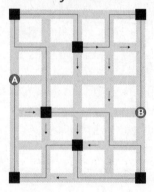

SOUND THINKING
AFFABILITY

PAGE 179
Take a Good Look

R	E	B	A		W	I	L	L	S		S	W	A	M
A	L	O	U		A	N	I	S	E		H	I	R	E
S	O	R	T		S	T	E	A	M		E	D	I	T
H	I	G	H	F	A	L	U	T	I	N		E	S	E
			O	L	D		S	T	A	B	B	E	D	
I	N	F	R	A	R	E	D		E	R	O	O		
L	O	A		T	A	L	U	S		Y	O	D	E	L
S	E	R	B		G	L	A	I	R		N	I	C	E
A	S	F	O	R		A	L	L	O	T		E	R	A
		E	R	I	C		S	T	O	R	E	D	U	P
I	N	T	E	A	R	S		M	I	R				
T	A	C		L	O	W	P	R	I	O	R	I	T	Y
S	O	H	O		W	I	L	E	E		A	M	I	E
O	M	E	N		E	P	E	E	S		T	A	R	A
K	I	D	S		D	E	A	L	T		A	X	E	S

PAGE 180

Straight Ahead

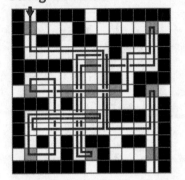

SAY IT AGAIN
BUFFET

PAGE 181

Star Search

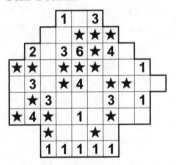

TELEPHONE TRIOS
KINGPIN, MANAGER, SKIPPER

PAGE 182

Sudoku

4	7	6	1	8	5	3	2	9
3	1	9	2	4	6	5	8	7
2	5	8	7	9	3	6	1	4
1	4	2	5	6	9	8	7	3
6	3	5	8	7	4	1	9	2
9	8	7	3	1	2	4	6	5
8	2	4	6	3	7	9	5	1
5	9	1	4	2	8	7	3	6
7	6	3	9	5	1	2	4	8

CENTURY MARKS
5 - 4 + 61 + 18 - 7 + 27= 100

PAGE 183

Terse Comment

PAGE 184

ABC

C	A	B		
	A		C	B
B			A	C
C		B		A
A	B	C		

CLUELESS CROSSWORD

B	O	B	S	L	E	D
U		L		I		E
Z	E	A	L	O	U	S
Z		B		N		I
A	M	B	L	I	N	G
R		E		Z		N
D	A	R	K	E	N	S

PAGE 185

Find the Ships

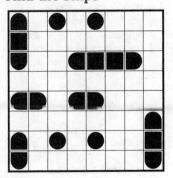

TWO-BY-FOUR
FARE (or FEAR), WARY
(or AWRY); WEAR, FRAY

PAGE 186

It's Only a Movie

PAGE 187

Arm Art
#3

THREE AT A RHYME
URGE, MERGE, SURGE

PAGE 188

123

2	3	1	3	1	2	1	2	3
1	2	3	2	3	1	3	1	2
2	1	2	3	1	3	2	3	1
3	2	3	1	2	1	3	1	2
1	3	2	3	1	2	1	2	3
3	2	1	2	3	1	3	1	2
2	1	3	1	2	3	2	3	1
1	3	1	2	3	2	1	2	3
3	1	2	1	2	3	2	3	1

SUDOKU SUM
3 2 7 + 6 1 8 = 9 4 5

PAGE 189
Fences

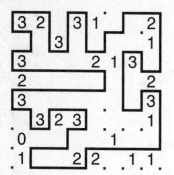

ADDITION SWITCH
3 7 6 + 2 8 8 = 6 6 4

PAGE 190
Ark-Ana

A	G	E	S		C	O	C	O		R	A	Z	O	R
L	U	R	E		O	P	E	N		A	W	A	R	E
E	R	I	E		P	E	L	E		N	E	G	E	V
C	U	C	K	O	O	C	L	A	R	K				
			S	M	U			M	O	L	A	R	S	
R	A	T		A	T	O	M		D	E	T	E	C	T
A	M	A	I	N		L	O	V	E		A	H	O	Y
C	O	M	B	I	N	A	T	I	O	N	L	A	R	K
E	R	A	S		E	V	E	N		E	L	S	I	E
D	A	L	E	T	H		T	O	P	S		H	A	S
	L	E	N	O	R	E			I	T	S			
			F	U	T	U	R	E	S	H	A	R	K	
A	L	O	O	F		U	S	E	R		I	V	A	N
G	A	B	L	E		D	I	O	R		N	I	N	E
O	X	I	D	E		E	A	S	E		E	D	G	E

PAGE 191
Hyper-Sudoku

9	1	5	6	8	2	4	7	3
6	7	3	9	4	5	1	8	2
8	2	4	1	7	3	6	9	5
3	8	6	5	9	7	2	4	1
5	9	2	4	6	1	8	3	7
7	4	1	2	3	8	9	5	6
1	6	9	3	5	4	7	2	8
4	5	8	7	2	6	3	1	9
2	3	7	8	1	9	5	6	4

MIXAGRAMS

A P P A L   S O U R
C O U P E   O K R A
F O R T E   U R G E
A R G U E   L O G O

PAGE 192
Split Decisions

TRANSDELETION
PAINTER

PAGE 193
Mixed Media

J	A	Z	Z		S	M	E	W		G	A	S	P	S
A	G	E	E		C	A	R	E		I	O	W	A	N
G	R	A	N	T	A	N	D	B	E	L	L	E	A	U
S	A	L		A	M	I	A	B	L	E		E	R	G
			P	U	P	A			A	A	A			
V	E	R	O	N	I	C	A	A	N	D	S	W	A	N
A	B	O	R	T			I	N	D		S	A	G	O
L	B	S		S	T	A	L	E	S	T		L	A	B
L	E	S	S		O	N	E			R	A	D	I	I
E	D	I	T	H	A	N	D	D	I	A	M	O	N	D
			P	A	T			E	N	V	Y			
S	A	W		D	E	L	U	I	S	E		A	H	A
P	E	O	P	L	E	A	N	D	P	L	A	C	E	S
A	R	O	S	E		K	I	R	A		Y	E	A	H
T	O	D	A	Y		E	V	E	N		E	D	D	Y

PAGE 194
Color Paths

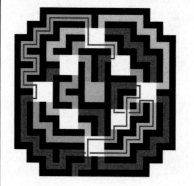

BETWEENER
SWEET

PAGE 195
Number-Out

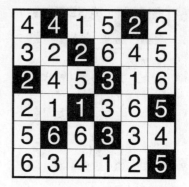

OPPOSITE ATTRACTION
ENTER, EXIT

PAGE 196
One-Way Streets

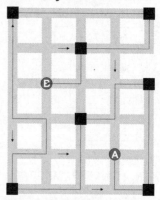

SOUND THINKING
WHODUNIT

PAGE 197
Say Cheese!

A	R	G	O	S		A	C	D	C		M	S	G	T
D	A	U	N	T		S	H	E	A		A	P	E	D
A	D	I	E	U		T	E	E	S	H	I	R	T	S
P	A	S	S	P	O	R	T	P	H	O	T	O		
T	R	E		E	V	A			W	A	C	S		
			I	F	I	L	O	O	K	L	I	K	E	
M	I	S	T	Y		P	R	O	S		E	A	T	
O	R	E	S		T	H	I	S	I		S	T	L	O
B	A	R		C	O	E	N		F	U	S	S	Y	
	N	E	E	D	T	H	E	T	R	I	P			
	I	N	C	R		V	A	N		U	S	A		
		G	L	O	R	I	A	S	W	A	N	S	O	N
S	T	E	A	M	E	D	U	P		G	O	U	L	D
A	N	T	I		D	O	D	O		L	E	A	V	E
S	T	I	R		S	L	I	T		E	L	L	E	S

PAGE 198

Sudoku

5	1	9	4	7	2	3	6	8
4	2	8	3	6	5	5	7	9
6	3	7	1	9	8	4	5	2
9	7	3	5	4	1	2	8	6
1	5	2	8	3	6	9	7	4
8	4	6	9	2	7	5	3	1
2	8	1	7	5	9	6	4	3
3	6	5	2	1	4	8	9	7
7	9	4	6	8	3	1	2	5

MIXAGRAMS

```
T O U C H      D R A T
A N N O Y      E V I L
P E R K Y      C O I L
E A T E N      K N O B
```

PAGE 199

Star Search

TELEPHONE TRIOS

CAPITAL, NEST EGG, SAVINGS

PAGE 200

Arf! Arf!

```
M A P L E S   M S E C   E L M
I M P A C T   Y E A H   P A O
D I D Y O U H E A R A B O U T
      A N N O Y     N A C R E
S L O W   T H E D O G T H A T
P I C A S S O     A L E S
O B E Y S     A R E     S P A
T R A   W E N T T O A   C A B
S A N     T O E     I T A L Y
    M A U I     S E R A P E S
F L E A C I R C U S   K E Y S
L A N C E     R I C H E
A N D S T O L E T H E S H O W
T A U     I N I T   E L O I S E
T I P   C O D E   W I N D E D
```

PAGE 201

Turn Maze

SAY IT AGAIN
DESERT

PAGE 202

Jolly Good

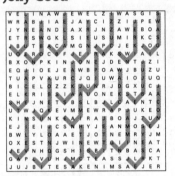

WHO'S WHAT WHERE?
Varsovian

PAGE 203

ABC

B	C			A
		A	B	C
C			A	B
	A	B	C	
A	B	C		

CLUELESS CROSSWORD

```
T R I C K E D
E   S   N   E
A N T H E M S
C   H   A   E
H U M I D O R
E   U   E   V
R E S I D U E
```

PAGE 204

Themeless Toughie

```
M I S S O U R I A N   C A S A
E N T E R S I N T O   U M P S
C H A L L E N G E R   R B I S
C A L V E   G R A N D D U K E
A L I E   C L E M   E L L E S
S E N S E L E S S   P E A L S
        R U T S   B O R N E O
M A L O N E S   P U N S T E R
A B I D E D   C O L E
L O B O S   T O O K S T E P S
A V E R T   A L L Y   A A R E
Y E L L O W S E A   A U R A E
S A L E   A T T R A C T I N G
I L E S   D E T E R R E N C E
A L E S   I D E A M O N G E R
```

PAGE 206

Find the Ships

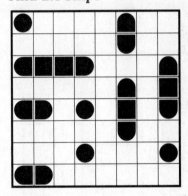

TWO-BY-FOUR

TUNA (or AUNT); MAUL
(or ALUM)

PAGE 207

Hyper-Sudoku

2	4	5	8	7	6	1	3	9
3	6	1	9	5	4	7	2	8
9	7	8	2	1	3	6	5	4
7	5	3	4	6	1	8	9	2
4	1	2	3	8	9	5	7	6
6	8	9	5	2	7	4	1	3
5	3	6	7	4	2	9	8	1
8	2	4	1	9	5	3	6	7
1	9	7	6	3	8	2	4	5

BETWEENER
STONE

PAGE 208
Themeless Toughie

```
V E T E R A N ■ S L I P P E R
A V A R I C E ■ H E R O I N E
S A L U T E S ■ E G O I S T S
S C O P E ■ T W A I N ■ T I P
A U N T ■ A L E R T ■ F O C I
L E E ■ A M I S S ■ M A N E T
S E D I M E N T ■ M O U S S E
■ ■ R A N G ■ P I L L ■ ■
A C C E S S ■ P A R T T I M E
R O A N S ■ C O N E S ■ T E M
R U B E ■ T O R O S ■ P A L E
A G A ■ P O W E R ■ S O L A R
N A R R A T E ■ A R I S I N G
G R E A T E R ■ M I L E A G E
E S T E E M S ■ A D O R N E D
```

PAGE 209
Crime Scene
#4

THREE AT A RHYME
LEAK, SEEK, CLIQUE

PAGE 210
Fences

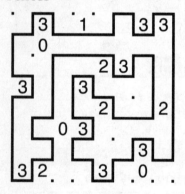

ADDITION SWITCH
3 9 0 + 3 1 7 = 7 0 7

PAGE 211
Themeless Toughie

```
W H A T T H E ■ S T R A F E R
H O M E R U N ■ T E A R O S E
A T A N E N D ■ E X P E R T S
C A N D Y ■ E D I T ■ S K I T
K I D S ■ M A I N S T ■ E V E
S R A ■ E A V E S ■ B R E A D
■ ■ A S C O T ■ G O U P T O
C L U B C A R ■ D I N E S E N
Y E L L O W ■ S I Z E S ■ ■
L A T E R ■ S E A M S ■ T V S
I N E ■ T U P E L O ■ B R I T
N O R M ■ S A M E ■ C L E A R
D N I E P E R ■ C O L U M B O
E M O T E R S ■ T W O F O L D
R E R A I S E ■ S E T F R E E
```

PAGE 212
123

```
2 1 3 2 3 1 2 3 1
1 3 2 1 2 3 1 2 3
3 2 1 3 1 2 3 1 2
2 1 3 2 3 1 2 3 1
3 2 1 3 1 2 3 1 2
1 3 2 1 2 3 1 2 3
2 1 3 2 3 1 2 3 1
3 2 1 3 1 2 1 2 3
1 3 2 1 2 3 2 3 1
```

SUDOKU SUM
3 1 9 + 5 2 7 = 8 4 6

PAGE 213
Number-Out

```
2 1 4 6 6 2
1 2 6 4 5 3
6 5 3 4 1 6
5 3 1 4 2 6
6 4 4 2 1 5
3 1 5 1 6 4
```

OPPOSITE ATTRACTION
SELDOM, OFTEN

PAGE 214
Themeless Toughie

```
P E T U N I A ■ C O U G H E D
I R O N O R E ■ U N L O O S E
C R U I S E R ■ C A N A S T A
C A R T E ■ A S K ■ A L T A R
O T I S ■ S T O O D ■ S I T E
L I S ■ O M I N O U S ■ L E S
O C T A G O N S ■ R A W E S T
■ ■ S L O G ■ P A R E ■ ■
C A C H E T ■ O R B I T E R S
A N A ■ S H E K E L S ■ D E E
T I P S ■ S L A T E ■ C U L L
E M I T S ■ A Y E ■ F O C A L
R A T A T A T ■ N A R R A T E
E T A G E R E ■ S W E A T E R
D E L E T E D ■ E N D L E S S
```

PAGE 215
Tennis Pro Jigsaw

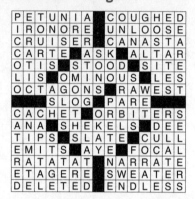

IN OTHER WORDS
BOYFRIEND

PAGE 216
The Sphinx

SAY IT AGAIN
EVENING

PAGE 217
Themeless Toughie

```
S U I T S M E █ A P O S T L E
I N N O C E N T S A B R O A D
C A L L A T T E N T I O N T O
█ W I L T █ R E E L S █ S I M
J A M S █ R E T R Y █ F I N I
O R B █ N O A H █ █ A L L O T
N E O P H Y T E █ M O U S S E
█ █ O L A Y █ P A R K █ █ █
C H A P E L █ P A R T Y H A T
H A L E R █ A S I A █ A R E
A R E S █ P E C A N █ D C I X
S P R █ T E P I D █ P I K A
S I T S O N O N E S H A N D S
I S L A N D C O N T I N E N T
S T Y L I S H █ A L L A Y E D
```

PAGE 218
ABCD

```
C B     A D
B A C D    
    B C A D
D C     B A
  D A   C B
A   D B   C
```

NATIONAL TREASURE
BANDAGES, HANDBAGS

PAGE 219
Sudoku

9	3	5	7	4	8	2	6	1
2	1	8	9	6	5	4	3	7
7	6	4	1	3	2	8	9	5
8	7	1	6	2	4	3	5	9
6	9	2	5	7	3	1	4	8
5	4	3	8	1	9	6	7	2
3	2	9	4	8	7	5	1	6
4	5	6	2	9	1	7	8	3
1	8	7	3	5	6	9	2	4

MIXAGRAMS

```
H A V O C   C I T E
A U D I T   C R O P
N U R S E   N E O N
D W A R F   O I L Y
```

PAGE 220
Themeless Toughie

```
W H I T T L E █ R E S P E C T
R U N A W A Y █ A T T A C H E
E N C L O S E █ M A U D L I N
A C H E S █ G R R █ B R I M S
T H I S █ S L O O P █ E P E E
H E N █ A L A D D I N █ S I S
E D G E W I S E █ C O V E N
█ G A D S █ T A R O █ █ █
M A O R I █ E A S T W A R D
B A M █ E N G L I S H █ S E E
E R O S █ G A L L O █ S I G N
A C U T E █ R A P █ B A N E S
D O N A T E D █ I M A G I N E
E N T I T L E █ P A R E N T S
D I S D A I N █ E V E R E S T
```

PAGE 221
One-Way Streets

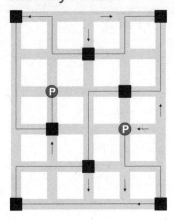

SOUND THINKING
JAWBONE

PAGE 222
Split Decisions

TRANSDELETION
SEA GREEN

PAGE 223
Themeless Toughie

```
P I C A █ J F K A I R P O R T
A N O N █ A R A B L E A G U E
S T A T █ M I Z Z E N M A S T
T O X I C █ G O U R D █ U S O
█ Q U A H O G █ A G I N
A D J U N C T S █ S A V E A S
V O L A N T E █ T O D O █
E M O T I O N █ H O O T E R S
█ I N N S █ I N P R I N T
G R A N G E █ P R E T E N S E
H A N G █ M A D R E S █
O N T █ F E E L S █ D A Z E D
S C H O O L M A T E █ N E R O
T H E D A K O T A S █ T A R P
S O R E L O S E R S █ E L S E
```

PAGE 224

Looped Path

SAY IT AGAIN
INCENSE

PAGE 225

Star Search

TELEPHONE TRIOS
FRAGILE, BRITTLE, RICKETY

PAGE 226

Themeless Toughie

```
C R O S S W A Y S   B A S I L
H E R E T I C A L   A D A N O
A C E T Y L E N E   T A L C S
F E L O N Y   K E G   M E A T
E N S U E   R E P O S   S M A
S T E T   S E E Y A L A T E R
      S E M I   B O G A R T
S A N A N T O N I O T E X A S
A R A R A T   G N U S
R E T I R E M E N T   D R A W
D A T   L E O N S   S A U D I
I C E D   S M U   J A M M E D
N O R A H   M I S E R A B L E
E D E N S   A T I T A G A I N
S E D A N   S Y N T H E S E S
```

PAGE 227

Number-Out

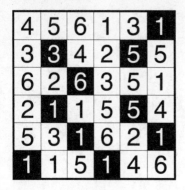

OPPOSITE ATTRACTION
HARDEN, SOFTEN

PAGE 228

Line Drawing

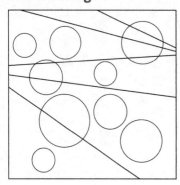

TWO-BY-FOUR
GATE, TUBE

PAGE 229

Themeless Toughie

```
C R U S O E   S P A N I A R D
R E N O I R   C O L A N D E R
I M P A L A   A N T I D O T E
T E R R E S T R I A L   R I A
I D O   D E A L E R   P E R M
C I V   W E S   H I D E S
S E E   L U N T   P U T
  S N E A K Y   M A N T I S
    A D E   V I N S   R E S
C A S T S   A A A   O P T
H E W S   P L U M P S   N A E
O N E   B I L L I O N A I R E
L E A V E O U T   R A S C A L
L A T I T U D E   C R E A T E
A S S E S S E D   H E A L E R
```

PAGE 230

Triad Split Decisions

TRANSDELETION
RIO GRANDE

PAGE 231

Wheels and Cogs
The charger

THREE AT A RHYME
SAWS, GAUZE, PAUSE

PAGE 232

Themeless Toughie

```
T R A P   A C C O R D A N C E
H E R A   C R A D L E S O N G
R D A S   C A N I S M A J O R
U M P S   R I C E   M O T E
S E A P L A N E   S L A K E S
T A H O E   L A T E N E S S
S T O R A G E S P O T
  S E T F O R   B U S T L E
    L E A N S T O W A R D
A N S W E R T O   F O Y E R
N O H I T S   S E L F S A M E
C H I P   P E R I   I S I S
H O N E S T L O O K   D I T S
O P E R A H O U S E   E D I E
R E D S P O T T E D   D E C S
```